AF763347

Concept Publishing Co.
Rs 750/--

Committees and Commissions in India
1974

Committees and Commissions in India
1974

Concepts in Communication
Informatics & Librarianship-48

General Editor : **S.P. Agrawal**

Committees and Commissions in India 1974

Volume 12

A Concept's Project

Compiled by a team of professionals
under the auspice of
VIRENDRA KUMAR

CONCEPT PUBLISHING COMPANY, NEW DELHI 110059

All rights reserved. No part of this work may be reproduced, stored in a retrieval system, or transmitted, in any form or by any means, electronic, mechanical, photocopying, microfilming, recording or otherwise, without the prior written permission of the copyright owner and the publisher.

ISBN 81-7022-476-4 (Vol. 12)

First Published 1993

© Publisher

Published and Printed by
Ashok Kumar Mittal
Concept Publishing Company
A/15-16, Commercial Block, Mohan Garden
NEW DELHI 110059 (India)

Lasertypeset by
Microtech Advance Printing Systems (Pvt.) Ltd.
H-13, Bali Nagar,
NEW DELHI 110015

GENERAL EDITOR'S INTRODUCTION

In the context of the changing world, the role of the government – be it at central, state or local level – is becoming more prevasive in the modern society. Everyday, it has to encounter new problems and face new issues which demand quite a new thinking and novel strategies to overcome them. Thus, the increasing role of the government in every sphere of people's life has broadened its functions and responsibilities tremendously and enlarged its activities to such an extent that the government machinery of its own can hardly manage its affairs. Moreover, its functions are becoming more complicated and complex requiring the assistance of outside specialists, technocrats and specialized agencies.

In view of this, the modern government has to set-up committees and commissions and working or study groups on various problems and issue from time to time. In the light of the recommendations of these committees and commissions, the government takes decisions on key issues and problems. Often the government is obliged to seek the assistance of a committee to evaluate some of its schemes in operation so that on the basis of the evaluation reports of the committee, it may either continue, modify or scrap the on-going schemes. In other words, the committees or commissions, etc., exercise a great deal of pivotal force in shaping the policies and programmes of the government and for this purpose submit a large number of reports.

In these volumes of *Committees and Commissions in India*, now being published under the *Concepts in Communication Informatics and Librarianship (CICIL)* series, an attempt has been made to cover the period from 1974 onwards. The volumes include the vital data about only those reports of the committees and commissions which have been constituted by the Central Government. We have made every endeavour to include the digest of all the important reports on various vital issues of great importance and on major areas of national development.

We have also an ambitious plan to publish the digests of the important reports of the committees and commissions appointed by different state governments, the semi-government organisations and the learned bodies as also the reports published during the period of the British Government.

The publication has been brought out under the guidance of Shri Virendra Kumar, specialist in his own right with vast experience of working in Government Documents Section in the Central Secretariat Library and having the privilege of the blessings of Dr. S.R. Ranganathan – the father of Indian Library Science. I also put on record the collaborative help provided by Shri M.W.K. Sherwani.

We are sure that this compilation will prove a very useful reference tool for researchers, serious students and scholars of the public administration and political science, administrators, policy-makers, educationists and historians.

S.P. AGRAWAL

PREFACE

This volume of *Committees and Commissions in India* attempts to understand the activities of the various Committees and Commissions during the period 1974.

A 'Commission' is a governmental agency created to perform a particular function such as special investigations or on governmental regulations of business. It is appointed mainly when it is thought that a matter involves some financial questions. There are other reasons for which a Commission is appointed, e.g., in matters pertaining to welfare of the State and its citizens and or improving the efficiency in an administration. The status of a 'Committee' is also the same as that of a 'Commission', but it does not possess as wide powers as are enjoyed by a Commission and has to limit itself to specific work assigned to it under its terms of reference. While arriving at decisions in the form of recommendations, a Commission or Committee ensures that such decisions arc representative of interests of various types of people and also a safeguard against abuse of power.

A Committee or a Commission comprises a Chairman, the Members and Member Secretary (sometimes there is also an Assistant Secretary). In some cases, there are even One-man Commissions and the enquiry in such Commissions is entrusted to an Officer-on-Special Duty.

The Chairman of a Commission is a person well-versed mostly in legal matters and is often a retired judge of a High Court or the Supreme Court of India. Occasionally, a Member of Parliament is also appointed as the Chairman of a Commission. On the other hand, the Chairman of the Committee is mostly a specialist in the subject of the Committee. He can be a Leader or a Convenor also, if he heads a Panel, a Study Group or a Delegation, etc.

The Members of a Commission, Committee, Panel, Study Group etc., are specialists in their respective fields and provide valuable guidance to the Commission or the Committee in making recommendations.

The Member-Secretary or Secretary is generally nominated from among the experienced officials who have the requisite competent knowledge of the subject on which the Commission or the Committee is appointed.

Committees and Commissions in India provides in chronological order vital information about Committees and Commissions appointed by the Government from time to time. Information for each Committee or Commission is presented in a compact form in four parts, namely; Constitution; Appointment; Terms of Reference and Recommendations.

CONTENTS

1

COMMITTEE ON ENGINEERING EXPORTS 1974 – REPORT[1]

Chairman Shri M. Sondhi

Members Brig. B.J. Shahaney; Dr. A.K. Ghosh; Shri M. Narasimham; Shri R. Tirumalai; Shri S.M. Ghosh; Shri R.K. Sethi; Chairman, Engineering Export Promotion Council; Chairman, Indian Engineering Association

The following were additionally co-opted as members of the Committee:

Shri B.C.B. Nath; Shri Mohd. Fazal; Shri Hari Bhushan; Shri M.M. Luther; Shri K. Rajagopalan; Shri G.K. Majumdar

M. Secy. Shri S.M. Chakravarty

Appointment

In order to consider the problems on the engineering industry relating to exports and to suggest concrete steps to stimulate exports, the Government set-up a Committee by its Resolution No.7(15)/73/TSW(II) dated the 2nd January, 1974 with the following composition:

Terms of Reference

The Terms of Reference of the Committee were the following:

(i) to plan export of engineering goods during the Fifth Plan

1. Delhi, Controller of Publications, 1974, 94 p.

period with reference to the exportable surpluses and the countries to be exported to;

(ii) to suggest concrete steps for quickening the processes of drawal and reimbursement of export incentives;

(iii) to formulate policies of allocation of materials against export order;

(iv) to formulate specific schemes of export finance;

(v) to formulate schemes for enhancement of capacity to generate surpluses for export; and

(vi) to formulate a complete industry-oriented and country-oriented export strategy in respect of specific items within a specific time period and also a package plan for input assistance and such policy correctives as are necessary to sustain the order of export including the financial arrangements and streamlining of procedures.

The Committee noted that, some time back, the Planning Commission had set-up several Working Groups to make recommendations with regard to the various aspects connected with engineering exports. In making their recommendations, the Committee have made use of the Reports of these Working Groups.

The Committee also had the benefit of associating Shri B.K. Sanyal, Secretary (Economic Division) in the Ministry of External Affairs, Dr. Arjun K. Sen Gupta, Economic Adviser in the Ministry of Commerce and Shri N.S. Vaidyanathan, Director (Export Production) in the Ministry of Commerce as well as the Member-Secretary of the Steering Group on Engineering Exports Instituted by the Planning Commission.

Contents

Appointment of the Committee of Engineering Exports Composition — Terms of Reference; Introduction, Broad Strategy, Enhancement of Capacity to Generate Surpluses for Exports; Export Obligations; Plan for Export of Engineering Goods during the Fifth Plan Period; Information System for Export Development and Export of Consultancy Services; Export of Turnkey Projects, Joint Ventures and Civil Construction; Export Incentives; Market Development Fund; Export Finance including Deferred Terms of Payment; Physical Constraints on Production of Export; Summary of Conclusions and Recommendations.

Recommendations

1. The recent oil crisis combined with inadequate production and much larger import bill has created a wider gap between our foreign exchange earning and expenditure. This requires a concerted and unified plan of action to increase exports and save on imports.

2. Our exports have no doubt shown an increase but partly this is an account of higher unit realization. Our share in world export has registered a decline.

3. Whereas the bulk of exports are accounted for by our traditional/agricultural produce, imports are mainly on account of capital equipment and raw materials for industry. In the larger term this is not tenable and Industrial Sector must export more.

4. Engineering exports particularly of capital equipment must contribute more to our export earnings.

5. An export target of about Rs. 600 crores for 1978-79 for engineering goods should be considered feasible. It should be backed up by a detailed development plan, market research and development after-sales services.

6. It has been increasingly apparent that the preference of the development countries would continue in favour of trade and exchange of technology with each other. Unless there are compelling reasons the developed countries would prefer to confine their imports from the developing countries to the agricultural produce and unprocessed raw materials.

7. Due to progressive industrialisation and exploitation of material resources by the developing countries and change in the ownership of mineral resources, there is today a greater complimentarity of the economies of the developing countries.

8. Due to the inflationary spiral combined with already high wages is the developed countries they may like to vacate the production of certain components, sub-assemblies, etc., where the developing countries have the advantage of lower wages or the availability of raw materials. We could use this opportunity to establish production of such components for exports.

9. Our efforts to balance our trade and to reduce dependence on economic aid has to be based on the solid foundation of increased production at cheaper costs combined with improvement in technology. A greater emphasis is needed to be laid on increasing production with minimum investment and in the quicker possible time.

10. Greater emphasis is necessary on regional and bilateral economic co-operation.

11. There would have to be greater effort by us to switch from the export of primary and unprocessed goods to more processed goods and capital equipment.

12. Every export order must be executed to the full satisfaction of the foreign customer else it mars the entire country's image. Government should ensure that the necessary inputs of raw materials are made available to the exporter on priority basis particularly steel.

13. The public sector units can play a significantly more effective role in increasing export of engineering equipment, consultancy, turnkey jobs and construction on the basis of pooling of their resources and experience. Hitherto, exports from public sector units are much below their potential. Greater efforts are needed to increase their exports.

14. The various procedures for disbursements of cash assistance, drawbacks, export obligation, etc., are complex and time consuming. There is a multiplicity of Government organisations dealing with various aspects. The procedures would need to be simplified. Perhaps in our anxiety to plug all loopholes we smother efforts and initiative. An additional aspect needing greater attention is that of import substitution and augmenting of production speedily in the core sector. For this purpose free foreign exchange or foreign exchange from easier sources should be made available to get the benefit of increased production in the quickest time.

15. While the arrangement for quality control and pre-shipment inspection of the notified engineering products has worked satisfactorily, there is pressure to relax them particularly from some of the small scale industries. We are not in favour of such relaxation. We would like to go farther and suggest that where sub-standard goods have shipped out despite inspection and where there are serious and genuine companies through investigation should be carried out and appropriate action taken against those responsible. Foreign buyers could be guided by TDA, EEPC, etc., with regard to the reliability of the exports with regard to quality. However, in the case of heavy engineering equipment, due to the wide variety and the nature of equipment as also due to the fact that the exporters are of proven technical competence with self-disciplined inplant quality control, it is our view that it is not necessary to bring them within the ambit of the Quality Control and Preshipment Inspection Act.

16. It is also our view that the Quality Control and Preshipment Inspection should not merely be regulatory but it should also help and guide introduction of proper inplant quality control procedures and equipment.

17. If we keep the main objective of improving our industrial production and increasing of our exports in view and have to function as a member of the international community there would be need for more automatic permissions and freedom of growth to industry, within broad guidelines.

18. Widespread diffusion of export obligation at various stages on various entrepreneurs is somewhat cumbersome and it has not brought about commensurate benefits. Export is a specialised activity. More important than the compulsory obligations are the basic policy incentives which can go much farther and lay a more solid foundation for a satisfactory growth of exports.

19. No industrial unit can afford to remain stagnant without undermining its viability. A minimal growth is essential both from the point of view of its viability, its competitiveness as also for generation of exportable surpluses at competitive cost. A production growth of 5 per cent per annum up to a ceiling of 25 per cent in a plan period in one, two or more steps in physical terms, should be automatically permissible to the manufacturing units in certain industries as illustratively mentioned. As a fall out of this measure the growth of ancillary industries would also be stimulated.

20. Any production for export, in excess of the minimum stipulated exports, should be freely permitted by all manufacturing units and that such production should be assisted by making available the required raw materials and other inputs. In such cases prior Government approval of the unit to produce more for export should not be necessary. It should suffice for the nit to simplify notify the Government.

21. Procedural delays have been observed in approving capacity even where the units proposed to set-up capacity for 100 per cent export production. In such cases the permission should be more or less automatic. For 100 per cent export-oriented industry our present policy regarding Indian participation should not be insisted upon and even 100 per cent foreign equity and the permitted subject to export prices being subject to Government surveillance.

22. Average exports of past three years, should be deducted from the total production/capacity of any unit for the consideration

of the dominance angle while considering the expansion of units with good export performance to their credit.

23. Government should consider working out a suitable formula for allowing export investment rebate on investment for export production on similar lines as the Development Rebate allowed to the industry in the past.

24. More liberal view should be taken in the case of export-oriented industries or those with a good record of export, with regard to foreign investment/collaboration and import of capital equipment.

25. Details of export obligations at various stages currently being stipulated on industries are enumerated.

26. Only in a small number of cases have the units, subject to general export obligation, been able to fulfil their obligation. The total value of export of the units in the industry against general export obligation may not add materially to the total export effort of the industrial sector.

27. Various suggestions made on export obligations. These have been listed.

28. There is considerable force in these suggestions. We felt that instead of a diluted and diffused export obligations on all and sundry, it will more effective if export efforts are directed selectively with regard to individual units, which have already shown a good performance or new entrants who are particularly interested in exports or where our products have inherent advantage and export potential.

29. As it is, our industrial units suffer from many handicaps of raw materials, power, lengthy and time consuming procedures for the entire gamut of economic activity, diseconomies scale of production and keen competition with well established and reputed large companies abroad with more advance technological base if production and exports have to receive due priority, questions of economic concentration, large houses, protection to small scale industries *vis-a-vis* exports should not be injected in our export policies when the only legs on which we can stand is competition in price and quality.

30. It is not intended to be little the role of small scale industries with regard to exports. Their contribution has been increasing progressively. Further encouragement to them need not be through curbing others but by alleviating their basic difficulties with regard to raw materials, guidance with regard to quality control, etc.

31. Those units who have already shown good export performance, when they come up for rehabilitation and modernisation,

should not be generally prescribed additionally of export as this would only convert an initiative into a compulsion, which is not to our advantage.

32. While giving permission for import of capital equipment for replacement and modernisation, we need not be rigid from capacity angle. In the very nature of modernisation, and rehabilitation when an obsolete or own outmachine is replaced by a new or modern one, it is inherent and desirable that capacity should improve.

33. There is need for Government to formulate more specific guidelines about the stipulation of exports at different stages namely Licensing, CG clearance and foreign collaboration.

34. Export obligation should not be so high as to be penal or impractical leaving the entrepreneurs inadequate manoeuverability to fulfil his commitment.

35. The industrial units already exporting a good part of their production should get preferential treatment over others in matters relating to capital goods imports, industrial licence and foreign collaboration.

36. The policy of reservation of items for development exclusively in the small scale sector and consequent fixation of export targets merits review particularly if there is a reasonably high farming of components to the small scale sector.

37. So far as the procedures of implementation of export obligation is concerned the present option of legal undertaking should continue.

38. In view the uncertainties of exports, export obligations need not be legally enforced for more than five years.

39. In the case of non-fulfilment of obligations it is unnecessarily harsh that twice the quantum of export commitment be made over to STC or other agency for export at whatever value it can fetch. It would be more equitable if instead, an equivalent quantum as per unfulfilled part of export obligation is handed over to the STC.

40. Due consideration needs to be given to evolve our strategy with regard to regionwise export such as:

(a) to the developing countries,
(b) oil producing countries, and
(c) developed countries.

41. India enjoys considerable goodwill with most of the

countries, particularly with the South East Asian countries and the oil producing countries. This can help to step up our exports.

42. There is considerable scope for us to participate in the projects financed by Asian Development Bank leading to the export of our equipment, consultant, etc.

43. Our technology and experiencc is particularly relevant to some of the developing countries in Africa. Giving due recognition to the aspirations and policies of these countries, our consultants could take initiative of suggesting suitable projects to them.

44. There is very good response from the oil producing countries towards closer economic co-operation with us. Money is no constraint with these countries who are anxious to accelerate their development and are likely to be highly selective with regard to the choice of technology and equipment. India can participate both directly as well as indirectly through reputed companies of the developed countries.

45. In view of spiralling prices and shortage of technical man-power the developed countries might like to vacate some of the areas of manufacture of components, sub-assemblies, etc., We can advantageously enter these areas and also share consultancy work, detailing of engineering, etc., for with the developed countries. Areas having potential development of export to these countries, identified by NIDC have been listed.

46. Engineering items which deserve to be given more attention for export to USSR and East European countries have been identified and listed illustratively.

47. It would be desirable, in the context of long-term programme of increasing bilateral trade to dovetail our economic development in a manner as to achieve complimentarity with the development plans, on a selective basis, with countries like Iran, West Europe, USSR, etc.

48. By and large, for the next two to three years our exports, particularly, of heavy engineering equipment, can be built up without any substantial investment/addition of new capacity. This can be largely achieved through better utilisation of capacity, diversification and through marginal additions of balancing equipment.

49. One of the important prerequisites for mounting export efforts is an information system which should serve our needs adequately.

50. While TDA, FIEO and EEPC can continue to collect infor-

mation relevant to their activities it would, nevertheless, be necessary to make use of organisations like MECON and EPI to collect the specialised data and information for heavy engineering exports, consultancy, turnkey projects, joint ventures, etc., In addition, NIDC, who have developed good contacts and credibility in certain countries might share this responsibility. Their expenses on this account should be met from the MDF and these agencies would make the informations collected by them available to the FIEO for use by others as and when required. This need not exclude data collection by large exporters or specialised agencies such as Railways, FCI, BHEL, etc.

51. There is need for concerted and continuing efforts on our part to familiarise the concerned authorities in other countries with our capabilities in the manufacture of equipment, in technology and consultancy. For the success of our export efforts, association of our consultants even at the stage of formulation of the project is essential.

52. Following the pattern of developed countries we should also encourage our consultants to take up preliminary and feasibility studies free of cost to the recipient countries where considered potentially rewarding. NIDC would be well suited to take up most of such studies and it could co-ordinate with the FIEO.

53. We have developed a strong base of design and engineering capability in many of our consultants; MECON, Dsturco, Railways, Department of Atomic Energy, NIDC, Fertilizer Corporation, Oil and Natural Gas Commission, etc. It should be our endeavour to bring these organisations into the mainstream of our export efforts and render them all necessary assistance. At the same time FIEO may also be strengthened and the consultancy organizations undertaking work abroad should keep FIEO posted with their assignments.

54. The area where complete consultancy services can be rendered by us have been listed on illustrative basis.

55. There are other areas for general consultancy services which can also be rendered by us. These have also been listed.

56. There are various constraints in the export of consultancy services which have been identified and enumerated. These should be remedied.

57. The Indian consultancy organisations where they feel it necessary, should be encouraged to establish links with similar organisations in advanced countries.

58. If the export of consultancy services by India is to be effec-

tive, whichever consultancy organisation is successful in getting order it has to be helped to bring together the best possible expertise available in the country. For this purpose Government should be prepared to relax its rules about deputation of its exports to other organisations.

59. A roster of top level experts and specialists in both public and private sectors should be prepared and kept up to date. A small committee under the Chairmanship of the Secondary, Export Production and heads of some of the public consultancy organisations be entrusted with the framing of such a roster and updating it periodically. Material for such a roster could be provided by NIDC, FIEO and others.

60. It is a time for us to bring out a detailed brochure, to international standards, on consultancy services obtainable in our country with a detailed reference of work done by them in India and abroad. Ministry of Commerce should take up their work on immediate basis.

61. The Venkataraman Committee had recommended the establishment of a proper institution which should control the development of consultancy services. Its implementation is overdue.

62. The consultants should also be encouraged to get themselves registered with the International Organizations.

63. If above measures are taken and financial constraints removed our consultants and experts can play a bigger role than higher to in stepping up our exports.

64. Many countries prefer to assign a turnkey project for various reasons; there could be such projects which India can secure directly for itself as prime contractor or there could be others where the prime contractor could be a developed country in which case we can act as sub-contractor and take a share of engineering work, supply of plant and machinery and construction.

65. Some of the traditional industries where we have considerable amount of expertise and where we have undertaken turnkey projects as prime contractors have been listed.

66. As our know-how and manufacturing base gets more developed and diversified it should be possible for us to take up turnkey projects in other sectors, either on our own or jointly with manufacturers and consultants of advanced countries.

67. In our effort to export turnkey projects, we would need to be selective and we must not default on satisfactory completion of a project where we are either the prime contractors or sub-contractors.

Areas where we can, in addition to the traditional industries listed earlier, concentrate in export of turnkey projects as prime contractors have been illustratively listed.

68. Other possible areas where we could try to secure a significant share as sub-contractors have also been listed.

69. Hitherto our exports of engineering equipment and turnkey projects have largely been due to incidental surpluses of capacity at a given point of time. It is emphasised that if exports have to be built-up on a long-term and sustained basis, export surpluses have to be planned and provided. For this purpose our industrial licensing policy should have sufficient flexibility so that any rise in domestic demand can be offset by increased production and yet leaving sufficient surpluses for export.

70. Whereas it may not be possible to dispense with the present stipulation of 25 per cent value added formula for export of engineering goods, cases which merit reduction of this percentage should be considered individually on merits, taking into account such factors as the availability of steel, differential between the JPC and international prices and domestic demand for engineering products. Government should be responsive to changes in the situation from time to time.

71. India has acquired a certain degree of competence to participate in the programme of industrial development in the developing countries and has implemented some of the joint ventures abroad such as listed.

72. Our investment in joint venture projects abroad is, however, small. There are still many areas where greater efforts for getting up joint ventures can be successful. There should be a systematic effort to collect and disseminate information on the prospect of joint ventures abroad.

73. There is need for certain modification in respect of the guidelines for joint ventures abroad. Suggestions in regard have been made.

74. Large companies can play a more significant role in setting up joint ventures abroad without any conflict with our economic policies.

75. There is a large scope for turnkey jobs particularly for civil construction works abroad. According to a rough estimate, jobs presently known to us, requiring to be completed in the next few years total about Rs. 1200 crores.

76. Our preparedness to take up construction works of large sizes needs much to be desired. The schedules prescribed for completion are very tight, the availability of local labour is difficult and their wages high. This requires construction through highly mechanized methods requiring large earth moving and other equipment not available with us. To take up such assignment abroad we have to pool our resources and rules for the grant of foreign exchange for the procurement of machinery abroad and, subsequently, their disposal after the work is completed have to be liberalized.

77. The only way we can take up large construction assignments in a big way abroad is to form a consortium with adequate resources, financial and man-power, at its disposal. Immediate steps should be taken to form such a consortium while making this recommendation it is not the intention to exclude other agencies from taking construction jobs abroad where there are competent to take them up.

78. Long delays are still taking place in disbursement of cash assistance. These should be removed. Any change in cash assistance should be effective only from a prospective date after allowing for a reasonable period. Cash assistance applicable at the time of securing the order should hold good till the completion of the order.

79. In the case of certain engineering goods where the bought out component in the product is high, there is a sizeable element of indirect taxes and levies for which the exporter is not compensated. This burden of indirect taxes going into cost of production at various stages should be compensated to the exporter in the same manner as 'Border Tax Adjustment' through suitable cash assistance. Ministry of Commerce who are examining this matter should expeditiously complete their examination keeping the above in mind.

80. As long as the scarcity of mild steel, special and alloy steels and non-ferrous metals continues or where the indigenous material is significantly more expensive a liberal policy in fixing import replenishment should continue.

81. Duty drawback is given to the exporter to compensate for the element of duty, customs and excise going into manufacture of the product. There are long delays in the payment of duty drawbacks. There is also a case for fixing of "All Industry" rates for duty drawback on a more rational basis so that the claims for fixing too many "Brand" rates are minimised.

82. There should be a mechanism to ensure automatic and expeditious adjustment in the rates of drawbacks on the basis of

changes of customs, excise duty and import component as well as on account of any increase in the imported prices of raw materials. In the case of sensitive items like cooper, zinc, etc., relevant data should be updated once every month.

83. A decentralized operation for the payment of cash assistance and duty drawback will be helpful and for this purpose the nationalized banking system should be entrusted this task. They would have a better orientative and culture to discharge this function.

84. Since import under advance licences are allowed for executing a particular export order there is no need to change import duty as long as satisfactory evidence is produced regarding the exports as committed on the basis of which advance licence was procured.

85. Supplementary to one recommendation No 83 above Senior Officers should be deputed in the offices of banks and other pertinent organizations exclusively to guide and help exporters at the spot with regard to the formalities, procedures, filling up of the forms, etc.

86. Use of modern business machines and computerisation should be seriously considered for a quick computation or duty drawbacks, cash assistance, import entitlement, etc., by the offices dealing with these matters.

87. Hitherto for want any source of funding, Indian consultancy organisations have been forced to ask for fees from recipient countries thus placing themselves and India a disadvantage in comparison to the advanced countries who take up preliminary and feasibility studies free of cost to the recipient countries. Our consultants should also be enabled to take up such duties free of cost and their cost should be reimbursed from the MDF. For the purpose of sanctioning allocations from the MDF against such studies, the sponsored cases should be put up to the Project Export Committee.

88. It would be necessary for us to publish annually a comprehensive directory, to international standard, detailing the capability and capacity of the more important of our machinery manufacturers. BHEL should be entrusted to coordinate this work and FIEO could be asked to update and publish the directory thereafter. The expenditure on this should be borne by the MDF. There is need for a continuous effort by Indian specialists to establish direct contacts with the concerned personnel in the recipient countries. Reciprocal visits will also be required to be made by the foreign personnel. These activities should also be financed from the MDF.

89. In the past export commitments of substantial order could not be executed or completed satisfactorily because of inadequate or untimely supplies and rising cost of raw materials. Once a commitment is made by any exporter, its satisfactory execution in the country's interest should be ensured, particularly through the timely supplies of raw materials and the continuance of incentives available at the time of securing the order.

90. Export Credit Guarantee Corporation has been set-up by Government to provide the exporters, the services not available from the commercial insurance companies. The services presently rendered by the ECGC have been detailed.

91. We noted the valuable services being rendered by ECGC but would like to make further suggestions for improving the services offered by ECGC to exporters. These have been detailed.

92. We noted that the list of capital goods qualifying for deferred payments has been recently revised and that it has been decided to review the list from time to time.

93. As we step up our exports, the need for third country purchases would increase rather than diminish. The Indian exporters have been facing certain difficulties in making commitments where the customer has specified a third country equipment but not provided foreign exchange for the same specifically, or the customer has not asked for particular equipment for the third country but the exporter finds it expedient to import the same either to make his offer more competitive and/or to match delivery schedule. It was noted that, as per Red Book, if the value of third country imports does not exceed 25 per cent of the FOB value of the Project, such imports would not be set off against the import replenishment due to the exporter. However, we feel that, in addition Government clearance should be prompt so long as such requirements are debited to the import entitlements. Where this is not adequate, release of foreign exchange should be promptly examined on merits.

94. We noted that the foreign exchange cover against fluctuations in the par value of four major currencies is now being operated by the RBI from June 1974. The cover is applicable for contracts with the proceeds payable in instalments not exceeding 10 years from the date of conclusion for the export contract.

95. We understand that the Government had accepted to extend the time limit of credit facilities beyond 180 days even for short-term export, where the regulations of the importing countries necessitate

this but, soon thereafter, this facility has been withdrawn.

96. RBI has agreed to relax certain rules regarding the visit of representatives of exporters abroad as detailed.

97. We recommend that there should be a provision of an annual blanket foreign exchange for any approved list of consultancy organisations and selected exporters on certain criterion for business development purposes. The amount could be limited to say 5 per cent of their turnover in the previous year.

98. We recommend that against each specific order, a blanket foreign exchange release be granted to the concerned Indian organisations to meet their commitments in respect of their specific orders; on the basis of their detailed foreign exchange budget to be furnished to RBI. This expenditure should be taken into account for the purpose of their net foreign exchange earnings.

99. Although the question of deferred terms of payment is no longer valid in the case of many of the importing countries, particularly the oil producing countries, for whom money is no longer a constraint, nevertheless, the need for deferred terms of payment in certain cases to other countries would continue. Government should formulate a long term policy for deferred terms of payment for turnkey projects, joint ventures, construction jobs and for the supply of capital equipment, etc. For this purpose a special cell should be created in the IDBI to handle this work exclusively.

100. In some cases the consultancy services and individual consultants may not bring immediate benefit to the export but they can play an important role in the long term promotion of export business. It is recommended that export of consultancy services, not necessarily connected with any specific export contract should also be eligible for medium-term credit facilities say not exceeding 5 years.

101. The Department of Economic Affairs, IDBI, RBI and ECGC should codify the existing guidelines and procedures for use by the concerned authorities/officers in order to expedite clearance from foreign exchange angle. These guidelines should also include the question of international bank guarantee.

102. It would be of considerable help if the IDBI, RBI and ECGC with the help of EEPC and FIEO bring out a comprehensive publication covering all procedural aspects as well as detailing the facilities available from RBI, IDBI and other banks, ECGC, etc., with regard to exports.

103. It is considered essential that a specialised bank which can

give concentrated attention to export/import financing can be established and that this will also ensure a more intimate coordination with other agencies like the ECGC and insurance exports. This should have necessary financial backing. Such a bank can better cater to the special growth potential of the export sector.

104. Among the difficulties faced by the exporters were fixation of limits with reference to the exporters financial standing, delays in decision-making in the banks, non-purchase of export bills and preference to take them on collection basis, etc. Such difficulties should be brought before the Standing Committee for expeditious solutions.

105. We were informed that the present credit squeeze is also seriously affecting the exporters. We recommend that in applying credit restrictions, the priority character of export finance should always be kept in mind and that the Exports section be provided with adequate credit.

106. A high level Standing Committee should be set-up in the RBI for coordinating and taking decision on the various problems in the field of export finance and insurance.

107. Physical constraints like non-availability of steel and non-ferrous metals, power shortage, difficulties with regard to transport and shipping have to alleviate for speeding up our exports.

108. The present procedures involved in obtaining steel supplies are complicated and time consuming and committed deliveries are impossible to have. The long time cycle for procuring even the sale/works orders for steel have been detailed.

109. The long lead time in the supply of steel and uncertainties in the supply of even small quantities is a serious handicap to engineering exporters as compared to their foreign counter-parts who obtain their supplies practically off the shelf.

110. The recent decisions taken by the Steel Priority Committee in regard to Steel allocation to the exporters as detailed would help and need to be implemented expeditiously.

111. In addition the following is recommended in regard to the allocation and supply of steel to the exporters:

(i) Steel allocation for export production should be made in bulk once every half year;

(ii) The pricing policy for exporters should pay due regard to the international level of prices and financial charges including internal transport and storage;

(iii) I&SC should be authorized to arrange minor modifications if the rolling programmes in the steel plant to meet urgent export requirements;

(iv) I&SC should meet fresh requirement even at short notice, if necessary, through certain adjustments and diversions from other allottees on request from the Ministry concerned; and

(v) SAIL International should take advance action for imported steel.

112. Considering the comparatively small requirement of power by engineering industries, we recommend that the power cuts as applicable to them should be less severe and can probably be applied by stipulating a ceiling on maximum demand/energy. Engineering units who want to set-up their own diesel generating sets may be allowed of do so with the subsidy from the states and they should be assured to adequate supply for diesel oil for the operation of the generation sets.

113. Government should consider the various recommendations made by the Baveja Working Group as well as by our Committee for removing the bottlenecks in regard to shipping of engineering goods and implement them speedily.

2

COMMITTEE ON RURAL ELECTRIFICATION IN EASTERN STATES, 1974 – REPORT[1]

Chairman	Prof. Siddheshwar Prasad
Members	Shri L.D. Kotoki; Shri Bhola Raut; Shri Yashpal Kapur; Shri A.P. Seethapathy; Shri B.N. Baliga (replaced by Shri H.R. Rao)
M. Secy.	Shri H.K. Bansal

Appointment

The Consultative Committee of the Members of Parliament for the Ministry of Irrigation and Power (now Ministry of Energy), in their meeting held on July 2, 1973, at Kodaikanal had recommended that a Sub-committee consisting of a few members of the Consultative Committee may be formed, so that it could meet the concerned officers of the Eastern States, to understand their problem and review the progress in regard to the Rural Electrification. Further the Estimates Committee in their 39th report have *inter alia* recommended that the Ministry of Energy and the Planning Commission may depute a study team to States which are backwards in the matter of Rural Electrification to impress upon and render necessary assistance to the authorities concern to take immediate steps in the matter.

Accordingly the Ministry of Energy, Government of India, con stituted a Committee on Rural Electrification in Eastern States *vide* their Notification No. 42(29)/73-P.E., dated January 21, 1974.

Terms of Reference

(i) To review the progress achieved in the matter of rural electrification in the States of Assam, Bihar, Manipur, Meghalaya,

---

1. New Delhi, Department of Power, Ministry of Energy, 1975, various pagination

Nagaland, Orissa, Tripura and West Bengal;

(ii) To identify the reasons for slow progress of rural electrification in these States and to recommend steps needed to be taken to accelerate the progress;

(iii) To examine the adequacy of the provision made by these States in their respective plans for rural electrification and the additional resources available from the institutional sources and make such suggestions as may be considered necessary.

(The Ministry of Energy, Government of India *vide* their Notification No. 42(29)/73 P.E., dated March 29, 1974, included the Union Territory of Arunachal Pradesh and Mizoram in the North Eastern Region within the purview of the Committee.)

Contents

Foreword; Summary and Recommendations; Introduction; Deliberations of the Committee; Review of the Progress; Reasons for Slow Progress; Investments and Provisions of Funds for Rural Electrification; Recommendations, Annexures from I to XXXIV.

Recommendations

1. Intensive efforts should be made in all developmental sectors, so as to provide necessary infrastructure for power development.

2. Some suitable agency may be created for coordinated development of tribal areas of Bihar, Orissa, West Bengal and Madhya Pradesh.

Power Development

3. Urgent steps may be taken to utilise the full plant capacities of the existing power stations.

4. Work on the power houses under construction should be expedited.

5. Expeditious action should be taken for investigating and planning the thermal and hydro-power potential in these States for phased exploitation.

6. Intensive efforts should be made for setting up micro-hydral units in remote and hilly areas of the North-Eastern region.

7. The excise duty on diesel oil used for power generation may be waived off for these States.

Transmission and Distribution System

8. Efforts should be made to expeditiously complete and commission the sanctioned transmission and distribution lines including inter-States lines.

9. Transmission systems of these States may be planned for long range power development.

10. For the entire North-Eastern region, planning of transmission system should be done for the region as a whole. Suitable agency for planning and construction of transmission lines in this region may be set-up.

11. Sub-transmission system in North Bihar, North Bengal and Orissa may be strengthened.

Load Promotion

12. Efforts should be made to change the agricultural pattern to avoid crop damage on account of floods and also to make use of fertiliser and high-yielding varieties of seeds.

13. The migratory nature of the tribals should be arrested by providing them with fixed habitats and by encouraging them to practise cultivation at fixed places.

14. Industrial development should be expedited; particularly the industries based on locally available raw-materials, such as forest-based industries and cottage industries, etc.

15. In hilly areas, intensive development of agriculture, horticulture, pisciculture and animal husbandry should be done to suit the local conditions, so that the economic conditions of the local masses improves. Efforts should also be made to develop tourism in these areas.

16. The mineral potential of these States may be assessed and long range programmes to exploit the same may be prepared.

17. In coastal areas, the fishing industry may be revitalised. Tourist resorts can also be developed in these areas.

18. Efforts to set-up industries related to rural electrification may be set-up for maintenance and repairs of agricultural implements, irrigation pump-sets, motors, etc.

19. A committee may be set-up to examine in detail the problems relating to rural industrial development and make suitable recommendations. This committee could also look into the load promotional aspects of rural electrification.

20. Efforts should be made to remove the complaints of the farmers about the procedures, terms and conditions, quality of service, etc., and also for improvement of power supply in rural areas. The recommendations of the "committee on rural consumers' complaints" should be adopted by the Electricity Boards without delay.

Material Shortage

21. Advance planning should be done for procuring materials, required for rural electrification, both on long-range and short-term basis.

22. Wood poles may be used wherever they are available. Jointed wood poles may also be used, so that shorter lengths of timber can be utilised. Timber treatment plants should be set-up so that treated wood poles could be used. Where wood poles are not available, extensive use of RCC and PCC poles should be made and factories for their manufacture established.

23. The rationalised specifications and construction standards as compiled by the Rural Electrification Corporation, should be adopted.

24. The procedure for obtaining allocation of steel, cement, aluminium, zinc and other scarce materials may be improved so as to remove the difficulties experienced by the States.

25. Geo-hydrological surveys should be completed on top priority basis and their results made available to all concerned. The Government of India should provide matching grants to the State Governments for the purpose.

26. State Governments should set-up suitable agencies for repurchase of diesel engines from farmers, so that they can go in for electrified pump-sets. Suitable facilities for providing loans to the farmers for purchase of electricity operated pump-sets may also be made available.

Organisational Aspects

27. The wings responsible for planning and execution of rural

electrification works in these States should be strengthened and made independent, preferably under the charge of a senior officer.

28. The States in North-Eastern region should be provided help in training their personnel in design, construction and maintenance of rural electrification works. The staff posted in difficult and remote areas should be properly compensated.

29. The authority for giving administrative and technical sanctions should be decentralised and quick clearance should be given to the projects.

30. There should be one coordination authority at central level, responsible for development of rural electrification in the country. Similarly, at State level also, there should be one authority responsible for this work, in each State.

31. State Governments should ensure coordination and rational development of all the areas in the States. Special assistance may be provided to areas suffering from natural calamities as geographical debilities. More central sector funds may be invested in such regions. If necessary, State Governments should provide subsidies to the concerned departments, for taking up developmental works in such backward areas.

32. Under the rural electrification programme of minimum needs, the states should concentrate their efforts in a large number of small schemes built around potentially good focal points of development.

Financial Aspects

33. Funds for rural electrification under the State plan outlay should be earmarked and the State Governments should release these funds in full and with utmost expediency. Continued out flow of funds should be ensured by the financing organisations.

34. Central sector funds should be routed more through the State Governments and less through the Rural Electrification Corporation.

35. Early decision may be taken by the Central Government regarding the advancing of funds by the financial institutions including public undertakings, to the Union Territories.

36. The loans under the Minimum Needs Programme for rural electrification may be given as out-right grants to the States of North-Eastern region, or significant concessions/relaxations may be

afforded in the loan-terms. The viability criteria for all rural electrification loans in the Eastern States have to be relaxed.

37. Fifty per cent cost of energisation of pump-sets should be given as subsidy by the concerned Agriculture Departments of the States to the Electricity Boards/Departments. Similarly, part of the cost of village electrification should be subsidised by the beneficiary departments.

38. The availability of Rural Electrification Corporation (REC) loans for rural electrification for each State should be quantified in advance.

39. Advance funds may be made available for purchase of materials for rural electrification for each year. The type of loan recently introduced by R.E.C., for this purpose, may be reviewed, after the reaction of the States to the same is available.

40. In case of rural electrification loans, the criteria of physical progress, for release of second and subsequent instalments, should be relaxed.

41. No prior approval should be considered necessary for minor deviations for sanctioned projects.

42. Additional loans should be provided to meet the increased cost of projects on account of rise in the cost of materials and labour, without affecting the scope of the projects. The relaxations recently introduced by the Rural Electrification Corporation need to be reviewed.

43. The off-working season in these States may be effectively utilised for planning, design, procurement and arrangement of materials and coordination with other organisations, so that the actual execution in the field can be done effectively.

3

COMMITTEE ON RECRUITMENT POLICY AND SELECTION METHODS, 1974 – REPORT[1]

Chairman Dr. D.S. Kothari

Members Prof. S. Chakravarty; Dr. M.L. Dhar; Prof. M.V. Mathur and Shri G. Parthasarathi

Secretary Shri D.R. Kohli

Under Secy. Shri S.K. Bose

Appointment

On January 19, 1974 the Union Public Service Commission held a meeting and a Resolution was adopted "Resolved that a committee be constituted to go into the existing system of recruitment to certain services and posts by the Union Public Service Commission and to recommend such changes as it considers appropriate". So the Committee on Recruitment Policy and Selection Methods was appointed by the Union Public Service Commission *vide* its Notice No. F. 26/21/72-E1(B) dated February 6, 1974.

Terms of Reference

To examine and report on the system of recruitment to the All India and Central Services Class I and Class II followed by the Union Public Service Commission and to recommend such changes in the scheme of examinations and in the selection methods as would give adequate emphasis to knowledge, skills and qualities appropriate to the role and functions of the service in the context of task of national development and reconstruction.

The committee will deal with the following matters in particular –

1. The desirability of having, instead of three examinations as

---

1. Civil Services Examinations, Delhi, Controller of Publications, 1976, 235 p.

at present, a single competitive examination for the All India and Class I services, recruitment to which is made through the I.A.S., etc., examinations;

2. The adequacy of personality test prescribed in the present scheme of the IAS, etc., examinations;

3. The desirability of including more subjects particularly Engineering, Commerce, Agriculture and other technical subjects, and excluding any of the existing subjects, as optional papers in the scheme of the IAS, etc., examinations, and of making any other changes in the scheme of the written part of that examination;

4. The number of chances that should be allowed at the IAS, etc., examinations;

5. The measures necessary to implement the decision of Government about the use of all languages included in the Eighth Schedule to the Constitution, along with English, as media for the IAS, etc., examinations;

6. The arrangements to be made for review at regular intervals of the Syllabi of subjects prescribed for the various examinations to take into account developments as regards courses of study conducted by educational institutions;

7. The system of direct recruitment to the central services and posts, Class I and Class II, otherwise than through the competitive examinations with particular reference to the measures required to speed up recruitment;

8. The feasibility and the procedure to be adopted for bringing down the proportion of candidates to the number of posts to which direct recruitment is required to be made through competitive examinations held by the Commission as well as through selection by interview;

9. Any special arrangements required in the Commission for efficient handling of recruitment to scientific and technical posts;

10. Any other matter which in the opinion of the Committee has a bearing on the aforesaid items or which may be referred to the Committee by the Commission.

Contents

Terms of Reference and Procedure of Work; Introduction and General Principles; Recruitment to All-India and Central Services: Brief History and Present Position; Civil Services Examination :

Proposed Scheme; National Academy of Administration; Summary of Conclusions and Recommendations; Appendices from I to IX.

Recommendations

1. The tasks and challenges which face the country are so colossal, and demand such close cooperation and interaction between people and Government, that it is not enough to have merely competent and skilled administrators. Apart from relevant knowledge and skills, which need to be continually renovated, socio-emotional and moral qualities for working for and with the community are essential. (1.3)[2]

2. We propose that the present method of selection be replaced by a comprehensive method taking into account our special requirements and conditions. The new method that we envisage is a combination of tests for the assessment of knowledge, and intellectual and personal attributes of candidates competing for entry into the higher civil services of our country. A test for intellectual ability alone cannot be regarded as adequate. (1.19)[2]

3. The system of selection for the civil service now in use in the UK is fundamentally different from the pre-war system. It is called method II [cf. Appendix (III)] to distinguish it from the earlier method, now referred to as Method I. We do not regard Method II (or its equivalent) as feasible or particularly advantageous for us. (1.10)[2]

4. We recommend that recruitment to the All India and Central Services (Class I) should be made on the basis of a unified scheme of examination common to all the services. We shall refer to it as the Civil Services Examination Scheme (CSE Scheme). (1.20, 3.3 and 3.17)[2]

The proposed scheme consists of three sequential stages, each making a significant and specific contribution to the total process.

These are –

(i) Civil Services Preliminary Examination (Objective type) for the selection of candidates for the Main Examination;

---

2. Relevant para(s) of the Report.

(ii) Civil Services Main Examination (Written and Interview) to select candidates for entry to the Academy; and

(iii) Civil Services Post Training Test to be conducted by the Union Public Service Commission, on completion of the Foundation Course at the Academy, to assess personal qualities and attributes relevant to the civil services.

5. There is need to devise a simple Preliminary Examination to serve as a screening test for the large number of candidates wishing to compete at the Civil Services Examination. This examination should at the same time be used to substantially widen the base of recruitment. We, therefore, recommend that the proposed Preliminary Examination should be held at a large number of centres dispersed throughout the country, say 100 centres, to begin with. (3.19)[2]

6. The Preliminary Examination is meant to serve as a screening test only; the marks obtained at this examination would have no other function or weightage in the selection process. (3.5 and 3.10)[2]

Question papers will be of the objective type. Question papers other than those for Indian Languages will be set in English. All papers would be of two hours duration.

7. The Preliminary Examination will consist of the following five papers: (3.10)[2]

Paper I –	Indian Languages – to be selected by the candidate from the languages included in the Eighth Schedule to the Constitution	... 300 marks
Paper II –	English Language	Do.
Paper III –	General Studies	Do.
Paper IV & V –	One subject covered in two papers from the list of optional subjects	... 300 marks for each paper

List of Optional Subjects:

Agriculture; Botany; Chemistry; Commerce; Economics; Engineering (Civil, Electrical or Mechanical); Geography; Geology; Indian History; Law; Mathematics; Philosophy; Physics; Political Science; Psychology; Sociology; Zoology.

8. The number of candidates admitted to the Main Examination should be about ten times the total number of vacancies to be

filled in a year in the All India and Central Services. This should determine the standard of the Preliminary Examination. Since candidates would be permitted two attempts at the Main Examination, the number qualifying in a year, on the basis of the Preliminary Examination, should be five times the number of vacancies, averaged, say over the past three years. This number should be mentioned in the annual notification of the examination. This number would be subject to suitable addition of Scheduled Castes and Scheduled Tribes candidates, to ensure that their number is not less than five times the reserved vacancies. (13.5)[2]

9. Civil Services – Main Examination will consist of written papers (2700 marks) and interview (300 marks). Candidates will have the option to answer the papers, except the language papers, in any of the languages included in the Eighth Schedule to the Constitution, and in English. Question papers other than the language papers will be set in English. All Papers will be of three hours duration. (3.11)[2]

10. The written part of the Main Examination will consist of the following papers (3.11)[2] :

Paper I –	Any one of the languages of the candidate's choice from the list of languages included in the Eighth Schedule to the Constitution.	... 300 marks)
Paper II –	English	Do.
Paper III –	Essay	Do.
Paper IV & V –	General Studies	... 300 marks for each paper
Papers VI, VII, VIII & IX		Do.

Candidates will offer two subjects out of the list of optional subjects. There will be two papers for each subject.

List of Optional Subjects

Agriculture; Botany; Chemistry; Commerce; Economics; Engineering (Civil, Electrical or Mechanical); Geography; Geology; History; International Relations; Law; Literature of one of the following languages: Assamese, Bengali, Gujarati, Hindi, Kannada, Kashmiri, Marathi, Malayalam, Oriya, Punjabi, Sanskrit, Sindhi, Tamil, Telugu, Urdu, Arabic, Persian, German, French, Russian and English; Management; Mathematics; Philosophy; Political Science; Physics; Psychology; Public Administration; Sociology; Zoology.

N.B. – Combinations not permissible are Political Science and Public Administration; Political Science and International Relations; Commerce and Management; and Public Administration and Management.

11. We recommend the adoption of the syllabi for the different subjects in the Civil Services Examination as given at Appendix IX. The scope of the syllabus for the optional subject papers for the Main Examination is broadly of the honours degree level, i.e., a level higher than bachelors degree but lower than masters degree. (3.49 and 3.28)[2]

12. The style of question papers also requires a major change. There should be greater emphasis on testing candidates powers of analytical and critical thinking, comprehension of fundamentals, and application of knowledge to meet national needs. (1.32)[2]

13. The list of optional subjects should be neither so restricted as to discourage promising candidates from taking the examination nor too large to seriously effect uniformity of standards. Generally speaking subjects which are of a highly specialised character or which are likely to be offered by only a very limited number of candidates should not be included in the list. The list should also take into account new developments in education. (1.13)[2]

14. The lists of optional subjects recommended for the Preliminary and Main Examinations should be reviewed by the Commission from time to time in consultation with the University Grants Commission and the universities. (3.29)[2]

15. Numeracy and ability to deal with quantitative aspects of problems also needs to be emphasised. (1.6)[2]

16. We recommend that the choice of medium of examination, now available for Essay and General Knowledge papers, should also be extended to subject papers. This is desirable educationally as well as from the point of view of equality of opportunity to eligible candidates. [1.35 and 1.40 (iv)][2]

17. To ensure a uniform standard of the marking of the answer books in different languages is not an easy problem. As a large proportion of answer books would be in English, at any rate for many years to come, these could serve as a kind of *norm* or comparison standard for answer books in other languages. If in any particular language the distribution of marks for answer books – the mean and standard deviation – differ greatly from those for answer books in English, statistical adjustments could be made, if considered neces-

sary by the board of examiners. (1.36)[2]

18. It is important to avoid systematic errors. By systematic errors we mean the tendency of an examiner to uniformally mark high or low answers in one language as compared to answers in an other language. The effect of systematic errors can be reduced by providing a board of examiners, which should lay down detailed guidelines and norms for evaluation of answers. It is desirable that as far as possible, there are on the board at least two examiners to evaluate answers in any given language. It is possible to substantially improve the objectivity of the examination with such as board of examiners and by the adoption of statistical tests and checks. (1.38)[2]

19. We recommend that the question papers should be set by a board of examiners – consisting of 3 members. We feel that the board should include eminent professors and where desirable and feasible, particularly in Science subjects, scholars from well known research institutions. Members of the board may be appointed for a period of 2-3 years with an arrangement that at least one of the members of a board is changed every year. (3.28 and 3.50)[2]

20. It is important that the paper setters for different subjects should set question papers of a more or less equal standard. For this purpose, standard briefing may be given to all members of the boards of examiners. The briefing should highlight the competitive nature of the examination and how a subject like Engineering or Mathematics has to be equated with Botany or Zoology or languages and how important, it is that the standard of various papers should be more or less equal. It will be equally important, when scripts of candidates are assessed, that outstanding scripts in various subjects score more or less equal marks. Further, the spread of marks in different subjects – provided the number in each subject are not too small – should follow more or less the same distribution pattern. (3.52)[2]

21. We suggest that while notifying the examination the Commission should make available to the candidates illustrative sample question papers. (3.53)[2]

22. The number of candidates to be invited on the basis of the results of written papers, to appear before the Interview Board of the Union Public Service Commission will be about twice the number of vacancies to be filled. If this number does not include candidates of the Scheduled Castes and Scheduled Tribes equal to twice the number of reserved vacancies, the Commission may invite an additional number of such candidates for interview by the board. (3.12)[2]

23. The Personality Test, which may now be called an Interview Test, should be regarded as a component of the Main Examination. We recommended that the interview test should carry 300 marks. (3.39)[2]

24. It would be a distinct advantage to have members of the Interview Board, representing a diversity of background and age spectrum. It would also be desirable to include women members on the board. Apart from experts and senior civil and foreign service officers, as far as possible, only serving members of the Union Public Service Commission may be appointed on the board. (3.39)[2]

25. It is important that the members of the boards are not required to sit on the Interview Boards for too long a period. We feel that the total period for interviews for any one board should not exceed one month. (3.40)[2]

26. The members of the Interview Board should be briefed on the techniques of interview so as to achieve a high degree of objectivity and uniformity in assessment. (3.41)[2]

27. We recommend that members of the Interview Board should individually rate intellectual and personal qualities of candidates on a five point scale (much above average, above average, average, below average and much below average). The qualities which could be rated on the Interview Impression Cards would be: clarity of expression, grasp of narrative and argument, reasoning ability, appreciation of different points of view, awareness and concern for socio-economic problems, range and depth of interests; and personal attributes relevant to interaction with people. An appropriate form of the Interview Impression Card may be devised by the Commission in consultation with experts. The final assessment by the board would be based on the discussion of individual assessments made by the members. (3.42)[2]

28. We are of the opinion that generally speaking candidates should be encouraged to answer questions at interviews, in English. Should in an exceptional case a candidate expresses a desire to speak in an Indian language, because of his inability to explain himself adequately in English, the Interview Board should put the candidate at ease and allow him to answer in an Indian language. (3.44)[2]

29. We recommend that no minimum qualifying marks may be fixed for the Interview Test. (3.43)[2]

30. In the compilation of the results for admission to the Academy, marks obtained by the candidates at the written part of the

Main Examination should be added to the marks obtained at the Interview Test. (3.45)[2]

31. The total number of vacancies in the All India and Class I Services in a given year, should determine the number of candidates deemed to have qualified for admission to the Academy. (3.45)[2]

32. The pre-Academy entry result sheet should not disclose the marks and order of merit of the qualifying candidates.(3.45)[2]

33. At the end of the Foundation Course, the trainees would take a Post Training Test conducted by a Board of the Union Public Service Commission. The board should be headed by a member of the Commission, preferably the Chairman. It should include senior members of the administrative and foreign services and three to five other experts. The board should have before it detailed individual reports, prepared by the Academy, on the performance of the trainees during the period of the Foundation Course, including field work. The board could meet at the Academy during the last two months of the Course, interviewing about 10 trainees each day. The Post Training Test should carry 400 marks. (4.6 and 4.7)[2]

34. Allocation of trainees to the various services will be determined by the total of the marks obtained at the Main Examination and the Post Training Test, taking into account their preferences for the services. (3.13 and 4.7)[2]

35. We recommend that the duration of the Foundation Course should be at least one year. The course should aim at developing in trainees a sense of social responsibility and help them to acquire and understanding of problems and tasks of development. The course should include field experience as an essential ingredient. (4.8)[2]

36. A committee of experts may be constituted to outline the detailed syllabus of the Foundation Course. (4.10)[2]

37. We are of the opinion that the Academy requires a complete reorganisation and that to implement our recommendations, this process should be taken in hand immediately. (4.2 and 4.5)[2]

The number of trainees at the Academy is likely to grow in the years to come and may, perhaps, reach a thousand in a decade or two. In planning the reorganisation of the Academy, this aspect should be kept in view.

38. The Academy should be a high level professional institution. It should have links with the Government at the highest level. It would be of great value to the Academy if the Prime Minister were associated with it as Chancellor. The governing body of the Academy

should have the Cabinet Secretary as its President and include senior officers of the All India and Central Services and eminent public men drawn from education, industry and public life. The membership of the governing body should be about 12 and the period of membership be of three years (one third retiring every year). (4.13)[2]

39. The Academy should be headed by a Director of the rank of Secretary to the Government of India. He should be a distinguished administrator or a foreign service officer, or an eminent scholar with administrative experience. The Director should be assisted by a Council of Management. The Council of about 25 members should include some faculty members, officers from the All India and Central Services, and experts from universities, Indian Institutes of Technology and Institutes of Management. (4.14)[2]

40. The Academy's faculty should be a proper mix of various age groups, of high quality administrators, senior foreign service officers and distinguished scholars. (4.15)[2]

41. In order to attract outstanding administrators and scholars to join the faculty, the emoluments and conditions of service of the staff should be adequate. The appointment should be generally on a contract basis and renewable wherever considered necessary. The total strength of the faculty should not be less than 50, to begin with, for covering adequately the wide range of subjects. (4.15)[2]

42. The minimum educational qualification for appearing at the Main Examination will be university degree. Candidates may, however, be permitted to take the Preliminary Examination while studying for their degree. (3.8)[2]

43. A candidate should not be less than 21 years of age and not more than 26 years on 1st July (or on any other date to be prescribed by the Union Public Service Commission for the purpose) of the year in which he appears at the examination, with the usual relaxation of the upper age limit for Scheduled Castes and Scheduled Tribes candidates and other categories as may be notified by the Government from time to time. (3.6, 3.56 and 3.58)[2]

44. We recommend that candidates (including those belonging to Scheduled Castes and Scheduled Tribes) will be permitted only two attempts for the Preliminary Examination and two for the Main Examination. (3.7 and 3.58)[2]

45. The CSE scheme should be implemented in two phases. The first phase should consist of the Preliminary Examination and the Main Examination. We recommend that the first phase be intro-

duced from the 1977 examination. (3.4, 3.46 3.48 and 1.45)[2]

Introduction of the third stage is expected to take more time as it involves reorganization of the National Academy of Administration. Till the introduction of the third stage, the allocation of the successful candidates to the various services will be determined by the marks obtained at the Main Examination (written examination and interview test) as at present. However, during the transitional stage the maximum marks for the interview test should be 500. We think that it should be possible to implement the full scheme by 1980.

46. For determination of the final ranking of candidates, the relative weightage given to the Main Examination and Post Training Test should be 70 : 30. To begin with, however, the relative weightage of the Post Training Test may be fixed at about 15 per cent and which may be raised over a period of 5 years to 30 per cent. (1.27)[2]

47. We recommend that commencing from the 1977 examination, candidates once appointed to All India or Central Services (Class I) should not be permitted to reappear at a subsequent examination without resigning from service. (On introduction of Phase II of the Civil Services Examination Scheme, candidates joining the Foundation Course will not be permitted to reappear at the Main Examination). (3.60)[2]

48. We are of the opinion that a fee of Rs. 30 may be charged for the Preliminary Examination and Rs. 50 for the Main Examination. For Scheduled Castes and Scheduled Tribes candidates, the corresponding fees would be Rs. 7.50 and Rs. 12.50. (3.61)[2]

49. A member of the board of examiners should be paid a fee of about Rs. 300 for the descriptive type question papers of the Main Examination. For setting of objective type question papers, a fee of Rs. 500 may be paid to each examiner. (3.62)[2]

50. We strongly recommend that candidates from weaker sections of the community, who qualify at this examination, should be provided with special counselling and guidance by the universities, and financial assistance by the State Governments to compete for the Main Examination. (1.21)[2]

51. Introduction of the objective type examination would need careful preparatory work by the Union Public Service Commission. There are also many other problems connected with competitive examinations which would require detailed study by competent research staff. An adequately staffed examination wing with facilities for research studies and computer work is essential for the Commis-

sion. It should be headed by an outstanding expert. (3.21 and 1.41)[2]

52. There should be a continuing review, by the Commission and the Personnel Department, of the standard of recruitment for the various services, using appropriate indices and statistical methods. If there is a noticeable lowering of standards, special steps should be taken by the Union Public Service Commission and where necessary by the Government, to remedy the situation. (1.41)[2]

53. Steps should be taken to promote dissemination of relevant information, visits to universities and colleges by members and senior staff of the Commission, opening of more examination centres, and in other ways to widen the base of recruitment, without lowering standards, so that large sections of the community and parts of the country which are at present under represented in the higher services have a more balanced representation. (1.41)[2]

54. A selection process or method used by the Union Public Service Commission should satisfy in our view certain basic requirements. These are (1.40)[2] –

(i) It should command the complete confidence and trust of candidates, of the Government and the public generally. Integrity is of the utmost importance.

(ii) It should provide to the maximum possible extent equality of opportunity to promising candidates irrespective of their assessment of relevant intellectual and personal qualities and attributes/motivations, irrespective social status, region and the university degree subjects.

(iii) It should be such as would encourage candidates with appropriate attributes and qualities to offer themselves for selection. Deliberate effort should be made by the Commission to widen continually the base of recruitment with special attention to deserving candidates belonging to the weaker sections of the community.

(iv) Candidates should have option to choose any of the Eighth Scheduled languages or English for the medium of the Union Public Service Commission examinations (written).

(v) The various tests of knowledge, skill and personality should make full use of new developments/techniques in the methods of assessment. Each part of the selection process should make a significant contribution towards the final selection.

More than ordinary care is necessary with regard to the

appointment of examiners and interviewers. They should be outstanding in their respective fields.

(vi) It should be clearly recognised that there are certain essential qualities which defy description in words but which a "good judge of men" can usually assess with a fair degree of reliability. An interview by competent board is an indispensable element of the selection process.

(vii) The method should be under continuous review and evaluation; continuing improvement in the light of experience and new developments is essential.

55. There are several important aspects of the work of the Commission for which it would be a distinct advantage to have a Standing Advisory Committee appointed by the Commission. The advice of the Committee would be of great value regarding policy and action on questions of examination reform, personality test, expansion of the base of recruitment and improvement in the opportunities open to promising candidates belonging to backward communities and areas. Such as Committee could meet two or three times a year. The Chairman of the Commission should be the Chairman of the Committee and the members, about 15, should be drawn from universities, industry and public life. The term of membership should be three years, a third of the members retiring every year. (1.44)[2]

4

COMMITTEE ON DRUGS AND PHARMACEUTICAL INDUSTRY, 1974 – REPORT[1]

Chairman Shri Jai Sukh Lal Hathi

Members Shri Yashpal Kapur; Shri Vasant Sathe; Dr. Ranen Sen; Shri K.S. Chavda; Shri C.M. Stephen; Dr. M.L. Dhar; Dr. B.D. Tilak; Shri S.S. Marathe, Shri Vinod Kumar; Shri P.S. Ramachandran; Dr. B. Shah; Dr. B.V. Ranga Rao; Shri M.K. Rangnekar

M. Secy. Dr. P.R. Gupta

Appointment

The functioning and growth of the Drugs and Pharmaceutical Industry in India over the past few years were engaging the attention of the Government for quite sometime, particularly with a view to finding out ways and means to meet the growing requirements and broad social objectives before the country. Questions about the performance of the public sector units, multi-national firms gaining stronghold in this field, prices of locally produced medicines, etc., were raised in the Parliament. Following a suggestion made in the Parliament, the Government of India in the Ministry of Petroleum and Chemicals, set-up a Committee by a Resolution No.3(26)/173-Ch. III dated the 8th February, 1974.

The Government of India appointed the above Committee to go into the various facets of the Drug Industry in India with a view to promoting growth of the Drug Industry particularly of the Indian and small sectors, improve technological development, taken effective Quality Control measures on drugs, reduce the prices of medicines, as well as to rationalise the price structure, provide essential drugs throughout the country, and make available raw materials to the in-

1. Delhi, Controller of Publications, 1975, 275 p.

dustry particularly to the small scale sector, . etc., Appointment of such a Committee was also felt necessary in the context of the large-scale expansion of the drug and pharmaceutical industry envisaged during the Fifth Five-Year Plan period, with a view to ensuring the regulated and rapid growth of drug manufacture.

Terms of Reference

(i) To enquire into the progress made by the industry and the status achieved by it.

(ii) To recommend measures necessary for ensuring that the public sector attains a leadership role in the manufacture of basic drugs and formulations, and in research and development.

(iii) To make recommendations for promoting the rapid growth of the drug industry and, particularly, of the Indian and Small Scale Industries Sector. In making its recommendations the Commission will keep in view the need for a balanced regional dispersal of the Industry.

(iv) To examine the present arrangements for the flow of new technology into the industry, and make recommendations therefor.

(v) To recommend measures for effective quality control of drugs, and for rendering assistance to small-scale units in this regard.

(vi) To examine the measures taken so far to reduce the prices of drugs for the consumer, and to recommend such further measures as may be necessary to rationalise the prices of basic drugs and formulations.

(vii) To recommend measures for providing essential drugs and common household remedies to the general public, especially in the rural areas.

(viii) To recommend institutional and other arrangements to ensure equitable distribution of basic drugs and raw materials especially to the Small Scale Sector.

The Committee will ascertain and take into consideration the views of the State Governments and other interests concerned, as may be found necessary.

Contents

Introduction; Progress Made and Status Achieved by the Pharmaceutical Industry Public Sector; National Drug Authority;

Development of the Drug Industry and the Indian Sector; Raw Materials for Bulk Drug Manufacture; Development and Flow of Technology; Pricing of Drugs and Pharmaceuticals; Quality Control of Drugs; Measures for Providing Essential Drugs and Common Household Remedies to the General Public especially in Rural Areas and Abolition of Brand Names for Drugs; Conclusion and Acknowledgement.

Recommendations (Public Sector)

With a view to streamlining the operations and achieving the basic objectives of producing distributing essential drugs to the largest number of people as economically as may be possible, the Committee recommends the establishment of a National Drug Authority (NDA) which will also lay down and co-ordinate the policies.

In appreciation of the fact that ill health has major socio-economic implications, the Committee feels that in welfare State, availability of prophylactics and curatives should receive the highest priority as per with food and shelter. Production and distribution of drugs should, therefore, constitute an important social responsibility of the State.

The Committee is of the opinion that trade aspects of this total industry should be divorced from the ordinarily accepted principles of trade for profit. Indeed, the Committee feels that trade aspects in this field should be limited only to the extent that the industry generates resources for its own growth and expansion through R and D, where necessary, to meet the increasing needs of the nations.

In order to achieve the above objectives, the Committee feels that leading role for production and distribution of drugs and pharmaceuticals should vest with the State. The Committee makes the following recommendations for providing to the public sector a leading role in the production and distribution of essential drugs and pharmaceuticals.

The public sector should be given the major role for the production of capital and technology intensive bulk drugs such as are needed in high tonnage quantities and where large scale production would be economically preferable.

The Committee feels that the basic data used by the NCST and the Task force appointed by the Planning Commission conforms to the existing pattern of market needs rather than the social needs of the country. There is urgent need to institutionalise data collection and base the national production targets in terms of the needs identified by such a system. The Committee also emphasise the necessity of fixing growth target and judging the growth rate in terms of individual quantities.

It is essential that raw materials for the production of bulk drugs arising out of the effort of either the public sector or the private sector units should meet the priority needs of bulk drug industry.

In the order of importance, the Committee has identified 14 plants having medicinal value, out of which 8, namely, dioscorcea species, cinchona, poppy, ergot, digitates, ipecac, dubesia (or atropa), and lemon grass are the sources for essential drug identified by this Committee.

The Committee strongly endorses the recommendations of the NCST for increased cultivation of the 14 plant materials and also production of active principles obtainable therefore with updated technology.

In view of the vital and growing importance of the drugs derived from the identified plant materials, cultivation of these plants, which is technology, finance, and labour intensive, should be taken up in a determined and business the manner under the public sector/joint sector.

IDPL should utilize the capacity that was originally created for the production of chlor-tetracycline, for the productive of tetracycline and oxytetracycline.

Although such antibiotics as erythromycin, ampicillin, etc., have not been identified as essential drugs, the Committee feels that it may be desirable to produce these in public sector because of their heavy imports. Ampicillin in Deoxy-oxytetracycline may be produced in the public sector particularly because the starting material for ampicillin and deoxy-oxytetracycline are already being produced in the public sector.

Public sector units should between themselves divide the responsibilities for the production of individuals illness so that they may attain the required level of specialisation and sophistication in their respective lines of effort.

The Committee stresses the needs for the creation of active centres for enzyme production to be preceded by the setting up of a strong centre for R and D in enzymology and enzyme technology.

Considering the importance of insulin production and utilization of the products available from the slaughter houses, the work of development of the sensitive items may be allocated to the bio-chemical units at S.V.P. Chest Institute, Delhi, Haffkine Institute Bombay and other Institutions like CDRI where facilities for such work exist.

The production of immunological agents at the State-owned institutions and in the private Indian Sector should be upsealed and streamlined to meet the needs of the country and also for exports.

The Committee noted that recovery of chemicals from coal-tar distillations products has been undertaken at Durgapur on a fairly large scale. New units should be established for the manufacture of bulk drugs at Durgapur to utilize the available downstream products.

While considering the licensing of new drugs manufactured abroad, the main consideration should be that the proposed new drugs have distinct advantages over the existing range of drugs, for which therapeutical character should be scrutinized by a Committee of experts.

Public sector has developed technological competence in the field of synthetic drugs and can be entrusted with the heavier responsibilities with confidence.

The Committee has identified 44 drugs derived purely from synthetic sources as essential drugs.

The public sector should take the responsibility of expending the production of analgin, piperzine, phenobarbitone, sulphadimidine, folic acid, vitamin B_1, and vitamin B_2, up to the quantities envisaged for the Fifth and Sixth Plan periods.

The Committee recommends that the first option for the production of nicotinamide, paracetamol, and PAS salts should be given purely to the Indian sector and if necessary, their production may be shared with public sector. In respect of sulphacetamide, the increased requirements should be met by public sector.

The following eight drugs, appearing in the essential drugs list and which are currently largely imported, should be produced in the public sector in quantities projected for the Fifth and Sixth Plan periods, taking into account the quantities for which capacities have already been licensed:-

1. Nitrofurantoin
2. Nitrofurazone
3. Fursemide

4. Pyridoxine Hydrochloride
5. Theophylline
6. Phthayl Sulfalthiazole
7. Aminophylline
8. Calcium Pantothenate

Immediate steps should be taken to co-ordinate the work already done in respect of developing production technologies of the eight drugs mentioned above, in the National Laboratories and the public sector, to upscale their processes through pilot-type large scale production within the next 24 months. If technology for any of the above drugs is found not to conform to economic working, such technology should be imported by the concerned public sector unit on priority basis. Licences for import of raw materials for these drugs, wherever necessary should also be given on a priority basis. The Committee feels that the production of Vitamin B_6 in particular should be expedited and recommends that the available indigenous technology should be assessed within next six months by the concerned Ministry/NDA and necessary decision to import or otherwise of the technology should be taken as early as possible.

Production of Metron-dezole should be undertaken in the public sector and high priority should be given to upscale the laboratory process and, if necessary, the relevant technology may also be imported.

While facilities should be provided to purely Indian Units to reach the licensed capacity for the production of Chloroquin, public sector should also undertake its production in a big way and fulfil the targets for 1978-79 and 1983-84.

No additional capacities for the manufacture of Methyl salicylate, Lignocaine, Dapsone vitamin D_2/D_3, Tolbutamide and Mepheritermine sulphate would be necessary at present and the existing licence-holder should be asked to work up to the licensed capacities.

Expansion in the capacities for Halogenated-8-Oxyquinolines, Acetyl Salicylic acid, pethidine, aspirin, and Vitamin C should be handled entirely between the public sector and Indian units to meet the national requirements.

Public sector should also take up the manufacture for Primaquin, Chlorpromazine, Succinyl choline chloride Thiopental, Adrenative, Noradrenaline, Oxytocin, Chlorpheniramine, Moleateand Hydro chlorthiazide. The Committee also recommends that Ephedrine should be manufactured in the Indian sector should be given the necessary licence to produce such quantity as may be required for the Fifth and Sixth Plan periods.

The public sector may produce sulphaemetheoxazole, indomethacin, ethambutol, diazepam, chlordiazepoxide, secobarbitone, trimethoprin and methyl dope, etc., which are currently largely imported.

At least 60 per cent of the bulk drugs produced by the public sector should be formulated by the Public Sector Industry itself. In the disposal of the remaining 40 per cent, first preference should be given to the Indian sector, particularly the small scale sector units.

The public sector should be required to manufacture 34 items of bulk drugs in quantities indicated against these for the Fifth-Five Year Plan by setting up additional capacities.

To ensure the production of 34 bulk drugs in quantities indicated in these two paras, the public sector will require an outlay of Rs. 51 crores in 1973 value of the rupee. For formulating, 60 per cent of their total production of bulk drugs, they will require another about Rs. 18 crores at the 1973 value of rupee.

Healthy industrial relation at all points in the production and management of the public sector should be developed to achieve the desired results.

The management should have a degree of freedom to act in every respect subject to the over all supervision by Government/NDA.

The present system of production and distribution of drugs needs revision to confirm to our social needs.

Working of the public sector plants at all levels should be carefully reorganized in respect of every step including purchase and standardization, production of bulk drugs and formulations, their storage and distribution, etc., Each unit should operate strictly on economic basis.

Raw materials and intermediates produced or manufactured indigenously in the public sector and such other units which come into existence hereafter should be made available to the Public Sector Units engaged in drug production on the basis of highest priority.

The R & D Laboratories of all the Public Sector drug manufacturing units should be strengthened immediately by reasonably liberal allocations in men, equipment and materials. A sound R & D base is the best insurance for the growth by the drugs and pharmaceutical industry.

Avoidable duplication of R & D efforts must be discouraged and the results available at each unit must be made available to the other related unit. There should be no secrets between the Public Sector Units. Any improvement in a strain or a process or a plant developed in the R and D laboratory of one unit should be freely available for use by the other units.

Public Sector Units must establish the closet liaison with the other R and D laboratories of the National Laboratories, State Institutions and other Educational Institutions under the supervision of NDA. Appropriate facilities should be created in the identified institutions wherever necessary, to permit time-bound completion of individual projects.

Public Sector should set an example in respect of R and D activity in the drugs field and to begin with should aside at least five per cent of their net turn-over for this purpose.

Public Sector should engage the indigenous engineering and designing units to meet their requirements of equipments, instruments and appliances of high precision.

To achieve increased production of Antibiotics expeditiously high yielding strains of micro-organism and the associated balancing technology should be allowed to be purchased as per conditions.

Public Sector Units should be allowed to use the Patents/invention as permissible under Section 99 and 100 of the Patents Act, 1970.

Early steps should be taken, with a time-bound programme to expand capacities and also instal new capacities, whenever necessary, to enable the Public Sector to fulfil the production obligations as recommended by this Committee.

Whenever possible Public Sector units should also produce bulk intermediates.

Additional formulation levels should be set-up in the country immediately. M/s. Smith Sanistreet, which is presently managed by IDPL should be taken over by IDPL and strengthened and converted into a modern pharmaceutical unit.

Distribution systems in the Public Sector should make use of unconventional agencies such as Primary Health Centres, Panchayats Dispensaries, Post Offices, Petrol and Kerosene Sales Depots, etc., for the distribution of household remedies. There is need to evolve a wide distribution system suited to our own socio-economic, ecological conditions.

All pharmaceutical units in the Public Sector should have strong Boards of Directors.

Additional Recommendations and Suggestions

Items which are the part of the approved productions programme of public sector units of items in respect of which public sector has the capacity to produce should ordinarily not be licensed to private sector units. However, in order to ensure that such a reservation of items does not result in shortages, or increased need for imports, an annual implementation programme should be drawn up in the first quarter of the calendar year. This programme will have to be kept under review; and on the basis of such a review twice a year, appropriate adjustments should be made in the items to be licensed to units outside the public sector.

Capital requirement for achieving the targeted figures for 1978-79 both for bulk and formulation (60% of bulk) production of antibiotics is estimated of Rs. 15 crores in terms of 1973 prices.

The Public Sector may farm out to the purely Indian Sector, particularly the units run by technocrat entrepreneurs, its needs for relatively low-cost tonnage intermediates. And, for this public sector should accept the responsibility to provide the basic technology to the entrepreneurs.

The public sector should be so planned that its constituent units for bulk production for basic drugs and their intermediates are set-up in different parts of the country subject to the desirability of centralizing single raw material or single/similar technology line products of one place for reasons for economy; the choice of the site for a unit being dictated only by economic compatibilities.

The State Governments and the Government of India should obtain all the governmental and Corporation needs of such of the drugs as are produced in the public sector from this sector at prices that may be fixed by a body of cost accountants, in consultation with the concerned public sector unit and the BICP. The ruling principle for determination of prices should be that the drugs must reach the largest number of people and profitability should be limited only to ensure progressive growth of the industry for meeting the increasing needs of the nation, with its own resources.

The existing public sector units should consolidate their technological gains and give first priority to the expansion of production of the items for which they have the necessary know-how skills. The magnitude of this expansion should be limited only by the magnitude of the estimated national needs in the next ten years. Simultaneously efforts must be made to improve, by innovation, the technologic or such other products as may already be within the production programmes of the public sector units and for which the present technologic need improvement.

Urgent steps should be taken to ensure employment of competent technologist and management experts and provide necessary in job training facilities for different cadres.

Constant appraisal and updating of the economics of in-plant operation as also of management procedures and practices and speedy implementation of improvements, as and when these occur, should be assured of both the plant and management levels.

In respect of the import of technologies concurrent purchase of equipment should be avoided. In every case of import of technology, the R & D units of the industry, and their collaborators should be associated from the very beginning. This would ensure that sophistication from the stage of import upwards may be brought about indigenously. Each imported technology should be freely available to all the relevant public and Indian sector units.

Development of the Drug Industry and the Indian Sectors

The Committee recommends that the restrictions stated to have been imposed at the Industry requiring the units having a turnover of Rs.2 crores and more to produce the bulk drugs required for new formulations, should be removed for the Indian Sector, and the foreign companies which have been producing formulations based on imported bulk drugs, should be made to manufacture the bulk drugs within a specified period.

As regards the Indian Sector of the Industry, more liberal policy is necessary to encourage. The Indian companies to make their contribution to the production of bulk drugs and formulations.

The Indian sector should maintain an effective dialogue with the medical profession regarding their products.

To encourage the Indian sector to take up the manufacture of bulk drugs, Government should impose ban on the import of such items, as and when it comes to the notice of Government. Expeditious decision should be taken by Government in this regard.

Highest priority has to be accorded to centrally directed research aimed at discovering newer drugs for the treatment of tropical diseases like malaria, filaria, etc., side by side, research for new drugs in the treatment of disease of cardio-vascular system, metabiotic disorders, etc., as well as for anticonceptive purposes, need to be accelerated.

Besides making the country self-sufficient in regard to drugs, medical service of a rudimentary nature in the remote villages should be introduced, where common house-hold remedies for cough, cold, fever, antacid preparations, etc., should be made available in pilfer-proof packings sufficient to meet 3-4 days treatment.

The Committee feels that in our anxiety to produce more drugs, we should not adopt a policy which places the Indian manufacturers of a disadvantage. On the contrary, if the choice were between the foreign companies and the Indian companies, encouragement should be given to the Indian companies which are technically competent.

The Committee suggests that the potentiality of foreign companies to exploit their names and smother the development of Indian sector of the Industry should be blunted and a more purposeful and positive policy to help the Indian sector should be simultaneously implemented.

The Committee recommended by a majority view that the multinational firms should over forthwith.

The Committee recommends that having regard to the present stage of development of the drug industry for the purpose of FERA guidelines, this industry should not be eligible for the preferential treatment given to items specified in the Industrial Licensing Policy of 1973. Foreign undertakings operating in this country should be directed to bring down their equity to 40 per cent forthwith and further reduce it progressively to 26 per cent. This however, is without prejudice to other concession to which they are eligible as a result of the industry being in the Industrial Licensing Policy of 1973. The Committee would further recommend that dilution of foreign equity should not take the form of dispersed holdings of the shares by large number of Indian nationals. It would be desirable for government to purchase these shares either by public sector undertakings which are directly or indirectly connected with the manufacture of drugs/chemicals, or by public financial institutions or by government itself.

The companies who are producing bulk drugs in excess of their licensed capacities, should be made to part with 50 per cent of their production beyond their licensed capacity, in addition to 50 per cent of their authorised production.

Those who are producing in accordance with the specified capacities should be made to part with 50 per cent of their production to non-associated formulations. In regard to new drugs which are developed as a result of research carried out in the country, there is no need to impose such a condition. This will automatically; negate the Government Notification No. 3(3)/65-Ch. III dated the 27th May, 1969.

Wherever manufactured of bulk drugs is carried as from penultimate stage, the companies concerned should be directed to manufacture the drug from basic stage within a period of two years.

In regard to the capacities approved for the manufacture of bulk drugs against permission letters and C.O.B. Licences, the Committee recommends that having regard to the national need for bulk drugs, the permission letters and C.O.B. licences issued to such firms, may be regularised on the condition that –

(a) all bulk drugs and manufactured from the basic stages; and
(b) fifty per cent of the production of basic drugs should be made available to non-associated Indian formulators.

So far as formulations covered by Permission letters/C.O.B. Licences are concerned, in order that there may not be a gap between production and market demand thereby creating a shortage in the market, the Indian firms applying for the manufacture of such formulations should be given licences liberally forthwith and the foreign firms should be asked to switch over within one year to the manufacture of bulk drugs and formulations to the extent of 50 per cent of the production of basic drugs by them, and the balance 50 per cent to be supplied to non-associated formulators.

In regard to bulk drugs for which no capacities have been fixed in the C.O.B. licences, capacities should be pegged at the level of production achieved in 1973. Likewise, the capacities of all formulations should be fixed.

In regard to formulations for which combined capacities have been fixed, the capacity for each formulation should be specified separately. Wherever, demand warrants, the firm may be permitted to exceed their capacity by 15 per cent, if needed in national interest.

Where foreign undertakings are producing in Indian drug formulations using imported bulk drugs, they should start and complete manufacture from the basic stage within a period of three years, failing which they should not be allowed to continue marketing the formulations after the said period. If, however, the manufacture of such bulk drugs have been assigned to the public sector limits, their manufacture should be taken up by the public sector. All research talents available in the academic institutions and the national laboratories should be mobilised and work on the production of bulk drugs in a time-bound programme should be undertaken. If for some reason, the public sector undertakings are not in a position to take up the manufacture of the bulk drugs, the Indian sector of the Industry should be offered the second choice, who, in turn, should take up this work on a time-bound programme.

Indian drugs manufacturers who are already engaged in the manufacture of the bulk drugs, identified by the Task Force, up to 10 per cent of their local turnover should be freely allowed to make all drug formulations, subject to their therapeutic being accepted by the Drug Control authorities.

Foreign companies which are already engaged in the manufacture of household remedies such as alcohol-based tonics, vitamin, preparations, etc., should not be granted any expansion in capacity, nor should they be allowed to take up such activity as additional items hereafter, nor be allowed to manufacture such items beyond the capacity mentioned in the Industrial Licence of application for registration.

The Committee suggests that penal action should be taken against branches of foreign companies or 100 per cent foreign equity holding units, manufacturing drugs without Government authority (Valid licence).

The Committee suggests that the NDA should review the norms for payment of research contribution, technical know-how fees, etc., by foreign companies.

The Committee recommends that a suitable machinery should be evolved to check that the conditions imposed in industrial and other licences are fulfilled by foreign firms before remittances broad are permitted.

The small scale should be a prohibited area for foreign companies.

The Committee recommends that excise duty should be levied on drugs sample distributed by manufacturers. All expenditure incurred on samples by drug manufactures should not be deemed to be business expenditure for purposes of corporate taxation. Supply of samples may, however, be permitted, as at present, for the first three years from the date of introduction of a product for the first time by an Indian company.

The Committee appreciates the importance of educating the people residing in rural areas about the use of household remedies, and advertisements of drugs may have to be permitted to serve this limited need.

The prices of imported bulk drugs, intermediates and raw materials should be screened by the NDA and wherever there are reasons to doubt that they are excessive, the prices should be brought down. If the directions, issued by Government in this connection are not complied with by the companies, the letter should be taken over by Government.

The NDA should look into the cases of all unimplemented licences, including those involving basic manufacture of bulk drugs in a phased manner, and should suggest necessary action.

Trade-marks registered in India by foreign firms for formulations should not be permitted to be renewed if similar formulations are processed in India by Indian firms. The provisions of the Trade and Merchandise Marks Act should be examined in this connection.

In regard to allotment of raw materials to Indian sector, the Committee recommends that liberal allocations of raw materials for essential new formulations and to new units should be made.

Indian firms should be given special consideration, in matters relating to exports, as follows: –

(a) wholly Indian companies should be exempted from the export obligation as applicable presently; and
(b) additional incentives like extra foreign exchange for import of raw materials and components should be provided in case they export their products.

The monetary limit for investment in plant and machinery for small scale unit in the drug industry should be raised to Rs. 20 lakhs.

The NDA should look into the difficulties by the small scale sector in obtaining import licences for machinery and equipment and a satisfactory solution be found. The Committee also wishes to point out that the recommendations made by a Committee appointed by the Ministry of Petroleum and Chemicals, soon after the price control measure cover drugs were introduced to help the small scale sector of the industry, should be implemented expeditiously.

Small scale manufacturers producing bulk drugs should be advised by the State Drug Control Authority to register their production capacities with the DGTD, Drug Controller (India), and the Ministry of Petroleum and Chemicals. Registration of capacities should be done on the basis of the information supplied by manufacturers through the State Drug Control Authorities regarding their potential capacity of production, the level of production achieved, the raw materials required for manufacture, the specifications of the drug and their sale prices. The capacities for production as registered should be taken into account by Government while granting Industrial Licences.

The NDA should maintain a comprehensive Drug Information Service.

The Committee recommends that a subject index should be prepared immediately and maintained by the Patent Controller's Office, regarding the pending applications to guide the intending entrepreneurs who after inspecting the same could decide the course of action themselves. It should also be helpful if the Patents Office brings out a list of patents applications which are rejected after examination by that office. The Committee would also recommends that wherever an Indian entrepreneur has set-up any basic production. Within a certain specified period which might infringe on the coverage claimed in the pending applications, a suitable solution should be found out whereby the concerned entrepreneurs could with their manufacturing operations.

Whenever foreign companies apply for manufacture of bulk drugs, Government should issue a notice about the application and its terms and ask the Indian companies and the public sector units to inform with a period of two months, whether they can take up the manufacture of such drugs. The applications should be considered in the light of the replies received from Indian companies and the public sector units. This, however, will not apply to applications received for bulk drugs manufactured in accordance with the recommendations made.

A special cell should be established in the NDA to process the representations received from the drug industry in connection with the availability of raw materials, solvents, etc., from indigenous sources. NDA should look into this problem expeditiously in consultation with the various agencies involved.

The Government should keep medical profession in touch with the policies and concepts on the development of drug industry. For this purpose, NDA should have a top-level Committee consisting of the representatives of the medical profession, Ministry of Health, various sectors of the drug industry and State Drug Controller.

Export of basic chemicals, solvents and bulk drugs which the imports are deficient in, should not be allowed.

Indian Council of Medical Research should concentrate its attention particularly on the discovery of the newer drugs for tropical diseases. NDA should be assigned the supervisory task in this regard. The Committee endorses the recommendations of the Task Force on the subject.

NDA should screen the import of technology required by the drugs industry. The import of drugs having low-volume turnover, like anti-career drugs, should be allowed for a period of two years. At the end of two years, if the sales value exceeds Rs.10 lakhs, the concerned units should be permitted to undertake the bulk manufacture of the drug, on payment of royalty up to 5 per cent of net sales realisation of the finished products, i.e., such value minus excise duty and trade commission. Export obligations need not be imposed in such cases.

Considering the vastness of the country, dispersal of the industry is essential. Within States, the industry should not be allowed to concentrate in or around towns and cities. States should provide sufficient incentives to the industry and help them to develop in the backward regions where the basic facilities are available.

State Governments should enlist the support of drug manufacturers, leading organic chemists, botanists, etc., and make a survey of the raw material, plant products, animal products solvents, etc., that are available in their regions.

States should also publish brochures setting forth the raw material position and the facilities and concessions that prospective manufacturers can hope to receive. They should also form Joint Sector Ventures in collaboration with well established companies or technical entrepreneurs. West Bengal offers good scope for development of phyto-chemical industry in that State in the Joint Sector. Joint Sector Ventures should also be set-up for the manufacture of glass containers, tubings for ampoules and other packing materials like aluminium foils, etc.

In view of the soaring prices and inadequate availability position of petroleum-based chemicals, greater attention should be paid on coal carbonisation, as abundant supplies of coal are available in the country. The coal carbonisation complex situated in Durgapur has already been developed to a certain stage and its potentiality should be explored fully by the Central Government. Similarly the coal reserves in Maharashtra and Andhra Pradesh should be utilised and coal carbonisation complexes be developed in those regions. The Committee would urge as the State Governments and Central Government to give serious consideration to the development and utilisation of these coal resources.

Uninterrupted supplies of electric power and abundant supply of water should be ensured to the drug industry.

Our recommendations for regularising production by foreign units in excess of their licensed capacity in subject to the overall condition that this should only be allowed if Indian Sector or the public sector is not manufacturing this or there is no scope of it being manufactured in the near future.

Raw Materials for Bulk Drug Manufacture

The Committee understands that several export bodies have examined in detail the possibilities of setting up of facilities in various parts of the country, like modern slaughter houses, facilities for collection and storage of glands, extraction of active principles, etc. The Committee is of the opinion that these valuable raw materials which are now being wasted in large quantities could be used profitably for biological products, sutures, etc.

In regard to manufacture of chemical intermediates scale industries especially those set-up by the technical entrepreneurs can play a very important role. Guidance from both the users of such intermediates as well as the Research Laboratories in the country are required in setting up units for their production. The State Governments and financial institutions who are offering special concessions to these young entrepreneurs need to be streamlined for all accelerating this development.

The Committee understands that the question of distribution of molasses for the production of alcohol has received the attention of the Central Government but because it happens to be a State subject, there have been difficulties in evolving a more rational and effective system of pricing/distribution controls, on molasses which would protect the supplies for industrial use. The Committee recommends that this question should be persued vigorously so that the essential requirements of alcohol, particularly of the chemical-based industries are met with, irrespective of the fluctuations in the output of sugar and, therefore, of molasses.

It has been brought to the notice of this Committee that different States charge different rates of excise duty on alcohol with the result that there is disparity in prices and availability. The Committee recommends that Government should examine this aspect and ensure that this disparity is eliminated.

Presently, there is only one source for Methyl-alcohol. It is necessary to have an alternate source to ensure regular supply of methyl-alcohol.

Valuable chemicals like Benzene and Toluene should be made available to the chemical industry and these should not be used as is done in the steel plants. Steps should also be taken to ensure that in the coke oven of the new Bokaro Steel Plant where 45,000 tonnes of Benzene and the corresponding amount of Toluene can be obtained from the coke ovens should be recovered and made available to organic chemical industries.

The acid sludge, obtained from the acid wash of coke oven gases contain valuable pyridine bases and this should be pooled from all the steel plants, for recovery of valuable items like pyridine, picolines, and quinolines.

Linking of basic chemicals with intermediates required by chemical-based industries not yet produced in the country is a continuous process and a challange will have to be taken up both by the industries and the R & D institutions in the country. Wherever, technologies are available in this direction, there should be no hesitation in obtaining the best and our efforts concentrated in improving them further. Harnessing the potentialities of the technologists that are coming out of the Educational Institutions, is another important factor in this direction. The integrated development of chemical raw materials and intermediates in the main factor that will increase the technical base of the country. Processing a large number of imported products does not build the required chemical base even if it be by mainly Indian owned firms but on the other hand only increases our dependence on other countries. All available facilities, in this direction, should be fully utilised to raise the technical base of the country.

All the naptha produced should be fully utilised by setting up recovery units near the refineries for recovering the aromatic chemicals like Benzene, Toluene and Xylene. This will enable more intermediates being produced for the drugs and other chemical based industries.

Although it would be desirable to regulate the import of raw materials for all formulations, a beginning should be made, whereby a central agency imports all bulk drugs and intermediates needed for the 117 essential formulations identified by the Committee. This should be done by the National Drug Authority, who will also import raw materials and the ingredients required for these drugs and distribute them to the concerned manufacturers. The NDA will also stipulate the quantities of formulations that should be produced by the firms out of the basic drugs supplied to them and ensure that the manufacturers utilise then properly. The Committee also hopes that as the NDA expands, it would progressively improve and expand its activity in this direction.

NDA would advise various manufacturers to regulate their production in accordance with the demand pattern and would also control the distribution of the drugs so produced among formulators. To begin with, the bulk drugs indigenously produced and the chemicals required for the production of 117 items as identified by this Committee, should be pooled by the NDA and distributed to the manufacturers according to their requirements.

NDA should take up the responsibility of coordinating the production and distribution of the chemicals which are required for the manufacture of drugs in the country. In the case of alcohol, this Authority should also persuade the State Governments to ear-mark the bona fide requirements of the drugs industry.

NDA should also lookafter the requirements of packing materials, like glass/plastic bottles, rubber stoppers, colophane/aluminium strips and such other essential packing materials required by the drug industry.

Development and Flow of Technology

There is need for increased productivity in a rationalised manner of all that we produce now and diversification of production to cater to national needs on a priority basis.

There are two broad areas where flow of technology is important in the field of Pharmaceuticals in our country. The first is with regard to the existing drugs, to produce the essential items in quantities adequate to meet our increasing requirements and maximise production from available resources and manufacturing facilities already established. Secondly, there are areas where existing drugs are not really very effective or where no curative drugs exist for certain diseases in the country. In this case, technology has to deal with research and introduction of better and more efficacious remedies for treatment.

Stepping up of production by the existing units by improvement of technology through R & D activities and efforts of the State owned research laboratories are very important. This should not, however, preclude obtaining from abroad – crucial technology for the purpose. Harnessing our limited resources of R & D facilities will definitely yield better results by concentrating on selected fields and also an improvement of imported processes.

Another important field where this country can take advantage of the special climate and soil conditions is the scientific cultivation of plants required for the drug industry.

The National Drug Authority should plan and supervise the development of indigenous know-how of natural products by utilizing the relevant National Laboratories, Educational Institutions, etc. on an economic scale. It should also plan and supervise the streamlining of production technologies. The National Drug Authority should also take over the responsibility for the production of an important drug Quinidine from cinebone febrifuge or from quinine itself.

It may be necessary to import the technologies for the economic production of ergot alkaloids and of the therapeutically active steroids if there are not washed out by the above group of laboratories within a period of two years.

There is need for the cultivation of menthol, eucalyptus oil bearing plants on a large scale.

The Public Sector Unit at Hyderabad in collaboration with the Department of Chemistry, Indian Institute of Science, Bangalore, Indian Institute of Experimental Medicine, Calcutta and Central Drug Research Institute, Lucknow, may develop the technology for ethinyl estradiol, nor ethisterone and norgesterel.

R & D efforts should be concentrated towards the development of technology for new drugs required for treatment of diseases prevailing in our country, such as (i) Authelimintics (ii) Anti-leprotics (iii) Anti-filarials (iv) Anti-malarials.

Indigenous technology should be worked out for succinyl choline chloride, chlorpromazine, adrenaline, metronidazole, furesemide, hydrochlorothiazide and nor adrenaline.

In addition to the R & D Laboratories in Public Sector the following laboratories may be involved in developing these technologies:

National Chemical Laboratory, Poona,
Central Drug Research Institute, Lucknow
Regional Research Laboratory, Hyderabad.

In regard to the drugs mentioned in paragraph 31, laboratory scale technology is available and it is expected that these processes will be put through pilot scale trials within the next 24 months. The results of these pilot plant trials should be awaited. Government/NDA, should, however, assess the availability of indigenous technology in respect of Vitamin B and take necessary decision on the import of technology. Technologies for the production of thiopental, primaquin, calcium pautothenate and chlorpheniramine should be imported.

There is an urgent need to obtain yielding strains of the micro-organisms. One of the public sector unit has obtained a high-yielding strain of streptomycin and the Committee recommends that urgent steps should be taken to optimise the production at other public sector unit also be making the new high-yielding strains available to them. It is immediately necessary to acquire high yielding micro-organisms for Penicillin and Tetracycline along with the associated balancing technologies.

In order to produce the quantities of chloramphenicol required in the country, steps should be taken to develop this complex technology indigenously starting four basic raw materials. This work should be entrusted to N.C.L. and the Indian Institute of Science, Bangalore and Central Drug Research Institute, Lucknow.

The public sector unit should set-up a formulation R & D unit as early as possible.

In order to reduce dependence on import of technology in general, urgent steps should be taken to equip the public sector units as also the laboratories already mentioned, with such R & D and pilot plant equipment as may be ... necessary for this work. This would include low temperature ..., high pressure and high-temperature equipment including ... the vapour phase reaction equipment. The Committee st... strongly recommends that in consultation with the above laboratories, the above specialised should be provided at least at two centres to begin with.

Early steps should be taken to strengthen the available facilities in the public sector units, care being taken that there is a strong design and engineering component established in the R & D structure so that a chemical process that may be developed may be indigenously tested and upsealed by employment of the necessary component of indigenous and competent design and engineering skill. Wherever necessary, the public sector units should seek assistance from other public sector or private design and engineering organisations in respect of upsealing of a given process. The proposed N.D.A. should coordinate all these Research and Development activities.

The Committee has identified areas where the technologies are existing and also such areas where there is need to develop and import technologies. The Committee, however, feels that, wherever it becomes necessary, at any point of time, for economic reasons or for pressure of time to import such a technology or an improvement thereon and/or it is available without onerous conditions attached to it, such technologies might be accepted.

Pricing of Drugs and Pharmaceuticals

If has been common experience all over the world that in most countries a large number of small firms which are locally owned account for roughly 20 per cent of the total sales of drugs and pharmaceuticals. The remainder of the market is controlled by mostly multi-national units which are much larger in size and resources.

An important characteristic of this industry is a quick product change or product adaptation technique which is only partly based on proven improvements in the effectiveness of production combinations. In large part, the product adaptation/innovation is essentially a marketing technique with a view of retaining or augmenting one's share, of the market for a particular Pharmacopocial product group. Such a marketing technique, of course, necessarily involves substantial selling costs in which in turn have to be added to the cost of the drug. In advanced industrial countries, the pharmaceutical industry also spends substantial amounts — around 10 per cent of total turnover — on drug research and product development. But these expenditures are relatively less significant in developing countries, including India, and by the large, the multi-national corporations use their research outlays in the parent countries to introduce new drugs/formulations by their subsidiaries in developing countries. The use of brand name as opposed to generic names also enables the industry to sell essentially similar drug formulations at widely varying prices. Quite often, it is difficult for the doctor and almost impossible for the patient to have, at their disposal, information which would enable them to compare prices of drug which are virtually identical. Advertisements rarely mentioned prices and, in general, the medical representatives convess the superiority of their particular brands of medicines with the doctor not on grounds of prices but on other grounds such as therapeutic effectiveness or advantages of the new or improved drug. In short, the success of the larger units in the modern pharmaceutical industry is dependent mainly on their ability to develop new products based on research and to create and sustain a demand for their product; and this is done by effective selling techniques and by product adaptation/innovation with a view to help the effective marketing.

There is some evidence to suggest that while the growth of the pharmaceutical industry over the past 15 years has been quite impressive in terms of growth of output, it has been less so, if one takes into account the product composition and the pricing policies of the industry.

The per capita consumption of modern medicine in India is currently estimated to be Rs. 6 per year and according to some estimates, if would appear probably below Rs. 30 per family where the family income is Rs. 4,200 per year. The Committee feels that the main objective of policy has to be to secure a better convergence of commercial considerations and social needs and priorities. The emphasis has to be on increasing the social utility of the industry particularly in the context of extreme poverty and the urgent need for extending as rapidly as possible certain minimum facilities in terms of preventive and curative medicines to the large mass of people both urban and rural.

While the operation of price control so far has certainly helped in presenting the emergence of very large or excessive profits by the drug and pharmaceutical industry, it does not appear to have contributed materially to the emergence of a product or price pattern which is more in consonance with social needs or national objectives.

An important element of cost which needs particular attention is the cost of packing. In some of the preparations like eye-drops, eye ointments, transfusion solutions, sterile, preparations, the cost of packing material could be much higher than the ingredients used because it is necessary to keep the ingredients free from even a trace of impurity. The Committee feels that greater attention should be paid, than at present, to standardization and economy in the use of packing materials consistent with the protection of consumer's interest.

It would be desirable to keep under continuous review the modes of packing and the materials used for packing purposes with a view to evolving appropriate packing standards, rationalising material usages and ignoring that competitive packing is not restored to as a sales promotion measure.

The administrative regulation and licensing should be geared to ensure that greater emphasis is laid on the production of the 117 essential medicines identified by the Committee. In this area, the policy objective should be to ensure that prices are fair and reasonable to the producer and to the consumer. But this will need to be supplemented by appropriate administrative action to strengthen the production base by ensuring adequate supplies of materials, both domestic and imported, and adequate arrangements to ensure that extraneous factors such as shortage of power, allotment of materials such as alcohol, etc., do not interfere unduly with production.

If these are accepted as the primary objectives of the regulatory framework, it seems necessary to have a certain shift of emphasis in regard to the existing regulatory arrangements including the present basis of price control. Firstly, in order to encourage the production of bulk drugs which are currently imported in significant quantities it would necessary to list out items which can and should be produced within the country in a specified period of time. To the extent that the public sector and/or the wholly owned Indian units are able and willing to produce these bulk drugs, they should receive preference. If, however, for any reason, production plans of these units do not materialise, other units in the industry including those with foreign equity may be permitted to set-up production capacity. As long as the country is dependent on net imports of a basic drug, the existing unit or a new unit may be free to determine the selling price provided it is not higher than the selling prices of STC which are based on average landed costs of imports and handling and other charges.

In the case of bulk drugs in which production is already established and in which imports are no longer necessary, greater attention should be paid to ensure that the cost of production is kept to the minimum. It would also be desirable to exempt from Price Control items in which there are no imports and which in terms of total sales of the basic drug do not exceed Rs. 25 lakhs annually.

In respect of other bulk drugs, a system of price regulation based as detailed cost investigation should continue, subject, however, to the price being so fixed that an efficient manufacture is able to get a return on his capital employed which is a little higher than is available on formulations for the industry as a whole.

The Committee after taking into consideration the question of the rate of return on investment required for production of bulk drugs, made by the Tariff Commission and also the Working Group headed by Shri N.N. Wanchoo, recommends that a return post-tax between 12 to 14 per cent as equity, i.e., paid up capital place reserves may be adopted as the basis for price fixation, depending on the importance and complexity of the bulk drug. For the purpose of determining the rate of returns, as this basis, taxation should be calculated on the basis of statutory rate of tax. Otherwise, the benefits of any specific corporate tax concession will be denied to the units in the industry

The Committee has come to the conclusion that more selectivity in the system of price regulation with a view to ensuring fair prices in respect of drugs and formulations would be desirable rather than on all drugs and formulations irrespective of their importance. As a first step, Committee recommends that the formulations based on 13 drugs, as identified by the Committee for the purpose of generic name usage should be free from Price Regulation.

In the case of other formulations, selectivity could be (a) in terms of size of the units; (b) in terms of selection of items, and (c) in terms of controlling the prices only of market leaders, in particular products, for which price control is contemplated. The Committee considers:–

(i) Units having annual turnover of less than Rs.1 crore, may be exempted from the purview of Price Regulation. This however, should not be applicable in respect of the units which were under the purview of MRTP Act.

(ii) Alternatively all formulations, other than those marketed under generic names which have an annual all-India sale in excess of Rs. 15 lakhs (including excise duty) should be within the ambit of price regulations whether or not the total annual turnover of the unit is in excess of Rs. 1 crore. If necessary Government may in exceptional cases decide to add any particular product to the list of price controlled items in public interest. The ceiling price will be determined taking into account the production costs and a reasonable return for the units which are the market leaders.

(iii) Another variant of selectivity, which could also be considered would be to identify product groups which individually are important and which collectively constitute the bulk of the output of the drugs and pharmaceutical industry. In respect of each item on this list, it would be possible to identify the leading producers who, between them, account for, say, 60 per cent of the sales. On the basis of the cost analysis in respect of those units, maximum prices may be prescribed and all other units may be free to fix their prices. On balance the Committee is of the view that this particular variant of selectivity may be administratively simpler.

The Committee feels that the recommendation of the Working Group on Drugs and Pharmaceuticals under the chairmanship of Shri N.N. Wanchoo, on formulation activity, under the alternative scheme of pricing, may be adopted with the revised rates of ceiling on profits, as 8 per cent to 13 per cent as sales turnover, by adding 2 per cent to 6 to 11 per cent to cover the recent increase in the cost of inputs, bank rates, etc., following the category of firms having the activities listed under the large, medium and small groups. Marginal adjustments would need to be made when an unit shifts from one class to another. In order to ensure that the profitability ceilings as above doubt work to the disadvantage of manufacturing units, particularly the Indian sector, the Committee would further suggest that, as an alternative criterion, the ceiling of profit may also be specified as between 10 to 12.5 per cent, post tax, on net worth, i.e., paid up capital and reserves.

In view of the flexibility allowed in adjusting the price structure of the products in line with those of market leaders, the range of products that come under direct price control will be limited, and the manufacturer will therefore have much more freedom to adjust the prices of other products according to market conditions. In some cases, the manufacturers may even be in a position to earn profits in excess of the ceilings suggested above. There should, therefore, be a provision, as at present, for finding the excess profits and these should be utilized for the purposes to be specified by the Government. However, the provision for adjusting the funded amount in the future profits or losses should be deleted as suggested by the Working Group.

Instead of the present comprehensive control as all products of each firm above certain size, the proposed system will be a much more selective and will be confined to the determination of fair prices in respect of important pharmaceutical product groups. Even in respect of these products, the basis for determination of fair price would be an investigation in the costs of production of two or three leading manufacturers which between them, account for say 60 per cent or more of the total sales of the product. Under the new system, fixation of ceiling prices for leader product will be on the basis of a more detailed cost examination. There will be no mark-up on costs but all costs including legitimate selling expenses, trade commission, freight, etc., will be taken into account. In addition, a return on sales on the lines suggested in para 40 will be permitted in arriving at the fair retail selling price. This price, as pointed out earlier, will be in the nature of a ceiling and all producers will be free to change their prices without prior approval of Government provided the retail price does not exceed the ceiling notified for that product.

In order to acquire that the Drug and Pharmaceutical Industry acquires adequate social content, the extensive of the public sector to acquire a dominant role in this industry is very important. In addition, however, the Committee feels that it is essential to evolve an effective and continuing system of monitoring in respect of this industry if social objectives are to be achieved.

The Committee recommends that high priority should be given to the building up of an information/monitoring system which should provide, on a continuing basis and with minimum time lags, all the relevant information regarding production and stocks, costs, sales, profitability, raw material availability and the emerging shortages, etc. This type of information will enable Government to act effectively and quickly.

5

SUB-COMMITTEE ON PERMISSION LETTERS, DIVERSIFICATION AND C.O.B. LICENCES, 1974 – REPORT[1]

Convenor Shri P.S. Ramachandran
Members Shri K.S. Chavda; Dr. Ranen Sen; Prof. B.V. Ranga Rao

Appointment

During the visit of the "Committee on Drugs and Pharmaceutical Industry" to various drugs and pharmaceutical units and also by written representations was brought to the notice of the Committee by the Indian Sector that the permission letters and C.O.B. licences were issued to many foreign firms to manufacture mainly formulations with the result that the foreign firms have attained dominant position in the industry to the detriment of the Indian sector. The question of permission letters and C.O.B. licences was raised on the floor of the Parliament on a number of occasions and the Minister, in reply to the question, stated that the Committee on Drugs and Pharmaceuticals Industry appointed by the Government will go into this question in detail. The Committee appointed a Sub-Committee.

Terms of Reference

(i) to look into the question of permission letters and C.O.B. Licences in detail.

(ii) to examine the provisions of the Industries (Development and Regulation) Act to ascertain whether the permission letters and the C.O.B. licences issued can stand the test of legal security.

---

1. Delhi, Controller of Publications, 1975, p. 141-143 (bound with The Committee on Drugs and Pharmaceutical Industry)

Contents

Introduction; Report; Recommendations.

Recommendations

On a proper interpretation of the IDR Act, permission letters could not be issued for new articles whether the firm has been given certificate or registration or a licence unless a new licence has been obtained by the firm for the manufacture of new article as defined under the Act and clarified by the Controller of Trade Marks;

Before granting C.O.B. Licences and D.G.T.D. or the authority should have verified whether effective steps have been taken by the firms in accordance with the provisions of Section 14, and

The issuance of permission letters and C.O.B. licences to foreign firms have given under advantage to these foreign firms to the detriment of the Indian sector.

The Sub-Committee, therefore recommends that so far as the bulk drugs are concerned, having regard to the national need for bulk drugs the permission letters and C.O.B. licences issued to these companies may be regularised on condition that –

(a) all bulk drugs are manufactured from the basic stage; and
(b) fifty per cent of the production of the basic drugs should be made available to non-associated Indian formulators.

So far as formulations are concerned, in order that there may not be a gap between production and market demand thereby creating a shortage in the market, the Indian companies applying for the manufacture of such formulations should be given licences liberally forthwith and the foreign companies should be asked to switch over within one year to the manufacture of bulk drugs and formulations to the extent of 50 per cent of the production of basic drugs by them and the balance 50 per cent to be supplied to non-associated formulators.

6

SUB-COMMITTEE ON QUALITY CONTROL OF DRUGS AND RELATED MATTER, 1974 – REPORT[1]

Convenor Shri P.S. Ramachandran

Members Dr. Ranen Sen; Dr. M.L. Dhar; Shri M.K. Rangnekar; Dr. B.B. Gaitonde; Dr. B.V. Ranga Rao

Appointment

The Committee on Drugs and Pharmaceutical Industry was constituted by the Ministry of Petroleum and Chemicals by their Resolution No. 3(26)/173-Ch III dated the 8th February, 1974 to examine various aspects of the Drug Industry. One of the terms of reference was also to recommend measures for effective quality control drugs and rendering assistance to the small scale units in this regard. While the work of the Committee was in progress, certain unfortunate and tragic incidents connected with the quality of drugs took place in the country which created a sense of urgency on the part of the committee to look into the specific terms of reference. The Minister for Health was also concerned over this unfortunate incident. He had discussions with the Chairman and requested him to go into the problem on a priority basis. He also wrote a letter dated 30th April, 1974 to the Minister for Petroleum and Chemicals to that effect. The Ministry of Petroleum and Chemicals desired that the Committee should examine this problem thoroughly and submit an interim report. Accordingly, the Committee which had already discussed this subject on 29th March, 1974, met on 2nd May, 1974 and appointed a Sub-Committee.

---

1. Delhi, Controller of Publications, 1975, p. 189-205 (Bound with "The Committee on Drugs and Pharmaceutical Industry")

Terms of Reference

To recommend measures for effective quality control of drugs and for rendering assistance to the small scale units in this regard.

Contents

Introduction; Scope of the Drugs and Cosmetics Act; Control Mechanism and Division of Responsibility; A Full-time Drug Controller with Necessary Qualifications and Experience; Adequate Number of Duly Qualified Inspectors on Attractive Pay Scales; A Full-fledged Testing Laboratory for Testing of all Categories of Drugs; Legal-cum-Intelligence Cell of for Carrying on Campaign against Spurious Drugs and for Processing Legal Cases; Spurious Drugs and Problems connected with the Campaign Against Them, "Spurious Drugs" Problems Assessed by Planning Commission's Task Force; Penal Provisions of the Drugs and Cosmetics Act whether these are Adequate or Not; The Role of the Central Drug Control Organisation; Financial Aid to the States; Coordination Between the Centre and State Drug Control Organisation; Amendment of the Drugs and Cosmetics Act; Hospital Purchases of Drugs; Quality Control and Small-Scale Units; Some General Observations, Recommendations; Appendix.

Recommendations

The officer incharge of the Drug Control in a State constitutes the king-pin of the organisation. He should be responsible not only for enforcing the quality control measures over drugs, but also for the development of the drug industry, having regard to the raw materials and natural resources available in the country. Lack of adequate technical knowledge on the part of the top officer with result in ill-equipped and ill-organised firms being licensed to manufacture drugs.

The check that is exercised over the first licensing or renewal of licence determines the quality of products that are turned out by the firm, though frequent inspections of the manufacturing firms are also necessary to ensure that the quality control discipline has become ingrained in all the personnel working in the firms.

As recommended by the Drugs Technical Advisory Board, the

qualifications of the Licensing Authority in each State should be laid down in the Drugs and Cosmetics Rules and if necessary an enabling provision should be introduced in the Drugs and Cosmetics Act for this purpose.

The overall authority in the State should also be the "Controlling Authority" for Drugs Inspectors and no Drugs Inspector should be permitted to institute a prosecution without the express order in writing from the "Controlling Authority".

The licensing of firms in each State should be done through a Licensing Board consisting of (i) Drug Control authority of the State concerned, (ii) Drug Control authorities of the States in the Region, (iii) A senior representative of the Drug Control Authority of India and (iv) if possible, one of the Drug Control authorities from Maharashtra, Gujarat or Karnataka. The Drugs and Cosmetics Act and Rules should be amended accordingly.

The manufacturers of injectables including glucose solutions, antibiotics (Schedule C) items should not be licensed to manufacture unless they have their own arrangements for testing them.

The present provisions permitting such firms to get their finished products tested by private laboratory should be withdrawn when the restrictions imposed on import of analytical equipments gets eased. Meanwhile commercial laboratories should be required to maintain efficient standards with regard to technical staff, equipment and environments and should be approved by the Drugs Control Organisation at the Centre.

The Drug Control Organisation should be divorced from the Directorate of Medical and/or Health Services and constituted into a separate department functioning directly under the Department/ Ministry of Health.

The States which do not have an adequate number of Drug Inspectors as per the scale recommended by the Committee on Drugs Control, should be helped to expand their Drug Inspectorate.

The salary offered to Drug Inspectors should be reasonable and sufficient to attract good talent from the profession.

Each State should have at least one Chief Inspector in the scale of Rs. 1100-1600 who would be well conversant with the manufacture of antibiotic preparations, injectable and vaccines, etc., including transfusion solutions. He should carry out the inspection of firms which apply for the manufacture of drugs also associating an inspector from the Central Government with the first inspection.

At the time of granting first licence for manufacture, utmost care should be exercised by the Drug Licensing Board/Drug Central Authority.

No inspector should be posted by State Government unless he has been trained. Training facilities for inspectors should be augmented and a second training course should be organised in Calcutta for Northern and Eastern Regions.

The Centre should assist the States in developing and/or expanding combined food and drug control laboratories by extending financial assistance to them.

In addition to the existing Central Drug Laboratory for testing Sera, Vaccines and Immunological products. The scheme of establishment of a Central Regional Standardisation Laboratory, should be given high priority in the Fifth Five-Year Plan.

The States should constitute legal-cum-intelligence cells for carrying on the campaign against spurious drugs. The Central Government should assist the States in organising this campaign by extending financial assistance to them.

Enlistment of the co-operation of the public, members of the medical profession, social organisations like Consumer's Councils, etc., in tightening Drug Control measures and in combating the menace of spurious drugs should be considered both by Central Government and State Governments.

Setting up of State Drug Advisory Boards consisting of medical profession, Police Department, social workers, the industry and the trade should be provided for statutorily in the Drugs and Cosmetics Act and that this should become mandatory on the part of deficient States to constitute such Boards. Public should be made aware of such organisations/boards.

As recommended by the Task Force on Drugs and Food Adulteration, 25 special mobile squads in the States should be organised for tracking down spurious drugs and food with 100 per cent financial assistance from the Centre.

Four special mobile squads should be established at the Centre for coordinating the activities of mobile squads in States.

A distinction should be made between offences relating to the manufacture and role of spurious drugs and those offences relating to standards of drugs. Punishment of life imprisonment may be provided for the manufacture, sale, stocking or exhibiting any drug which is deemed to be misbranded of any drug that is adulterated under Section 17 or for manufacture of a drug without a valid licence.

The complement of the Central Drug Inspectors should be augmented to at least 50 immediately, and the Zonal Officers in Madras and Ghaziabad should be senior enough in status to enable them to discuss with the State Drug Control Authorities and Health secretaries the problems relating to drug control.

The facilities for screening 'New Drugs' should be reinforced by the inclusion of a medical officer with post-graduate qualifications who should be able to advise on the conduct of clinical trials with 'New Drugs'.

The Central Government should have a fully equipped toxicological laboratory for carrying out toxicity as well as teratology studies with new drugs in particular.

The library facilities should be augmented at the Zonal Offices and these facilities should be made available to drug manufacturers and State Drug Control Authorities.

The facilities for training Drug Inspectors (two such courses are recommended in Bombay and Calcutta) and Drug Analysts should be made permanent and whole-time senior officers should be appointed to conduct them.

The Drug Standard Cell for publication of Pharmacopoeia and National Formulary should be strengthened immediately to keep them up to date.

The Central Drug Standard Control Organisation should have its own library of books and journals. Adequate provision should also be made for this organisation towards travelling allowances and to improve the tone of drug control measures in the country.

The Central Government should have its own publicity wing to enable it to give suitable guidance to the States.

Four mobile squads equipped with fast transport radio communications, police assistance and plain clothed watching staff should be attached to the four zonal offices to help the States in the campaign against spurious drugs.

Drug Inspectorate in the States and arrangements for keeping their technical competence up to date such as provision of journals, pharmacopoeias, technical books, etc., should be augmented. Transport facilities at least to the senior inspectors should be provided.

Financial assistance should be provided to the States in establishing top grade combined Food and Drug Control Laboratory.

As recommended by the BICP, a cess of one per cent should be levied on the pharmaceutical industry and the funds so collected which are estimated to be of the order of Rs. 3.5 crores should be utilised primarily for the construction of the Toxicological Laboratory at the Centre and the balance of funds should be utilised for strengthening the Drug Control measures at the Central and State levels, as well as for financing approved schemes of research.

The standards of first inspection of manufacturing firms and inspection at the time of renewal of manufacturing licences must be stringent. Joint inspections by the Central and State Drugs Inspectors should be carried out before licences are granted or renewed.

States should draw up priorities for frequent inspection of drug manufacturing units and firms which execute orders of Government departments and those which manufacture Schedule 'C' drugs including 'blood banks'.

Inspection of hospital stores and pharmacies throughout the States should be frequently done.

The Centre should concentrate on repeated inspections of firms manufacturing Schedule 'C' drugs and also take out for test samples of life-saving drugs on a planned basis.

The licences of the drug manufacturers who have been given licenses and who are unfit to carry on the manufacture in the opinion of the Central Drug Control authorities should be cancelled in consultation with the State Drug Control authorities.

The prosecution for offences under Drugs and Cosmetics Act should be initiated by States. There should be a close liaison between the States and the Centre to ensure quick effective prosecution.

The present provision which permits the court to award imprisonment for a period not less than one year has been amended and imprisonment for a minimum period of five years has been recommended. Further amendments as recommended are suggested for implementation.

The States should have their own centralised arrangements for purchase of drugs. The tenderers should be screened with reference to good manufacturing practices observed by them and enrolled as prospective supplies.

The procedure adopted by Maharashtra should be followed for purchases of drugs by other States. Hospital pharmacy services should be re-organised.

The drugs should be subjected to a thorough visual examination at the time of receipt in hospital and where there are reasons to suspect their quality, samples should be got examined.

In smaller towns and rural areas and Public Health Centres, frequent inspection of drugs is all the more necessary.

The Drug Control Authorities should frequently inspect the firms which supply drugs to hospitals.

Most of the small scale firms find it difficult to get their drugs tested. The State Government should place the testing facilities available with their analytical laboratories at the disposal of the small scale firms on payment of prescribed fees.

The Central and the State Drug Organisations should conduct special seminars, technical lectures and issue bulletins emphasising on manufacturers the various aspects that have to be taken into consideration in maintaining quality control measures.

Talks on subjects such as maintenance of sterile areas in drug manufacturing units sterilization procedures for drugs, etc., should be held.

An organisation where prospective manufacturers of drugs particularly those whose financial resources are limited could be initiated into the substitutes of quality control measures in regard to drugs should be started.

As recommended by the Drugs and Equipment Standards Committee, the Central and State Drug Control Organisations should be independent of the Directorate of Medical and Health Services. The Centre should adopt this immediately to act as an example for the State to follow.

Industrial units which are engaged in the production of drugs which are thermo lable and are sensitive to heat such as sero, vaccines, other immunological products and antibiotics should not be subjected to power cuts as their production would be seriously hampered.

A joint inspection by the local and Central Drug Control authorities should be undertaken immediately and completed within a period of two months for all units in the small scale sector in respect of Schedule 'C' items.

The general public in their own interest should also be aware of the precautions to be taken while purchasing drugs. They should also bring to the notice of the Drug Control authorities whenever the existence of any spurious drug comes to notice.

The question that naturally arises is how should a consumer

protect himself from this menace of spurious drugs. While there can be no fool-proof protection, nevertheless there are certain precautions which if taken by consumers could not only ensure their protection but also assist the Drug Control Organisation in their investigational activities. These precautions are: –

1. Buy drugs only from a reputed chemist preferably one known to you.
2. Insist on a cash memo while purchasing the drug. The Drugs and Cosmetics Act requires a chemist to give a cash-memo and it is an offence for a chemist to refuse to grant a cash-memo.
3. Compare the price charged by the chemist with that indicated on the label. If the price charged is considerably lower than that indicated on the label then there is a possibility that the drug supplied may not be genuine.
4. Beware of any shop which sells drugs at prices considerably lower than other competitors.
5. Examine the labels of the drugs purchased and do not buy drugs which have crossed the expiry date.
6. If the package of the medicine purchased appears different from that purchased earlier, forward the package to the nearest Drug Inspector for investigations. Similarly, if a medicine purchased tastes differently then report along with a sample of the medicine all to the nearest Drug Inspector.
7. Destroy all used containers of medicines particularly those where the name of the medicine or the manufacturer is indelibly marked on the container.
8. Associate the Drug Control Organisation in meetings of the Citizen Committee where quality control of drugs, is being discussed.
9. Inform the State Drugs Controller of any cases of spurious drugs that have come to your notice. While furnishing this information please ascertain the fact correctly so that the time of the Drug Control Officer is not unduly wasted in fruitless investigations.

The steps set out above if followed by consumers would ensure not only protection but also assist the Drug Control Organisation in investigation cases of spurious drugs.

7

PANEL TO RECOMMEND MEASURES FOR PROVIDING ESSENTIAL DRUGS AND COMMON HOUSEHOLD REMEDIES TO THE GENERAL PUBLIC, ESPECIALLY IN RURAL AREAS, 1974 – REPORT[1]

Convenor Dr. B.B. Gaitonde

Members Dr. Ranen Sen; Shri P.S. Ramachandran; Dr. B. Shah; Dr. A.B. Choudhury; Dr. B. Ray Chaudhury; Dr. K.L. Wig; Dr. S. Padmavati; Dr. K.G. Nair; Dr. B.J. Vakil; Dr. K.V. Thiruvengadam; Dr. P.R. Gupta (Dr. B. Shah and Dr. K.L. Wig informed their inability to work on this panel)

Appointment

The Committee on Drugs and Pharmaceuticals Industry was constituted by the Ministry of Petroleum and Chemicals by the Resolution dated the 8th February, 1974 to examine the various aspects of the drug industry. One of the terms of reference was "to recommend measures for providing essential drugs and common household remedies to the general public especially in rural areas."

The Committee during the course of their discussions, particularly on the availability of essential medicines in larger quantities, felt that although the question of substitution of brand names of the medicines marketed by the industry by generic names was not a specific terms of reference for this committee, the subject follows clearly from the other terms of references, such as reduction/ rationalisation of prices of formulations for the consumers, making the essential drugs available to the general public, attainment of

---

1. Delhi, Controller of Publications, 1975, p. 251-258 (Bound with The Committee on Drugs and Pharmaceutical Industry)

leadership role by the public sector, promoting the growth of the Indian sector, etc. Besides, the question was also directly linked with many important facts of the industry such as drug patents, irrational practices of medicines, excessive use of ingredients in multi-drug formulations, proliferation of such preparations and baneful influence on the medical profession, etc., of medicine marketed under brand names. Keeping the above aspects in view, the Committee decided that this question should also be looked into by the Committee. The Committee also felt that the views of eminent medical personnel from the different parts of the country should be obtained in this regard. Accordingly, a penal was set-up.

Terms of Reference

(i) To recommend measures for providing essential drugs and common household remedies to the general public especially in the rural areas, and

(ii) Whether it would be in national interest to substitute brand names by generic names and if so, the manner and extent to which it should be done.

Contents

Introduction; Supply of Essential Drugs and Common Household Remedies; Substitution of Brand Names of Drugs by Generic Names; Summary of Recommendations.

Recommendations

(1) *Essential Drugs and Common Household Remedies –Supply Thereof*

In order to make the essential drugs as identified by the Committee, available in large quantities and at a reasonably low price throughout the country, the Committee recommends following measures:

Production

Production of those medicines should be expanded or taken up in adequate quantities, giving top priority for the manufacture of the relevant bulk drugs/active ingredients.

The Ministry of Petroleum and Chemicals should take all such measures, which will increase the production of those drugs expeditiously. Special assistance, priority for power supply, other incentive schemes, etc., may be given to entrepreneurs, preferably the National Sector, who come forward to undertake production of these essential drugs. In short, if there are any impediments, these should be immediately looked into and removed.

Technology

In cases of some drugs, the technical know-how is already available, but there is a production shortfall. More entrepreneurs should be encouraged to take up the production of such drugs. In case of these drugs for which technical know-how is not available in the country, special incentives may be given to national laboratories to develop the know-how on a time-bound basis. If necessary, the foreign technical know-how may also be obtained immediately.

Distribution

To make these drugs available in rural areas, the distribution system must be nationalised and decentralised, in regard to household remedies and commonly used medicines which do not require the prescription of doctors. Assistance should also be sought from the postal department, Indian Oil Company Depots, Kerosene Depots. Cooperative societies should be encouraged for the distribution of drugs in rural areas.

Packing

Packing details should be looked into. Tablets should be supplied in strip packings, liquid preparations should be in bottles fitted with pilfer-proof closures.

Exports

Export of the bulk drugs required for the production of medicines identified by the Committee, as well as their formulations should be so regulated that there is no shortage of these essential drugs in the country at any time.

(1) *Dispensing*: At present, there are a number of difficulties, especially in small towns and rural areas, to establish pharmacies for dispensing of drugs. To obviate these problems, immediate steps should be taken to revise the present syllabus of training of the pharmacists. The Pharmacy Council should be approached to tailor the course to suit the needs of the country. An intensive, need-oriented course of a short duration after matriculation should be instituted for training of dispensers, who then could be licensed to establish pharmacies and drug stores for distribution of these medicines in smaller towns, rural areas and remote parts of the country.

Primary Health Centres should be given adequate financial assistance for purchase of drugs, so that the rural population also gets the same quality drugs in adequate amounts as in urban areas.

(2) *Substitution of Brand Names of Drugs by Generic Names*:

(i) Brand names should be abolished in a phased manner.

(ii) A beginning should be made for a change-over to generic names starting with the drugs as identified by the Committee. These drugs are mostly being marketed under generic names and their generic names are quite elegant.

(iii) Drugs which are to be exported may be allowed to bear brand names.

(iv) All supplies of single ingredient drugs included in Indian Pharmacopoeia for Central and State Government distributions and local bodies should be tendered and supplies made under generic names. At present, drugs, though tendered under generic names, are supplied under brand names, and this should be discouraged.

(v) All drugs (other than those listed in the Annexure III) should bear labels displaying prominently, the generic names. Brand names may be shown on labels in a less conspicious manner.

(vi) The Drug Controller should, while granting permissions, be requested not to give recognition to brand names of new drugs. New drugs should not be allowed to be marketed under brand names, when first introduced into this country.

(vii) Multiple drugs combinations often containing drugs, particularly vitamins, in amounts for in excess of what is required are presently marketed in India. The majority of such combinations are irrational. There is a colossal national wastage of drugs because of such combinations. The Drug Control Administration should immediately go into the various drug combinations and take prompt measures to eliminate irrational drug combinations. No firm should be allowed to incorporate excessive quantities of any drug over and above what is required to go into the formulations for therapeutic and prophylactic purposes. Pharmacopoeial Committee should be requested to give new/generic names for multiple-ingredient preparations. New types of multi-ingredient preparations should not be allowed to be marketed hereafter unless they are mentioned in the National Formulary or Pharmacopoeia and approved by the Drugs Controller of India. If any amendment of the Drugs and Cosmetics Act and Rules in considered necessary, this should be carried out.

(viii) Non-propriety names as recommended by W.H.O. from time to time should be adopted.

(ix) Bio-availability studies are important in cases of a few drugs, although this factor has recently been overplayed not always an rational basis. Facilities should be created in different parts of the country, so that the industry, both large and small scales, can take advantage of such facilities to plan and conduct bio-availability and pharmaco-kinetic studies.

(x) In order to keep the medical profession, particularly the general practitioners, well-informed about new drugs and also to popularise the generic names it is essential to take the following steps immediately:

(a) To revise the Indian National Formulary and make it up-to-date.

(b) To publish journals on the lines of *Prescriber's Journals*, U.K., *Medical Letter*, U.S.A., or *Formulary Notes* of Sri Lanka. Such publications will have to be under the control of an Editorial Board comprising leaders of the medical profession in the country contributed by the Ministry of Health, Government of India.

(3) *Periodic Review*: A periodic review of the impact of this step on the drug industry, prices and availability of medicines is necessary

so as to take suitable connective measures, if required.

(4) *Availability of Medicines*: Government should take steps for early implementation of the recommendations made above with regard to measures for providing essential drugs and common household remedies especially in the rural areas.

(5) *Quality Control*: The Committee emphasised that the recommendation regarding the change over from brand names to generic names has to be implemented continuously and on a phased basis ensuring. Simultaneously the necessity of enforcing quality control on drugs and in particular the concerned recommendations made in the Interim Reports of Committee on Quality Control of Drugs.

8

OIL PRICES COMMITTEE, 1974 – REPORT[1]

Chairman Dr. K.S. Krishnaswamy
Members Shri N. Krishnan; Prof. Ajit Das Gupta
M. Secy. Shri M. Ramaswami

Appointment

The Government of India Resolution No. 1(78)/69-PPD dated May 11, 1970 sets out the pricing arrangements for petroleum products which has been in force since June 1, 1970, initially for a period of three years, to be extended for a further period or periods at the discretion of the Government. The period of validity of the present pricing arrangement which was to expire on May 31, 1973 has been extended up to May 31, 1974.

The Government of India has now decided to set up a new Oil Prices Committee to examine, in the light of developing world trends in the availability and pricing of crude oil and petroleum products and the existing practices in India and recommend a pricing policy that would be practicable and flexible enough to meet extraordinary situations that may arise, simultaneously taking into account the impact of product prices on the critical areas of the industrial and agricultural sectors. So the Oil Prices Committee was appointed by the Government of India in the Ministry of Petroleum and Chemicals vide its Resolution No. J-11011/8/72-PPD dated March 16, 1974.

Terms of Reference

(i) (a) The determination of the ex-refinery prices of refined petroleum products including paraffin wax, MLO, TDO,

---

1. Delhi, Controller of Publications, 1977, 269, II p.

NTO and JBO/SBP spirits produced by the refineries whether on the basis of import parity as hitherto or by the adoption of any other appropriate method with due regard to the capacity/facilities at the various ports to receive oil tankers of different sizes;

(b) the determination of the price at which indigenously produced crude oil should be transferred to the refineries, as the pooled price of the imported and the indigenously produced crude oil would be one of the determinants for the price of the refined products;

(c) determination of shrinkage allowance on Motor Spirit/High Speed Diesel Oil at high altitudes;

(d) need for reimbursement of inland transportation cost of imported crude for the use of inland refineries (like Mathura, Barauni, Koyali refineries) and if it is considered necessary, to suggest an equitable method of reimbursement; and

(e) in case prices are to be based on the import parity basis, whether the monthly freight variations to be adjusted through C and F Account should be on a national basis as hitherto or at actuals for each refinery and whether this freight adjustment should be given to any refinery purchasing indigenous crude on other than import parity basis, i.e., at a price lower or higher than import parity prices;

(ii) With reference to (i)(a), the feasibility of introducing uniform price on all India or on a regional basis;

(iii) The determination of landed prices in respect of similar products which may be imported and whether any compensation in C and F prices, etc., is required to be given in respect of imported products;

(iv) The need for additional pricing points, e.g., Mangalore, Tuticorin, Port Blair, etc., and the need for retention of existing pricing points like Okha, Goa, etc., togather with a review of the existing pricing zones;

(v) The determination of marketing and distribution charges and profit on the marketing operations and there allocation to the products mentioned in (i)(a) above, due account being taken of the experience of Assam Oil Company Limited and Indo-Burma Petroleum Company Ltd.;

(vi) (a) The determination of ceiling selling prices in respect of lubricating oils, greases and specialities either individually or on gradewise basis, e.g., premium grade, secondary grade, etc., including that of transformer oil; and

(b) with reference to (a) above to review existing block control mechanism taking into account the latest *inter se* companywise position of cumulative over-recoveries/under-recoveries and examine the feasibility of evolving an equitable/suitable alternative method.

(vii) Rationale of levying "devaluation" duties (additional Excise duties) at the same rate on refineries established before and after devaluation of the rupee in 1966 and suggest modifications, if considered necessary;

(viii) Method of adjustment in respect of product prices as a consequences of variation in the rate of exchange of US Dollars, Pound Sterling and rupee occurring during the pricing period;

(ix) Movement of products by pipelines and the fixation of the transportation cost by the same inclusion in product prices at Stations fed by them;

(x) The need for continuance or streamlining of the freight surcharge scheme for reimbursed of the under-recoveries on account of out of zone/coastal movement, etc., of petroleum products and norms for reimbursement of under-recoveries;

(xi) The question of reimbursement of all under-recoveries arising from levy of sales tax (central or local)/Purchase tax/Octroi/ Entry tax on inter-company or inter-State transactions in respect of imported as well indigenously produced products;

(xii) (a) Reimbursement of the cost of the Bitumen drums and 18.5 litre kerosene tins taking into account the cost of steel sheets/tin plates made available to concerned oil companies by MMTC/STC, etc.;

(b) Bulk-packed differential for bitumen to encourage distribution of bitumen in bulk thereby save foreign exchange on import of steel sheets for drums;

(xiii) The determination of the rate of commission to dealers in respect of Motor Spirit, High Speed Diesel Oil , Kerosene and Light Diesel Oil with due regard to the views of the interests concerned;

(xiv) The determination of rate of commission in respect of kerosene to (a) agent; (b) dealers and (c) retailers taking into account the losses, expenses incurred by them on account of leakage, handling charges, godown rent, establishment charges, with due regard to the views of the State Governments and other interests;

(xv) The need for the continuance of the transportation cost by "flat rate" system in respect of motor spirit and kerosene in the existing "Assam Area" and if continuance is considered necessary to determine the extent of the area to which this rate should be made applicable in future and the manner of dealing with remaining areas;

(xvi) Determination of (a) the cost of transportation of products from refinery to main installation and at transhipment points, e.g., siding and shunting charges, etc., and the manner of reimbursement of the same to refinery/marketing companies incurring such charges, and (b) the quantum of MI charges to be allowed to the refineries when refining installations are used by the marketing companies for direct despatch of products in tank wagons, tank trucks, pipeline, etc., to consuming points;

(xvii) Need for adjustment of variations between national rail freight and freight actually incurred;

(xviii) Need for relating Time Charter or other freight rates of tankers carrying imported crude oil with the freight element included in the price build-up and the question of prospectively or retrospectively adjusting variations, if considered necessary;

(xix) The manner in which construction and all other costs for additional crude oil tankage should be recovered from the concerned refineries as well as in respect of subterranean caverns for storing crude;

(xx) The need for continuance of the present informal price control of petroleum products and the method of maintenance of various accounts by the oil companies on an industry basis, e.g., C and F Adjustment Account, Block, Control, Freight Surcharge Pool, etc.;

(xxi) Adventitious gain/losses on account of duty increases/ decreases on stock of petroleum products held by oil marketing companies and the need for additional remuneration to be given on account of increase in working capital during the pricing period;

(xxii) (a) The determination of the manner of pricing of L.P. Gas supplied in Cylinders for domestic use as well as for supplies of L.P. Gas in bulk; and

(b) Determination of loading/unloading, handling and filling charges, etc., for L.P. Gas Cylinders for domestic use taking into account the actual experience of Cochin Refineries Ltd./Madras Refineries Ltd. in this regard.

Contents

Introduction; Demand Estimates; Indigenous Crude Oil – Production; Indigenous Crude Oil – Pricing; Imported Crude Oil; Transportation of Crude Oil; Pooled Price of Crude Oil; Pricing of Petroleum Products – Ex-Refinery; Marketing and Distribution; Proposed Selling Prices; Pricing Points and Uniform Pricing; Period of Price Fixation and Provision for Adjustments; Oil Industry Pool Accounts; Dealers' Commission on Motor Spirit, High Speed Diesel Oil, Kerosene Oil and Light Diesel Oil; Lubricating Oils and Greases; Pricing of Special Products; Other Important Pricing Matters; Summary of Recommendations and Conclusions; Acknowledgement; List of Tables from 1 to 19; Annexures from I to XVIII, Statements 1 to 23; Resolutions.

Recommendations

Our recommendations and conclusions are summarised below:

1. The question of reorganising the oil industry with a view to optimising the use of assets and facilities and rendering more efficient service to the public is engaging the attention of the Government. We considered various alternative arrangements for the reorganisation of the oil industry. We do not favour any reorganisation of the industry on regional basis. We are of the view that there should be 3 all-India companies with at least two companies to serve any single region. This could perhaps be achieved by (i) IOC, (ii) HPCL plus BRL and (iii) Caltex together with AOC and IBP as the three operative all India organisations. (Para 1.13)

2. Keeping in view the measures taken or proposed to be taken to curb consumption of petroleum products, the pace of substitution of Fuel Oil (FO) by coal in different industries, the Committee has placed the demand estimates of petroleum products at 27.91 million tonnes in 1978-79 and 31.70 million tonnes in 1980-81 as against Planning Commission's estimate of 28.50 million tonnes and 31.68 million

tonnes for the two years respectively. (Para 2.2)

3. On current reckoning the total refining capacity available in the last year of the Fifth Plan period would at maximum be about 31.50 million tonnes per annum and by 1980-81 about 37.50 million tonnes. (Para 2.5)

4. The imports of crude would be maintained at the level of around 13 to 14 million tonnes per annum by 1980-81 and even subsequently thereafter. The increasing supplies from offshore areas would be used to meet additional demand for petroleum products. (Para 2.8)

5. (a) It is necessary to enlarge the domestic component of crude oil supplies as rapidly as possible.

(b) Should the availability of indigenous crude turn to be larger than anticipated, such additions should be applied to replacement of imports rather than to enlarge domestic offtake. (Para 2.9)

6. Exploration, development and production of crude oil, onshore and offshore should be intensified. (Para 2.10)

7. (a) Measures — administrative as well as fiscal — should continue to be taken to restrain the growth of consumption of petroleum products, especially of HSDO, SKO and FO which form the bulk of consumption of petroleum products.

(b) There is scope for greater efficiency in the use of HSDO through better maintenance and speed regulation of both passenger and goods vehicles and rationalisation of road and rail services, as has been suggested by the Committee on Transport Policy and Coordination (1966).

(c) Steps should be taken to make available the prototype kerosene stove brought out by the oil industry which is expected to improve efficiency and reduce consumption.

(d) In addition to measures to contain the demand of kerosene and ensure better distribution efforts will have to be made to enlarge the supply of soft coke and accelerate the pace of rural electrification. (Para 2.11)

8. More systematic steps should be adopted for economising the consumption of fuel oil and the substitution of fuel oil by coal. (Para 2.13)

9. Refining of the Bombay High crude would generate additional Naphtha and LSHS the utilisation of which has to be programmed in advance. The full production of Bombay High crude will yield substantial amounts of associate gas and its utilisation will

also require to be reorganised. (Para 3.8)

10. The price of indigenous crude should in our view be based on the long-run social marginal cost of domestic crude. (Para 4.2)

11. The long-run social marginal cost of onshore crude oil has been assessed by us at Rs. 33.30 per barrel inclusive of the enhanced royalty rate of Rs. 42 per tonne but exclusive of the cess of Rs. 60 per tonne. (Para 4.4)

12. The price of Bombay High crude oil may be fixed at Rs. 45 per barrel for 34° API, exclusive of the cess of Rs. 60 per tonne and royalty. A review could, however, be made in about 3 years' time when a clearer picture of the productivity and costs should be available. (Para 4.10)

13. It will not be rational to price associate gas from Bombay High on the assumption that all common overhead expenditure will be included in the price of crude oil. It is important that during the next review of the price of Bombay High crude, the pricing of associate gas should also be adequately covered. (Para 4.13)

14. The surplus funds generated by Oil (India) Ltd. at the recommended price of onshore crude oil which accrue to the Government under the Second Supplemental Agreement, should be credited to the Oil Development Fund. (Para 4.14)

15. It will be necessary to provide supplementary funds to ONGC from sources other than the budgetary allocation by the Government. With this end in view we recommend the present ceiling on cess of 100 per tonne of crude oil should be raised to Rs. 150 per tonne. (Paras 4.14 & 4.22)

16. The existing gravity escalation formula (2 cents per barrel equivalent to 18 paise per barrel) for every degree variation up or down from the base (34.0°—34.9° API) should continue to be adopted. (Para 4.15)

17. There is no need for sulphur premium for indigenous crude. (Para 4.16)

18. The credit period for ONGC and OIL crudes should not exceed three weeks. (Para 4.17)

19. Sales tax on crude oil should be borne by the refinery and not by the producers of crude. (Para 4.18)

20. The cost of delivery of the crude by pipeline should be borne by the refinery and it should be based on actual operating cost plus 15 per cent return on capital employed. The quantity delivered should be determined on the basis of dip measurements of crude oil at the

refinery tanks. (Para 4.19)

21. Similarly the cost of transporting Bombay High Crude to the coastal refineries including the cost of providing special equipments and facilities has to be borne by the oil industry (refineries). (Para 4.20)

22. The rate of interest on the amount invested from the funds of OIDB in ONGC, IOC, etc., should not be lower than those prescribed by the Government in the case of loans sanctioned to other public sector undertakings as budgetary support for plan projects. The interest accrual in the Fund may be exempted from income tax. (Para 4.23)

23. The current average FOB cost of imported crude works out to $ 11.65 per barrel; any impact of subsequent increase in the price of imported crude oil prices would have to be reflected in product prices. (Para 5.6)

24. The most urgent consideration should be given to the proposals for the fourth oil berth with improved draft at Bombay, the super tanker oil jetty at Cochin and the oil berth at Visakhapatnam outer harbour. More immediately every effort should be made to ensure that the LR-II tankers are used in a year round basis at Bombay Port and night piloting facilities at Cochin are provided. (Para 6.2)

25. (a) We would like to emphasise that lighterage cannot be considered as a long-term solution. In the interest of optimising tanker utilisation and reducing overall transportation costs as also from the point of view of safeguarding against pollution in the coastal waters, the need to develop facilities in the ports and for direct receiving and handling of these tankers — at least up to 87,500 DWT — should receive the highest possible priority.

(b) The actual costs of ocean transportation including the cost of lighterage should continue to be reflected in the price of petroleum products and the refineries should be reimbursed on this basis. Any extra cost on account of demurrage, dead-freighting (other than that specifically directed by the Government on operational grounds) and additional terminal time should not be allowed for reimbursement. The existing mechanism of reimbursement of freight charges through C & F Account should continue. In the case of CRL, their present contract rate of affreightment with Norse Shipping Company should be taken into account for reimbursement. (Paras 6.3 and 6.4)

26. The actual cost of ocean transportation should be extended

to the tankers acquired by SCI, specifically for transportation of crude to the Indian refineries and their contractual rate should be in rupees per tonne. (Para 6.5)

27. The actual pipeline operating costs plus a 15 per cent return on capital employed for transporting the indigenous crude from the field head (CTF) to the refinery installations should be paid by the refineries. Certain norms of utilisation (of not less than 75 per cent of the capacity in initial 3/5 years of commissioning) should be stipulated periodically by the Oil Coordination Committee. The same principles should be applied to the transportation of imported crude oil to inland refineries, of Bombay High Crude Oil to onshore installations and of products to depots/terminals. (Para 6.6)

28. The concept of a pooled price of imported and indigenous crude oil should continue to be adopted for determining the price of petroleum products. The pooled f.o.b. price works out to Rs. 84.60 per barrel or Rs. 623.50 per tonne at Rs. 9=1 US Dollar. (Para 7.2)

29. With the increasing proportion of indigenous crude in the total crude processed by the refineries, the price of indigenous crude (rather the cess on crude oil) should be further increased so that the average pooled price remains at Rs. 84.60 per barrel to give a measure of stability to the prices of petroleum products. (Para 7.3)

30. Only the quantity of crude oil attributable to the products for which we have fixed the retention prices will be eligible for adjustments through the COPE Account and the differential in respect of imported crude should be calculated on the basis of telegraphic transfer (TT) selling exchange rate. (Para 7.4)

31. There is a qualitative change in the situation pertaining to the oil industry in India inasmuch as all the units comprising the oil industry would be soon under the Government ownership. This should enable the Government to bring about optimum utilisation of the assets of different oil companies and eliminate wasteful duplication. (Para 8.7)

32. The import parity concept for determining the ex-refinery prices should be given up and a flexible system of pricing of products at the refinery level, keeping in view the overall energy policy, the demand for petroleum products in the country and the refinery economics should be evolved. (Paras 8.8 and 8.9)

33. We have evolved a set of relative weights (indices) for allocating the total cost of a refinery to individual products. One tonne of kerosene oil which is an article of mass consumption, is taken as

the base equal to one and other products in terms of tonnes are related to kerosenes. These indices are based on the considered judgement of the Committee which took into account various factors like present and prospective demand and supply, ability of individual products to bear additional charges, their end use patterns, refinery economics and other related factors. The Committee would like to stress that these indices have a strictly limited role, namely, they are a devise for the allocation of total refinery costs to individual products. (Paras 8.9 and 8.10)

34. The retention prices of petroleum products for each refinery as worked out by us, taking into account the levels of crude throughput, pattern of production, the delivered cost of crude, the cost of processing/refining and a reasonable rate of return on capital employed, are indicated in Annexures VII and VIII. (Para 8.11)

35. (a) The ocean loss should be kept at the minimum possible level in view of the high cost of imported crude oil.

(b) HPCL has switched over to bank guarantee scheme whereby the bank charges per tonne of imported crude have been very much reduced. Other oil companies should take immediate steps to follow this scheme. (Para 8.12)

36. We are satisfied that the operating levels of the coastal refineries assumed by us can be achieved within the crude imports envisaged. Hence no adjustments on account of shortfall in throughput should be necessary. (Para 8.14)

37. For any incremental throughput of the companies' own crude over the level indicated by us, a refinery should get the incremental refining cost together with the return on working capital. The marketing company lifting these incremental products should pay the full price to the refinery and the refinery should credit to the pool account the excess of such price over the cost of crude oil, incremental costs and the return on working capital. (Para 8.15)

38. In case a refinery processes incremental crude supplied by another company in addition to its own crude, so that the total crude processed does not exceed the operating level assumed by us, that refinery is entitled in respect of the additional crude to retain an amount calculated at the average refining cost and the unit return on net fixed assets. The cost of crude oil together with return on its working capital should accrue to the crude supplier. The balance, if any, should be funded to the Pool Account. In case the total crude including that from another company, is in excess of the operating level

assumed by us, the processing refinery will be eligible for reimbursement of only the incremental refining cost. (Para 8.16)

39. (a) The refineries should be compensated through an adjustment in the Pool Account for any shortfall in realisation due to variation from the standard production pattern on account of a specific directive from the Government. Similarly the refinery should credit any surplus of the Pool Account if the production pattern given by the Government has a favourable effect on realisation. However, any deterioration in the production pattern on account of plant deficiency, operational defects or other factors not be compensated from the pool.

(b) In case a refinery processes crude oil below the level indicated by us and attains a better pattern of production as compared to the standard pattern adopted by us, (as may be modified by the Government direction) that refinery is entitled to recover from the product prices the cost of crude oil, the return element on the working capital and the refining cost up to the actual level of throughput but the return on fixed assets will be only upto the maximum levels indicated by us. The balance/excess should be funded to the All India Pool Account. (Para 8.17)

40. The Government should set-up an Oil Coordination Committee (OCC) for deciding on allocation of crude oil and monthly production patterns based on oil imports and exports and national and regional demands, logistics of transportation and other allied matters. The OCC should also administer pool accounts and coordinate the transportation arrangements for crude imports and coastal movements. This should be an industry Committee with a separate secretariat and the expenditure of this organisation should be borne by the C & F Account. In order that the OCC performs these functions effectively, the Government should ensure that it is endowed with adequate legal powers and status. The OCC should also have sufficient autonomy in the matter of employment of expert staff. (Para 8.18)

41. The Committee stresses that refineries should take effective measures to bring down the incidence of refinery fuel and loss in view of the high cost of crude. The OCC should undertake a periodical review of the refinery fuel and loss percentage, taking into account refineries product pattern, throughput level, change in crude mix, etc. (Para 8.19)

42. The cost of renewals and replacements of fixed assets in ex-

cess of the depreciation allowed by us in the retention prices may be reimbursed from the C & F Account after the claims of the oil companies are scrutinised and cleared by the Oil Coordination Committee. (Para 8.21)

43. We are convinced that a 15 per cent return on capital employed is a fair and reasonable rate for both refineries and marketing companies. (Para 8.22)

44. Any under or over recovery on account of the variations of actual conversion factors (kilolitres/tonne ratios) from the standards adopted by us will be eligible for adjustment in the All India Pool Account. These adjustments may be given effect to from 14th July, 1975. (Para 8.23)

45. We had recommended in our Interim Report certain differentials for different refinery locations. But the Government considered that the ex-refinery prices should be uniform. Though we do not see eye to eye with the Government in this matter for practical considerations we have adopted the concept of uniform ex-refinery prices. (Para 8.24)

46. The difference between the ex-refinery prices and the retention prices to the refineries should be funded to the All India Pool Account. (Para 8.24)

47. With the structural change in the oil industry in India it would no longer be appropriate to restrict the market shares of BRL, HPCL, Caltex and AOC and allow unrestrained growth of IOC. BRL, HPCL, Caltex and AOC should also have the rightful shares of the current market and an equitable share in future growth rate. Their spell of stagnation should be ended. (Para 9.5)

48. The products from the refinery could be allocated to all the marketing companies on the basis of their available facilities and not on the basis of the ownership of the refinery. Similarly, the imports of products may be allocated to various oil companies and need not be earmarked for a particular company. We do not visualise any difficulty in the sale and/or exchange of assets and facilities on the basis of the written down value as per income tax method amongst the oil companies. (Para 9.8)

49. We have visualised that IOC should play a leading role in the oil sector. But its present share of 61 per cent should be gradually reduced over the next 4 years to 57 per cent. Thereafter IOC's share would stabilise at around 55 per cent and all the oil companies would be allowed uniform growth rate. But during the intervening period

(1977-78 to 1982-83) market share of BRL, HPCL, Caltex, AOC and IBP would be fixed on the basis of 1976-77 levels indicated by us. (Para 9.9)

50. In case the oil industry is reorganised into three all-India companies, as suggested by us the market shares of the three restructured oil companies could easily be determined by simple addition of the market shares of the individual companies. (Para 9.10)

51. After giving due allowance for the likely increase in the costs of marketing and distribution we have estimated the companywise unit costs for the period 1976/79. (Para 9.11)

52. We have adopted a return of 15 per cent on capital employed for the marketing operations. (Para 9.12)

53. (a) We have given careful consideration to the views expressed by all the oil companies and examined the pros and cons of the concept of retention marketing margin. We see no rationale in continuing the system which gives undue advantage to one and adversely affects others.

(b) Retention price or margin does not mean that all costs are recognised and reimbursed. Any deterioration in marketing efficiency or shortfall in the volume of sale from the levels anticipated by us would not call for any adjustment of retention margin. In fact we have provided a built-in mechanism where inefficiencies and deficiencies would be penalised and operational innovation would be rewarded. (Para 9.13)

54. We have allocated the entire marketing expenditure (after excluding the expenditure attributable to lubes and greases and LPG) to the individual bulk refined petroleum products on the basis of the quantity of the products sold. The stock loss has been assessed separately for each product on industry basis. The variation in the total marketing margin inclusive of return per KL/tonne from one product to another is only in respect of stock loss and return on working capital. (Para 9.14)

55. The weighted averages of the retention margins of all the oil companies for each product have been adopted for build up of basic ceiling selling prices. The difference between the retention margins and average marketing margins included in the price build up should be adjusted in the All India Pool Account. (Para 9.15)

56. For successful implementation of the scheme of retention marketing margin, it is essential that appropriate quantities of the specified products should be supplied to various oil marketing com-

panies by the refineries and the imports are allocated so that the oil companies are able to reach the levels of volume indicated by us. In case an oil company sells additional products over and above the levels indicated by us or the levels determined by Government from time to time (denying supply to other oil companies resulting in shortfalls in their sales) the total retention marketing margin of this oil company on such additional sales should be restricted to 5 per cent over the levels authorised by us and the extra realisation towards these margins on sales in excess of this 5 per cent should be surrendered to the Pool. (Para 9.16)

57. As we have derived the retention prices of petroleum products for each refinery on the basis of cost plus reasonable return rather than import parity, the continuance of the non-recoverable devaluation duty is not warranted. To offset the resultant loss to Government revenue a part of existing selling price of lubes and greases should be converted into basic excise duty. We have maintained the existing rates of customs and basic excise duties. (Para 10.2)

58. The existing surcharge of Rs. 15 per KL/tonne towards Freight Surcharge Pool should be continued. (Para 10.3)

59. A C&F Surcharge of Rs. 25 per KL/tonne should be imposed on all petroleum products. (Para 10.4)

60. We have recognised separately the cost of bitumen drums and filling charges assuming consumption of 65 kg of sheets per tonne of bitumen. Variations in the delivered price of 24 G drum-sheets from Rs. 2,750 per tonne is eligible for adjustment in the C and F Account. (Para 10.5)

61. (a) The average filling, loading and unloading costs of Rs. 80 per tonne of LPG is payable to the refinery company irrespective of the size of cylinder. If the bottling or filling of LPG is done by the marketing company, it should retain the filling charges for the quantity filled.

(b) A filling charge of Rs. 30 per tonne is payable to the refinery for bulk LPG filling and loading.

(c) We feel that the question of sharing the agents commission of Rs. 3.37 per cylinder of LPG between the agents and sub-agents has to be settled by the parties concerned.

(d) LPG should also be subject to the general C & F Surcharge of Rs. 25 per tonne and FSP Surcharge of Rs. 15 per tonne.

(e) Government should make a detailed review of the existing transportation costs and pattern of movement of LPG to fix the transportation charges for each pair of stations.

(f) In regard to the supply of LPG to industrial and commercial consumers (including hotels and restaurants) either in bulk or in packed cylinders, an additional C & F Surcharge of Rs. 400 per tonne should be levied to restrain consumption. (Para 10.6)

62. Prices of bunker fuels for vessels on coastal services should be fixed at the same level as for inland sales ex-storage points; in respect of international bunker supplies prices should be comparable to those prevailing at nearby ports. (Para 10.7)

63. A comparison of the basic ceiling selling prices of petroleum products developed by us and the current basic ceiling selling prices at the oil companies' storage point shows that the current prices of naphtha for fertilizer industry, bitumen, JBO, MTO, SKO, HSDO and LPG (domestic) are lower than the prices built up on the basis of norms evolved by us. On the other hand the existing prices of FO, MS, ATF, solvents, etc., are higher than those formulated by us. The oil industry will be sustaining a net under-recovery of about Rs. 38 crores per annum at the present level of crude and product prices. Keeping in view the impact of any increase in the prices of specific products on the industry and economy in general and the need under the present circumstances to hold the price line, we feel that the existing prices should be brought in line with the prices formulated by us in a phased manner. We have recommended only moderate increase in the prices of mass consumption items such as SKO, HSDO, LPG (domestic). Our recommendations are:–

(i) The price of naphtha for fertilizer industry be increased by Rs. 100 per tonne;

(ii) The price of Fuel Oil for fertilizer industry be reduced by Rs. 60 per tonne;

(iii) In case fuel oil is used as a feed stock, the excise duty may be further reduced so as to bring down the price of naphtha and fuel oil (per tonne) on par. It would not be appropriate to reduce the price of fuel oil further to take care of the higher incidence of capital and operating costs of a fuel oil based fertilizer plant. This could be achieved through a system of retention prices for fertilizer plants;

(iv) The price of naphtha for non-fertilizer use could be increased by Rs. 120 per tonne;

(v) To partially offset the net under recovery to the oil industry on account of reduced price of naphtha for fertilizer use a surcharge of Rs. 94 per KL on MS is proposed, without affecting the existing price of MS;

(vi) In order to prevent diversion and encourage more judicious use of LDO, we recommend an increase in its price by Rs. 100 per KL as and when the price of imported crude is hiked up. This increase by economising the use of LDO will not materially affect agricultural operations and small scale industries;

(vii) An upward adjustment in the price of ATF by Rs. 100 per KL could be given effect to when the price of imported crude is increased. The price of ATF for international airlines including Air India may continue to be determined on the basis of prices prevailing in neighbouring countries. The surcharge on ATF and Avgas for international airlines could suitable be adjusted from time to time;

(viii) In order to conserve the valuable steel sheets, there should be an incentive for the users to switch over from packed to bulk bitumen. Keeping in view the additional costs to users and other relevant factors, the Oil companies could give a price reduction up to Rs. 100 per tonne. The quantum of incentive may vary from place to place and from time to time. These amounts could be adjusted in the C & F Account subject to approval of the oil Coordination Committee;

(ix) Even after the recent increase of 12 paise per litre in the price of HSDO with effect from 1st December, 1975 consequent upon the increase in the price of imported crude oil by about 10 per cent from October 1975, the current price of HSDO is lower than the price worked out by us (Rs. 34 per KL). The price of HSDO could be increased by Rs. 20 per KL in the first instance and the balance (Rs. 14 per KL) in the second phase;

(x) Similarly the current price of kerosene is lower by Rs. 41 per KL. Keeping in view the current economic situation, the price of kerosene may be increased by Rs. 20 per KL in the first instance and the balance (Rs. 21 per KL) in the next phase;

(xi) The price of LPG has also not risen at a rate commensurate with the rise in the price of crude oil. To restrain the further growth of demand, the price of LPG can be increased by 70 paise per cylinder; and

(xii) The prices of Aviation gasolene, MS, ATF, LDO, bitumen, SBP spirits, hexane, solvents, MTO, JBO and LPG (Industrial) may be retained at the current levels. (Para 10.9)

64. The Government decided that the ex-refinery prices should be uniform at all the refinery locations. However, in actual practice uniformity has been brought about as the ceiling selling prices of some of the products were frozen at the pre-July 1975 levels and the ceiling selling prices of some others were given increases of 5 to 8 paise per litre. Thus the current basic ceiling selling prices of many products reflect certain price differentials resulting from the import parity concept. We have removed these differentials. Ceiling selling prices at Bombay have been adopted for all the primary pricing points (refinery locations). The prices recommended by us for immediate implementation are indicated in Table 18. (Paras 10.10 and 10.11)

65. We have developed the prices of petroleum products on certain norms of performance and efficiency and economy in operation. Any reduction in the ultimate selling prices cannot be effected without seriously impairing the efficiency and viability of the oil industry. We have not examined the question of adjustment in the excise duties levied on petroleum products. This aspect should be considered by the Government before any increase in the prices of essential petroleum products is contemplated to meet the additional inescapable expenditure to the oil industry. (Para 10.12)

66. The distortions in the current prices of some products should be removed in stages and not accentuated by more arbitrary changes. Across-the-board increase in the prices of various products so as to reflect the increase in the price of crude oil is more appropriate than selective increases in the prices of a few products. Further, adjustments in prices should be made promptly and not postponed, as time is of the essence. (Para 10.13)

67. The refineries will be the primary pricing points. Prices in the main installations and upcountry depots should be determined on the basis of prices at the nearest refinery point plus the cost of transportation (including shunting and siding charges or wharfages) by the cheapest means (rail, coastal, barge or pipeline). (Para 11.1)

68. (a) Prices at Calcutta should be based on Haldia plus rail freight for Budge Budge and for Mourigram. The existing free

delivery zone of Calcutta should be served by Mourigram and Budge Budge as focal points.

(b) The prices at Goa, Kandla and Okha will be related to the prices at Bombay plus the transportation cost by coastal tanker movement.

(c) The price of naphtha for Mangalore should be based on Bombay price plus coastal freight (including export and import wharfages) from Bombay to Mangalore. For other products, prices should be worked out on the basis of Cochin prices plus railway freight. Prices of FO and naphtha for Tuticorin are to be based on Cochin prices plus coastal transportation (including export and import wharfages) from Cochin to Tuticorin and prices of other products at Tuticorin be based on Cochin prices plus railway freight. Position should be reviewed periodically to ascertain the cheapest mode of transport and the relevant charges to be recovered from consumers. The difficulties of fertilizer plants at these locations should be solved in some other way and not through an exception to the general principle we have evolved for determining prices at upcountry stations.

(d) The prices of petroleum products at Port Blair should be linked to those of Madras plus the actual cost of transportation.

(e) One of the marketing companies should explore the possibility of setting up depot facilities in Lakshadweep. Prices in Lakshadweep should be determined based on Cochin prices plus the actual transportation charges including the export and import wharfages. Meantime the prices of SKO and HSDO may be fixed at Rs. 1.50 per litre in Lakshadweep and Minicoy islands and any short recovery by the oil companies adjusted in the All India Pool Account as is being done for the border areas in North-East region. (Para 11.2)

69. We recommend the following transportation charges for products through pipeline:–

Station	per tonne
Ahmedabad	Rs. 15 from Koyali.
Patna	Rs. 15 from Barauni.
Mugalsarai	Rs. 35 from Barauni.
Allahabad	Rs. 45 from Barauni
Kanpur	Rs. 60 from Barauni.

The foregoing rates are for SKO, HSDO, LDO and FO. For MS,

naphtha and other hazardous products, in view of the higher railway freight rates, these charges should be escalated by a factor of 1.66. The Indian Oil Corporation should submit to the Oil Coordination Committee periodically audited statements to indicate the recovery at the foregoing rates and match these recoveries with their actual cost of transportation by pipelines, inclusive of a return of 15 per cent on capital employed. (Para 11.3)

70. In view of the high transportation costs in the border States/Union Territories in the North-East Region there should be a flat surcharge of 5 paise per litre on kerosene and HSDO and 7 paise per litre on MS with Digboi and Gauhati as primary pricing points. The subsidy on the operation of this scheme should be adjusted in the All India Pool Account. The flat transportation surcharge scheme in respect of MS and kerosene which was applicable to all the places in Assam State should be abolished and the prices of these products should be determined in the same manner as in other State subject to the condition that such prices (exclusive of sales tax, local levies, etc., charged for SKO, HSDO and MS) at any point or station in the State of Assam do not exceed those specified for the States of Meghalaya, Mizoram, Nagaland, etc. (Para 11.4)

71. (a) We do not favour a system of uniform/pool prices of all or specific products, throughout India or over specific regions.

(b) Apart from the practical administrative problems and the possibility of abuse there are no special circumstances to warrant the adoption of a scheme of dual pricing in respect of MS and HSDO. (Para 11.5)

72. (a) The retention prices and margins as evolved by us should remain valid for a period of 4 years from the date of implementation subject to adjustments for certain factors.

(b) Any variation in the pooled price (the weighted average of imported crude oil and indigenous crude oil in respect of production of bulk refined petroleum products) from the level of Rs. 623.50 per tonne would require adjustment in the retention price/basic ceiling selling price of individual petroleum products.

(c) Difference in the actual transportation costs as compared to the estimated costs should be adjusted in the C and F Adjustment Account. There is no need to either increase the ex-refinery price or the basic ceiling selling price on this account.

(d) Similarly variations in the auxiliary duty on imported crude oil, octroi/sales tax on indigenous crude oil, wharfage and statutory landing charges, rates of electricity and duty thereon, any new tax or R and D cess levied by the Centre or by the States should be eligible for adjustments in the Pool Account.

(e) The actual impact of any long term settlement in the course of the next 4 years may be assessed by the Oil Coordination Committee and allowed for adjustment in the Pool Account.

(f) The oil companies would be called upon to set up a large number of kerosene distribution centres/depots at Taluk headquarters and farm fuel outlets. Their capital cost and operation costs could be adjusted in the All India Pool Account subject to the approval of OCC.

(g) The oil companies may be required to construct additional storage tanks for crude oil and products and provide services which may not be remunerative but are essential on strategic consideration and considerations of socio-economic policies of the Government. The under recoveries sustained by the oil companies on such projects and services should be eligible for reimbursement from the All India Pool Account.

(h) Minor debottlenecking may be necessary in certain units to improve the pattern of production and/or reduce the incidence of own fuel consumption and loss. Minor modifications of some of the refineries may be required for processing a mixture of different types of crude oil. The expenditure in these regards should also be eligible for adjustment in the All India Pool Account. (Chapter 12)

73. The refineries processing indigenous onshore crude oil would credit to the COPE Account the difference between Rs. 305.42 per tonne of crude of 34° API and Rs. 623.50 per tonne assumed in the calculation of retention prices. Similarly, the refineries processing indigenous offshore crude oil would credit the COPE Account with the difference between Rs. 391.64 per tonne of crude of 34°API gravity and Rs. 623.50 per tonne. Refineries processing imported crude oil would be eligible to recover the difference between the f.o.b. price of imported crude oil, as approved by the Government and Rs. 623.50 per tonne. The f.o.b. value of imported crude oil should be converted to rupees at the actual telegraphic transfer rate of exchange as obtaining on the date of remittance. (Para 13.2)

74. We understand that OCC has evolved certain norms and parameters for coastal and inland movements and adjustments are being effected to the FSP with reference to these norms. We recommend that these norms and parameters should be reviewed peri-

odically by OCC. (Para 13.3)

75. The more important items that should be taken by the oil companies for adjustments of debits or credits in the C and F surcharge account are indicated in this para. (Para 13.4)

76. The prices recommended by us for immediate implementation are different from the prices developed on the basis of norms and parameters. These differences (plus or minus) should be continued to be adjusted in the product price adjustment Account (PPA). (Para 13.5)

77. As the prices of petroleum products recommended by us are based on cost, levy of non-recoverable sales tax or surcharge would seriously affect the financial viability of the oil companies. The various sales tax surcharge schemes should be continued. The long term solution for this problem is that the State Government should levy recoverable sales tax. (Para 13.6)

78. The octroi on crude oil may be withdrawn. In case this is not done, the present octroi surcharge scheme should be continued. (Para 13.7)

79. (a) We are aware of the increase in the workload of the oil companies in the maintenance of a large number of pool accounts, of the auditors in checking and certification and of OCC and Government in exercising proper scrutiny of these accounts. Time is of the essence and the distribution of workload amongst the auditors appears to be inevitable. Some of the pool accounts or some items of the pool account could be checked and verified by the companies internal auditors, some others by statutory auditors and the balance by practising chartered/cost accountants.

(b) The Oil Coordination Committee should obtain all the relevant data for proper scrutiny of the accounts. Test checks should be conducted. The formats of the statements and accounts should be prepared in consultation with the Government auditors. (Para 13.8)

80. As the surcharges are elements of prices to cover the variations in certain elements of costs, the pool accounts should be maintained as oil industry's accounts. There is no need to keep each account in isolation and increase the product prices to cover the deficit in particular pool account. The OCC should judiciously deploy the surplus funds either in short term bank deposit or as advances to the oil companies as authorised by the Government. Annually a review of the balances in each account should be made and surplus, if any, after taking into account the likely debits of the oil industry, could be

credited to the Oil Industry Development Fund administered by the Oil Industry Development Board. The interest on the pool balances should be exempted from payment of income-tax. (Para 13.9)

81. The dealers' commission on MS, HSDO, SKO and LDO should be specific, expressed in rupees per KL and not on an *ad valorem* basis. (Para 14.13)

82. The licence fees recovered from the dealers by the oil companies should be frozen at the existing levels at least for a period of 2 years (*i.e.*, end of December, 1978) during which a detailed review should be made by the oil industry in consultation with the dealers for formulating mutually acceptable guidelines for determination of licence fees. (Para 14.15)

83. The security deposit should in no case exceed Rs. 1,000 per outlet without lube bay and Rs. 1,500 per outlet with lube bay. Any amount in excess should be viewed as a public deposit on which the oil companies should pay appropriate interest. (Para 14.16)

84. A sliding scale of commission is necessary to ensure the viability of low and medium throughput retail outlets and at the same time avoid giving unintended benefits to either medium or high throughput outlets. In view of the frequency distribution and higher average throughput of HSDO dealers, bands of volume of sales per annum for HSDO need not be the same as those for MS. Rounding off benefit need not be taken into account in the determination of the sliding rates of commission as this element varies from time to time and from place to place. (Para 14.21)

85. The Committee recommends the sliding rates of commission as under:

Band	MS
	Rs/KL
1 to 480 KL per annum	80
481 to 1080 KL per annum	50
over 1080 KL per annum	35

Band	HSDO
	Rs/KL
1 to 600 KL per annum	50
601 to 1200 per annum	25
over 1200 KL per annum	20

(Para 14.22)

86. Economy in the scale of operation is not so perceptible in

retail trade of MS. High volume retail outlets are predominantly in the metropolitan areas involving higher cost of operation. There is need for effecting economy in some areas such as entertainments, gifts, sales promotion, conveyance expenditure, etc. Keeping this in view we suggest that the average rate of commission for outlets with very high throughputs for MS should not be less than Rs. 50 per KL. (Para 14.23)

87. We do not find any justification in applying the rates separately on the volume of sale of MS and HSDO. (Para 14.24)

88. With the sliding scale of commission recommended by us there is no need for continuance by outlets of the levy of unauthorised service charges. Consequently there should not be, in general any increase in the ultimate price charged to the consumer. (Para 14.26)

89. A pooling mechanism has been evolved by us to disburse the appropriate amount of commission due to each dealer. (Para 14.27)

90. Since the shrinkage allowance are specific to pairs of supply and consumption stations, and we have not been able to assess the precise difference in the average temperatures we can only recommend for the present an increase of 5 per cent over the existing shrinkage allowance for MS and 30 per cent for HSDO. We also suggest that the Oil Coordination Committee should examine this aspect in greater depth in consultation with the meteorological department at Poona. (Para 14.29)

91. Taking all factors into consideration and the broad functions performed by agents/wholesalers/retailers, we recommend a total commission of Rs. 55 per KL on kerosene in addition to actual transportation charges. The above rate of commission does not include shrinkage allowance and other extraordinary expenses peculiar to individual locations depending upon the terrain and altitude. In arriving at the transportation and other such charges peculiar to individual locations, the rounding off benefit accruing to the dealers or agents should also be borne in mind. (Para 14.33)

92. The Committee recommends a margin of Rs. 25 per KL on LDO in addition to actual costs of transportation as applicable to kerosene. (Para 14.34)

93. (a) It should be possible to determine the ceiling selling prices for certain grades of lubricating oil such as automotive lubes (blended with additives) and secondary grade non-additive lubes. The industrial oils with additives, marine lubricants and aviation

lubes do not seem to be amenable to a set of price formula. The prices could be brought under the block control system. We have developed certain norms for blending, marketing and distribution, etc., for effective control. This, in our view, would be adequate.

(b) In respect of industrial lubricants the industry should make efforts to reduce their number to the extent possible by standardising the specifications for each end application. The oil industry should also undertake a revision of current prices of the industrial lubes and greases so as to find out whether restructuring of their prices is required on the basis of current cost of raw materials and chemicals. (Para 15.10)

94. The import parity concept of determining the ex-refinery prices of lube base stocks should be given up. (Para 15.11)

95. We have developed the retention prices for each lube base stock for the individual lube refinery on the basis of the cost of reduced crude, operating cost, production pattern and a return of 15 per cent on total capital employed. (Para 15.12)

96. The lube base stocks are grouped under 3 broad categories, viz., LVI, HVI/Bright Stock and Turbine Oils. The ex-refinery prices have been worked out for each category. These prices would be uniform at all the five lube refineries. (Paras 15.17 and 15.26)

97. We have recommended a pricing formula for determining the ceiling selling prices for automotive lubricants and general purpose secondary grade non-additive lubes. These account for about 70 per cent of the total volume of lubricants and greases sold in the country. On the high volume and commonly used lubricants the price formulated by us would result in some reduction in their prices. (Paras 15.18 and 15.19)

98. (a) Keeping in view the latest changes made in the excise tariff and our recommendations in regard to the levy of non-recoverable devaluation duty on fuel products, we recommend that the basic excise duty on lubricants and greases at the 11-A stage may be 20 per cent *ad valorem* plus Rs. 2,000 per tonne and at the 11-B stage be specific at Rs. 1,000 per tonne.

(b) The basic excise duty on TOBS and spindle oil may be kept at Rs. 1,000 per KL and the flushing oil should be subject to 11-A and 11-B excise duties.

(c) The additional excise duty on lube base stocks and wax should be withdrawn. To simplify the matter further, the Committee recommends that the basic excise duty on lubricants and greases should be levied only at one stage, i.e., 11-A stage and should be specific at Rs. 3,400 per tonne. This recommendation could be considered by the Government at the appropriate time.

(d) With the implementation of these recommendations the surcharge of Rs. 3,000 per tonne levied from 2nd March 1974 would be reduced on an average to Rs. 500 per tonne. (Para 15.20)

99. The industrial oil and greases (the balance 30 per cent) which are not amenable for such pricing formulation should continue to be in the lube block control system. For effective control of this system we have recommended certain norms and ceilings. The prices are to be frozen at the current levels subject to certain specific escalations. (Para 15.21)

100. The actual expenditure of the R&D Centre of IOC attributable to lubes and greases should continue to be debited to the Block Control Account. The benefit of the work done by the R&D Centre of IOC should be made available to all the marketing oil companies. (Para 15.22)

101. The expenditure for institutional advertising campaign for educating the customers in the proper application of the approved brands of lubricants and greases and also warning them against hazards of using unknown and spurious grades, should be eligible for adjustment in the Block Control as approved by the OCC. (Para 15.23)

102. To ensure proper working of the scheme the oil companies (IOC and HPCL) having captive lube plants should be directed to supply adequate quantities of lube base stocks to the other oil companies. In case an oil company sells additional lubricating oils and greases over and above the levels indicated by us or the level determined by the Government from time to time (denying supply of the essential lube base stocks to other oil companies resulting in shortfalls in their sales), blending and marketing margin of this oil company on such additional sales should be restricted to only 5 per cent over the level authorised by us and the extra realisation towards these margins on sales in excess of this 5 per cent should be surrendered to the pool. (Para 15.24)

103. Prices of finished lubricants and greases should be the same at Bombay and Madras; a small differential of Rs. 30 per KL has been recommended for lubricants and greases ex-Calcutta taking into account the additional cost of transporting the lube base stocks from Haldia to Calcutta. (Para 15.26)

104. The minor oil companies (Castrol, Tide Water and Gulf) who are marketing and distributing lubricants and greases may be kept outside the lube block control system. But these companies would be required to sell the automotive lubes and secondary grade non-additive lubes at the ceiling selling prices recommended by us. In view of their higher unit cost of operations, these oil companies may be given a refund of Rs. 250 per KL on the sale of automotive and secondary grade non additive lubes. The long-term solutions to their problems lie in the major oil companies acquiring controlling interests in these companies. (Para 15.28)

105. The IBP having a network of retail outlets may continue to be in the lube block control. (Para 15.29)

106. On the general issues we have recommended that the production of lubricants and greases should be confined to the organised sector; fiscal incentives which help the emergence of unregulated small scale units in the production and sale of lubricants and greases should not be continued; and the rubber spray oil, aluminium oils, etc., produced from HSDO and other fuel products should be subject to appropriate excise duty. (Para 15.30)

107. With the processing of Bombay High Crude in BRL and with an increase in the proportion of north Gujarat crude processed by the Koyali refinery the production of LSHS will go up to 2.5 million tonnes in 1978. Till the commissioning of the secondary processing facilities at Koyali for converting the LSHS into high sulphur heavy residue and middle distillates, disposal of LSHS would pose a serious problem to the oil industry. Allout efforts should be made to market the large quantities of LSHS expected to be produced in the next 4-5 years. (Para 16.3)

108. The prices of LSHS supplied to thermal plants may continue to be determined in terms of the existing contracts, but the relevant quantities of LSHS should be taken into account for adjustment in CCPE, C&F and other pool accounts. The exemption of LSHS from the levy of excise duties should be continued up to 1980, when the problem of LSHS disposal would be greatly reduced. In respect of new contracts the price of LSHS should be the same as recommended for general trade. (Para 16.7)

109. The price of LSHS as fertilizer feedstock should be on par with the price of naphtha or fuel oil per tonne. Here again LSHS as feedstock should be exempted from the levy of excise duty as in the case of fuel oil. The price of LSHS supplied to fertilizer industry for

general heating purpose may be fixed at Rs. 760 per tonne inclusive of excise duty of Rs. 68 per tonne. (Para 16.8)

110. We recommend a price difference (reduction) up to Rs. 100 per tonne for LSHS used by general trade customers as compared to FO. The price of LSHS would then work out to Rs. 727 per tonne. The additional excise duty on LSHS may be withdrawn. (Para 16.9)

111. (a) Taking into account the higher sulphur content and other characteristics, we have adopted a lower index in developing the ex-refinery price of Hot Heavy Stock (HHS). The selling price works out to Rs. 684.21 per tonne exclusive of duties. We recommend that the additional non-recoverable excise duty of Rs. 38.89 per tonne should be withdrawn.

(b) The transfer price of LSHS transported from IOC refinery at Koyali and supplied to HPCL should be the ex-refinery price. The quantity of LSHS processed in the HPCL refinery should be included in the average throughput of the refinery for calculating the total retention prices/margins. (Para 16.10)

112. We have developed the ex-refinery/basic ceiling selling prices of carbon black feedstock produced by BRL and HPCL and phenol extract by the IOC refinery at Barauni. (Para 16.11)

113. The basic ceiling selling prices of refinery gas has been developed by us after giving due allowance for the calorific value of the refinery gas *vis-a-vis* fuel oil. (Para 16.12)

114. In developing prices of benzene and toluene we have taken into account the cost of naphtha feedstock and the cost of Udex plant (both capital and operating). The prices recommended for these two products are about Rs. 500 per tonne less than their current prices. Prior to effecting this reduction it has, firstly, to be ensured that the price reduction is actually passed on to the ultimate consumers and not retained by the intermediaries; secondly, other producers of benzene—Union Carbide, NOCIL and Steel Plants—should also reduce their prices. (Para 16.13)

115. Ceiling selling prices for other special products are also worked out by us. (Para 16.14)

116. The adventitious loss or gain for the refinery and marketing companies on the special products *vis-a-vis* costs (including the 15 per cent return on capital employed) should be adjusted in the All India Pool Accounts. (Para 16.16)

117. (a) There should be a premium of Rs. 50 per tonne in the price of low viscosity grade and Rs. 20 per tonne in the price of

medium viscosity grade of fuel oil over the high viscosity and high sulphur fuel oil for which the price has been determined by us.

(b) In respect of special cut naphtha from Koyali refinery for IPCL, the additional cost of production, storage and supply should be recovered from the consumer. The Committee has not fixed any price specifically for such products. (Para 17.2)

118. The Committee has not made any recommendation regarding the price of transformer oil but steps should be taken to ensure that the reduction in the price of transformer oil base stocks (about Rs. 500 per KL) recommended by the Committee is passed on by the manufacturers of transformer oil to the ultimate consumers, namely, the electricity boards. (Para 17.3)

119. The marketing companies should make payments to the refineries on the basis of cash on delivery. A grace period of 3 days may be allowed. (Para 17.4)

120. Refineries are not eligible for any extra payment on account of main installation charges. (Para 17.5)

121. Railway shunting and siding charges should legitimately form part of the transportation cost (freight and costs) and not included in the main installation charges. (Para 17.6)

122. The refinery fuel and loss should continue to be exempted from the levy of excise duty. (Para 17.7)

123. (a) The volume of petroleum products sold to the marketing companies should be based on the refinery tankage dips/tankage wagons dips, tank truck dips.

(b) The variations between the volume of sale as billed by the marketing companies to the consumers and the volume as estimated for 29.5°C, above 1 per cent (+ or −) should be adjusted in the sale volume of petroleum products despatched directly from the refineries. This applies to individual bulk supplies of 10 KL and above. (Para 17.8)

124. There is no rationale in allowing the refineries to retain the marketing margin included in the ceiling selling prices of products marketed directly by them. (Para 17.9)

125. (a) To ensure regular supplies to essential petroleum products and optimum utilisation of larger capacity tankers it is essential that the coastal refineries construct adequate crude tankage to store 21 days' crude throughput. In case the oil companies are called upon for strategic considerations to construct additional crude tankage (subterranean caverns or overland tanks) over and above the

norm indicated, the required funds should be made available from the oil industry pool account.

(b) The adequacy or otherwise of the storage tanks for essential products should be assessed by the OCC and the concerned oil companies should provide the required storage capacity as part of their normal obligations. Any failure to comply with this norm should attract penalties by way of reduction in the return on working capital entitlement. (Para 17.10)

126. The informal price control should be continued except in the case of SKO, FO and LDO, the prices of which are being controlled under the Essential Commodities Act. (Para 17.11)

127. The adventitious gains should be mopped up only when there are substantial variations in the price of crude oil or in excise duties. (Para 17.12)

128. We strongly suggest that the incidence of stock/product loss should be carefully examined by the OCC and adjustments, if any, may be made in the marketing margins. (Para 17.13)

129. With the acquisition of practically the entire oil industry by the Government the product exchange, ullage assistance and other hospitality arrangements should be further developed in a systematic manner under Central direction. A mechanism to facilitate product exchange of dissimilar products has been suggested. (Para 17.14)

130. An incentive scheme has been recommended for saving in refineries own fuel and loss through managerial efficiency. (Para 17.15)

131. It is necessary to have adequate machinery within the Ministry of Petroleum to keep track of developments and analyse their impact on the oil industry as well as on the multiplicity of consumers of petroleum products. It would also be necessary to monitor continuously the changes that occur in the cost structure of the oil industry. For this purpose the Economic and Statistics Wing of the Ministry should be substantially strengthened through addition of technical personnel consisting of Economists, Statisticians and Cost Accountants preferably with experience and knowledge of the oil industry. (Para 17.16)

9

RAILWAY ACCIDENT INVESTIGATION REPORT ON DERAILMENT OF 662 UP MIXED TRAIN BETWEEN SILLIPUR AND BIRPUR STATIONS ON SHEOPUR KALAN GWALIOR NARROW GAUGE SECTION OF JHANSI DIVISION ON CENTRAL RAILWAY ON 9th MARCH 1974

March 9, 1974 – August 12, 1974[1]

One Man Commission Shri D.G. Divgi

Officers Present Shri F. Dacosta; Shri O.P. Srivastava; Shri N. Appukuttan; Shri B.V. Joshi; Shri R. Balasubramaniam

Appointment

The Commission was constituted under Rule 4 of the Statutory Investigation into Railway Accidents Rule 1973 issued by the Ministry of Tourism and Civil Aviation vide their Notification No. RS 13.T(8)/71 dated 19th April, 1973.

Terms of Reference

To inquire into the derailment of 662 Up mixed train between Sillipur and Birpur Stations on Sheopur Kalan–Gwalior Narrow Gauge Section of Jhansi Division on Central Railway on 9th March, 1974.

Conclusion

Cause

After full consideration of all the factual, material and circumstantial

---

1. Ministry of Tourism and Civil Aviation, Commission of Railway Safety, Government of India, New Delhi, 1979, [i] + 14 p.

evidence, I have reached the conclusion that the derailment of 662 Up Mixed Train on the 9th March, 1974 at km 1355/5-6 between Sillipur and Birpur stations was caused by the train being driven at an excessive speed on the falling gradient of 1 in 80.

Responsibility

Driver Ahmed Ali has been acquitted by the court of Railway Magistrate, Indore (a) I hold Driver Ahmed Ali responsible for the accident in that he did not keep the train under control (para 34) thereby contravening General Rule 89(b). The extenuating circumstances which rendered his task difficult were the absence of the brakes on the tender, which rendered the train control oversensitive to variations in speed, in the range beyond about 25 km p.h. (Para 51) and the absence of the speedometer (Paras 43 and 48).

(b) Driver Ahmed Ali aged 50 years was appointed on 1-6-1942 as Cleaner and was later promoted on 1-1-1944 as Fireman and on 1-7-1951 as Driver. He had passed the periodical medical examination on 26-5-1973 and was declared fit for 'A' Class without glasses. He attended the Safety Camp at Jhansi in November 1972 and the Refresher Course in 1967. He has had 14 penalties. They include fines, censure and withholding of increments for causing engine failures, hot boxes, time loss and non-submission of journal.

Relief Measures

Emergency calls were made within the least possible time considering the difficult communication arrangements in the area and they were met with prompt response. I am satisfied that the Medical Aid and Relief Measures were as efficient as could be expected in the circumstances.

Recommendations

The Driver's ability to retrieve the situation by bringing the train under control back from excessive speed was severely curtailed owing to the non-functioning of the brakes on the Tender.

The staff responsible for letting the engine leave the Shed on 7-3-1974 without attending to the slackness of the brake year should be taken up with as also those responsible for not fitting at all a portion of the Tender brake rigging in February 1974.

The absence of brake power on the Tender reduces sharply the safety margin in train control particularly on the steep gradients. It should be ensured that engines which are equipped with brake power on Tender are not allowed to run without the full complement of the brake power in working order. It is also recommended that such of the engines as do not have the steam brakes on the Tender should if possible be equipped with such brakes.

In respect of the engines which did not have the brake power working on the Tender, the maximum prescribed speed of 30 km p.h. down the gradient of 1 in 80 required long emergency braking distance. On such gradients an appropriate speed restriction or load restriction should, therefore, be imposed so as to enable the train to be stopped within about 450 metres.

The work of fixing speedometers on the engines should be expedited.

Both the Driver and the Guard of the train were found to be not quite conversant with the procedures to be followed for calling for assistance of Guard's hand brake and for applying the hand brake. Measures to ensure that their knowledge in such matters is up-to-date should be taken.

No norms for variations in versines and superelevation have been laid down for the section. It appears desirable to lay down working norms in respect of such variations.

The Permanent Way maintenance should be tightened up so as to avoid abnormal variation in track parameters. The supervisory staff responsible for allowing the superelevation to go down to 6 mm from 24 mm specified and for allowing the kink in the alignment should be suitably taken up with.

10

ONE MAN COMMISSION OF INQUIRY INTO THE SADAR BAZAR DISTURBANCES 1974 – REPORT[1]

One Man Commission Shri R. Prasad
Officer Present Shri S.K. Magon

Appointment

On 5th May, 1974, serious communal disturbances broke out in certain localities within the jurisdiction of the Sadar Bazar Police Station, Delhi and a few adjacent areas. As a result of these disturbances 10 persons lost their lives on that day and one died later. The riots caused a great deal of anxiety to the public and were the subject-matter of much press comment as well as discussion in Parliament on the 25th of June 1974, the Government of India in the Ministry of Home Affairs appointed a Commission of Inquiry for the purpose of making an inquiry into a definite matter of public importance, to wit, the communal disturbances that occurred in the area falling within the jurisdiction of Sadar Bazar Police Station, Delhi on the 5th day of May 1974 vide its Notification No. II-14011/9/74-NID (B) dated June 25th, 1974.

Terms of Reference

(a) to inquire into the causes and course of the disturbances which took place in the area falling within the jurisdiction of Sadar Bazar Police Station, Delhi and the areas adjoining it, on 5th May 1974;

(b) to enquire into the adequacy of the administrative measures taken to prevent and to deal with the said disturbances;

---

1. New Delhi, Ministry of Home Affairs, 1975, 2 Vols (bound in one), 219 p.

(c) to recommend measures which may be adopted to prevent the recurrence of such disturbances in the special conditions of the Sadar Bazar locality; and

(d) to consider such matters as may be found relevant in the course of the inquiry.

Contents

Constitution of the Commission – Its Terms of Reference and Course of Inquiry; Causes and Course of the Disturbances in the Sadar Bazar Area and the Areas Adjoining on 5th May, 1974; Administrative Measures Taken in Connection with These Disturbances; Official Account of the Disturbances; Evidence of Additional Officials Called by the Commission and Evidence of Public Witnesses; Commission's Findings in Regard to the Causes and Course of the Disturbances and the Adequacy of Administrative Measures Taken (Causes of Disturbances); Course of the Disturbances; Findings of the Commission in Regard to the Adequacy of the Measures Taken; Riot Damage and Relief Assistance; Summary of Conclusions of Findings of the Commission in Chapter II (Causes of Disturbances); Course of the Disturbances; Adequacy of the Administrative Measures Taken; Measures Recommended for Prevention of such Disturbances and Other Relevant Matters; Suggestions Made by selected Public Witness; General Communal Situation in Delhi and Measures of the Administration; Public Co-operation; Citizens Volunteer Force; Home Guards; Independence in Investigations and Prosecutions; Police Set-up and Administration (Use of Powers Under Section 15 of the Police Act, 1961, and Misc. Matters); Delhi Armed Police and Central Reserve Police Force; Police Intelligence; Recruitment of Muslims in Delhi Police; Fire Arms and Arms Act Licenses; Fire Fighting Arrangements; Problems of Urban Redevelopment and Social Improvement in Sadar Bazar; Summary of Recommendations of the Commission in Chapter III; Concluding Observations; Acknowledgements; A Map of the Main Riot Affected Areas it at the End of Volume I; Vide Volume-II for Appendices and Annexures.

Recommendations

The observations of the N.N. Tandon Report on clashes in Bara

Hindu Rao on the 12th and 13th June, 1973, in regard to the use of the provisions of Section 110 of the Code of Criminal Procedure and of the Bombay Police Act rather than Section 107 of the Code of Criminal Procedure are endorsed. While action under the preventive sections of the Criminal Procedure Code is important it should not be a substitute for appropriate action under the substantive provisions of the law and wherever such substantive provisions of the criminal law can be invoked in regard to the facts of a particular case, regular charge-sheet for the offence or offences should be filed. Though action under the preventive sections of the Criminal Procedure Code has been stepped up in Delhi from June 1973, it would still appear, however, that there is room for further vigorous action in this direction in the Sadar Bazar area as that area probably accounts for substantially a higher proportion of the bad characters of Delhi than one-tenth. There is also much greater scope for externment of persons under the Bombay Police Act in that area.

More liberal use should also be made of different provisions of the Bombay Police Act and the Punjab Security of the State Act in force in Delhi. (Paras 3.13 and 3.14)

While it is necessary to have the members of elected bodies on the Sub-Divisional Committees formed to secure public cooperation for the maintenance of law and order, from the present composition of the Sadar Bazar Sub-Divisional Committee it would appear that it is not adequately representative of the minority community and that the recommendations of the Tandon Report regarding Ekta Samitis or Integration Committees have not yet been implemented properly. It is suggested that regular Committees should be constituted both at the Sub-Divisional and at the Thana level bearing in mind the observations of the Tandon Report and the advice given by the Home Minister to States and Union Territories in regard to their composition. (Paras 3.16 and 3.17)

The idea of a Citizens Volunteer Force is a good one but it must be activated and also cultivated so that the members of this Force have a sense of participation and do not lose interest otherwise the scheme will become moribund. (Para 3.18)

The suggestions of the Commandant of the Delhi Home Guards that Battalion Commanders of the Home Guards and also some other select suitable personnel in the organisation even below the Battalion Commander level, be made special police officers for their respective localities under Section 17 of the Police Act, 1861, is supported and this can be extended also to suitable persons in the Delhi Civil Defence Organisation. This step can be taken in sensitive areas where unlawful assemblies or riots or disturbances had taken place or are reasonably apprehended. (Para 3.19)

An independent machinery to supervise investigations and prosecutions is recommended to be set up under a Director of Prosecutions who may be of the rank of a Chief Judicial Magistrate and be appointed in consultation with the High Court. The power to take any decision contrary to the view of the Director of Prosecutions should vest only in the highest authority of the Delhi Civil Administration, viz., the Administrator or the Lt. Governor who should record his reasons for such a decision. (Para 3.20)

A full up to date review of the Police strength may now be made, without further delay, in terms of the Khosla Commission's recommendations which were accepted in principle by the Government and some very necessary adjustments be made accordingly even though there are financial constraints. In the meantime, some *ad hoc* sanctions should be given in cases which are very urgently required and obviously cannot wait. (Para 3.21)

The Delhi Police should have a P.A.B.X. or P.B.X. system connecting all police stations, police posts and supervising officers. (Para 3.22)

Increase in the number of mobile vans in Delhi requires urgent attention in the light of what has been urged by the Department and the observations of Shri K.F. Rustamji. (Para 3.23)

A separate police station is recommended to be be set up for the Division-I localities of the existing Sadar Bazar police station with staff for it sanctioned according to the yard-sticks of the Khosla Commission. There should be adequate strength to allow for beats/patrols round the clock in three shifts. If a suitable building cannot be leased or requisitioned, semi-permanent construction of the hutment type may be done by the C.P.W.D.

The beat and patrol staff of the two bifurcated police stations in Sadar Bazar should be provided with walkie-talkie sets or BEL talkies. (Para 3.24)

The Sadar Bazar area appears to qualify for a declaration by proclamation in exercise of the powers under Section 15 of the Police Act, 1861. Government may consider whether such a declaration should not be issued and half of the additional police force to be sanctioned regarded as "additional police force" to be quartered in the area and the cost thereof borne by the inhabitants. If this is done, say for three years, it will have a salutary and sobering effect. (Para 3.25)

The arrangements in the deployment of an Emergency Reserve/Striking Force in the Union Territory should be made permanent and the required strength for this force should be separately sanctioned immediately in advance of the general review of the Delhi Police establishment, as recommended earlier. (Para 3.26)

The requirement that public address systems should be there in police vehicles which carry men to trouble spots should be strictly enforced. (Para 3.27)

It is suggested that on occasions where intensive rioting is taking place in any localities of Delhi as roundabout Kishanganj Mohalla on the 5th May and there is no direct or easy means of communications with the inhabitants of such affected or threatened localities, use should be made of the All India Radio to broadcast police messages at very frequent intervals. (Para 3.28)

The Commission endorses the suggestions made by Shri K.F. Rustamji, (W. No. 145), Special Secretary to the Government of India, that (i) under effective action, should be included proper training of all officers and men on the police side and annual exercises and proper understanding between the magistracy and the police regarding the action to be taken in such riotous situations of a communal nature; and (ii) on the equipment side apart from the shortage of vehicles, there is a serious deficiency in the supply of tearsmoke and this is an important item which ought to be produced indigenously.

Shri Rustamji has also referred to a riot-gun which, instead of bullets, uses plastic pellets which can injure but not kill and which is still in an experimental stage. The Commission suggests that experiments with this riot-gun may be concluded early and it may be made one of the standard equipments for the police force. (Para 3.28)

When arrangements are made to deal with a serious intensive riot or disturbances like that in Kishanganj with the tendency to spread, the police and the magistracy at the top level must devise something like a general staff approach, namely, take stock from time to time of the situation as developing in the various areas and threatening to spread further, that is, not only survey the anti-riot operation at the place where the trouble has broken out but also its likely tentacles. (Para 3.29)

Officers and men of the police force and also magistrates should be prudent enough on such occasions when lethal missiles are being thrown, and more especially when fire arms are being used, to have helmets and shields ready and take advantage of the maximum cover possible while directing operations. (Para 3.29)

A convincing case has been made out by the I.G.P. for the strengthening of the Delhi Armed Police and for reduction of the degree of dependence on outside forces and specially on the C.R.P.F. This dependence on the C.R.P.F. in Delhi has been carried a little too far and from the evidence that has come before the Commission in connection with the disturbances of the 5th day of May, the present arrangements do not appear to be working as smoothly as would be required. (Paras 3.30 and 3.31)

It appears that obtaining of the "firing orders" by the C.R.P.F. officials from magistrates and police officers has, at present, become just a routine or even a meaningless formality. The correct procedure and forms in regard to these firing orders were not followed during the riots of 5th day of May and such firing orders were obtained even from police officers which is not warranted by law. If this form-filling business is to continue at all it should be in a streamlined and rationalised way with a different form devised for police officers and some clearer instructions to the Magistracy and Police of States/Union Territories as well as the officials of the C.R.P.F., appear to be called for.

It also seems clear that even though the impressions formed by many public witnesses and also press reports in regard to the attitude of the C.R.P.F. units on 5th May were exaggerated and the unit commanders did comply with the directions given without unreasonable delay, the C.R.P.F. units do not appear to have been fully integrated in the law and order organisation of Delhi so as to enable the totality of the force available to work together as a well oiled machine in unity of action. This experience by itself, apart from the other detailed reasons given by the Inspector General of Police, would be sufficient ground to suggest strengthening of the Delhi Armed Police and reduction of the present degree of reliance on an outside force like the C.R.P.F. (Paras. 3.32 and 3.33)

Taken in conjunction with what the I.G. has reported about the effective strength of 4 C.R.P.F. battalions available in Delhi, being only about 1,900, the total actual strength of the 5 Delhi Armed Police and the 4 C.R.P.F. battalions together when mobilised for field duty will not be much more than 4,500 in all, which is inadequate for Delhi. It is, therefore, recommended that the Delhi Armed Police which now has 5 battalions may be made 7 battalion strong as the first step with the two additional battalions to be raised as early as possible. The C.R.P.F. may be used more like an armed force providing the necessary backbone or strengthening as a second line to the ordinary local armed police. (Para 3.34)

The suggestion of the D.I.G. (Range) Shri Marwah, that each Police District should have some armed police sections within the district itself instead of all the armed police units being centralised in a single police lines is supported. (Para 3.34)

Since the authorities in Delhi have been twice taken by surprise within the course of 12 months in two different localities of Sadar Bazar police station, viz., Bara Hindu Rao in June, 1973, and Kishanganj in May 1974, it behoves them to make a critical re-examination as to whether some further improvements in the machinery and modes of gathering intelligence, both at the Thana level and in the C.I.D., are not called for. At the Thana level it should be possible to do this much more effectively with the beats or patrols from the bifurcated police stations organised round the clock in three shifts. The C.I.D. must also endeavour to perfect its own machinery so that even minor or trivial incidents in communally mixed localities are not overlooked, paying special attention to pan and tea shops and cinemas. (Para 3.35)

While there are no reservations for any community in Central Government services, apart from Scheduled Castes and Scheduled Tribes, it seems that greater effort has to be made to bring in a larger number of persons of the minority community into the Delhi Police Force. Cooperation of local leaders of the community should be sought and army recruitment methods should be studied. (Para 3.36)

There is evidently much room for tightening up of the rules and procedures in respect of All India Arms licences or licences issued outside Delhi where the weapons are being kept in Delhi by persons who are now staying in Delhi without intimation being given to the authorities. Whenever such a case comes to light, a severe view should be taken and prosecution launched irrespective of the standing of the defaulter. (Para 3.38)

A high level review of the entire policy and the legal and constitutional position in respect of issue of arms licences and possession of fire arms is recommended to be taken up so that it becomes possible for the Licensing Authorities to follow a much more restrictive and selective approach in the grant of Arms Act licences. (Para 3.39)

The Chief Fire Officer has suggested that it would be helpful for fire-fighting purposes if the various reservoirs of the Delhi Water Works have direct telephone extensions from the Fire Service Central Control Room so that the Control Room can contact the required extension at any time and issue continuous directions for adequate water supply to any particular affected area. The implementation of this proposal, at an early date, is recommended as it would help to control and fight a serious fire more effectively in any locality.

The Delhi Fire Service has also just drawn up a special scheme in outline for the Sadar Bazar area providing for a greater capacity of underground water storage and a network of pipelines to cover the interior of the market, which is estimated roughly to cost something between Rs. 10 to 15 lakhs. The Delhi Corporation may give early consideration to this scheme and take it up for implementation as early as possible with liberal financial assistance from the Government. (Para 3.40)

It is recommended that a fresh and activist approach to these problems of urban re-development and social welfare should be brought to bear by the powers that be, namely, the D.D.A., the Municipal Corporation, the Delhi Administration and the Central Government and within the basic policy and its objective of reducing the congestion of population and promoting its shift to new areas, every effort should be made under the provisions of different laws and also in administrative practice, to penalise strictly illegal or non-conforming activity to the maximum degree and also to give every possible incentive which promotes the basic objective. In particular, no further time should be lost in taking up the scheme of transfer of the slaughter house in Motia Khan and in initiating the shifting of wholesale markets and noxious and hazardous trades out of the area of Sadar Bazar. A high level coordinating committee may be set up to oversee this programme with the Lt. Governor who is also the Chairman of the Delhi Development Authority, as its head. (Para 3.46)

11

TECHNICAL COMMITTEE ON ECONOMY IN THE USE OF CEMENT AND STEEL IN BUILDING CONSTRUCTION, 1974 – REPORT[1]

Chairman Shri M.S. Bhatia

Members Shri V.R. Vaish; Brig Harish Chandra; Shri J.M. Benjamin; Shri Kulbir Singh, Shri K.R. Ramaswamy; Shri Rabinder Singh; Shri D. Ajitha Simha; Shri B.G. Baljekar; Shri K.G. Salvi; Shri K. Rama Verman; Shri T.M. Thomas; Shri B.V. Kulkarni (replaced by Shri V. Narayanan)

Convenor Shri R.G. Gokhale

Jt. Convenor Shri P.C. Khanna

Appointment

The country has been facing shortage of essential construction materials like cement and steel for the past few years and the position has been gradually deteriorating. In a meeting held under the aegis of the Planning Commission in May 1974, it was decided that a Technical Committee be set up by the Ministry of Works and Housing to go into the matter and suggest measures that should be adopted for bringing about economy in the use of essential construction materials like cement and steel in building industry. In pursuance to that decision a Technical Committee was set up by the Ministry of Works and Housing vide their order No. N-16012/1/73-PS, dated July 8, 1974.

Terms of Reference

(i) To study and recommend changes required in architectural

---

1. New Delhi, Ministry of Works and Housing, 1974, 47 p.

concept, structural designs and space standards for ordinary buildings to allow for greater use of local materials like lime, *surkhi*, stone, tiles, timber, etc., to ensure economy in the use of cement and steel and measures for getting these changes accepted and implemented;

(ii) To recommend operational measures which would allow for immediate use of fly-ash in civil works of PWDs, public section undertakings and other Government works;

(iii) To recommend amendments to PWD and departmental specifications, rules and procedures to allow for greater use of local materials referred to in (i) above;

(iv) To examine and suggest measures for implementation of the recommendations of the committee on economy in consumption of steel in the country insofar as they concern building construction;

(v) To study the technical feasibility and suggest use of present building components like channel units, cored units, battens and hollow blocks and cellular units, with a view to reducing consumption of cement and steel *vis-a-vis* conventional RCC construction; and

(vi) To recommend amendments to National Building Code so as to include provisions for greater use of local materials and simplification of the relevant parts of the code to facilitate their adoption by local authorities.

Contents

Preface; Architectural Concepts, Space Standards and Structural Designs; Measures to Promote Use of Fly-ash in Building Projects; Amendments to Specifications, Rules and Procedures of Public Works Departments; Measures for Implementation of Recommendations of the Committee on Economy in Consumption of Steel in the Country relating to Building Construction; Use of Precast Building Components; National Building Code; Building Materials; Follow up Action on the Report; Summary of Recommendations; Appendices from A to F.

Recommendations

Architectural concepts be such as to give the most economical structure; maximum use of local materials should be made in the construction; non-functional elements should not be provided; use of expensive materials and rich specifications for finishes should be avoided as far as possible.

Efficiency in site planning and design of individual building unit can considerably add to economy. The recommendations contained in COPP Reports, viz., 'Report on Multi-storeyed Buildings' and 'Report on Residential Buildings' should be adopted with such modifications as may be necessary. N.B.O. should update these recommendations as early as possible.

Up to three storeys, load bearing structures should be adopted; where bricks of higher crushing strength are available load bearing structures up to five storeys may be constructed. If higher structures are unavoidable in Metropolitan cities, 7-8 storeyed construction would generally be economical.

Number and size of doors and windows should be kept to the minimum consistent with functional requirements. Area of windows may vary from 10 to 20 per cent of floor area depending upon the climate. Use of steel and aluminium windows should be avoided as far as possible simple window for security be provided.

Principles of standardisation and modular coordination should be followed while planning and designing of buildings. Wherever a large number of units of any particular type of building are to be constructed a prototype may first be constructed to decide upon the most suitable design and details.

Adoption of minimum floor areas prescribed in the National Building Code, subject to modification suggested in para 6.2 in low cost housing, will result in economy. For non-residential buildings, areas should be as per prescribed norms where available or should be based on the analysis of activities be performed so as to avoid provision of unnecessary space. Width of corridors and staircases should be decided with reference to the occupancy of the building.

Floor heights in building may be limited generally to 2.75 metres (floor to ceiling). For buildings where central air-conditioning is to be provided, the height may be such as to obtain clear head room of 2.25 m below false ceiling in corridor and 2.4 m in rooms. Where there are deep beams, a clearance of 2.25 m below the soffit of the beam should be provided.

Load bearing masonary structures should be designed according to National Building Code. Such buildings should be carefully planned so as to utilise the strength of all walls to the best advantage. Ultimate strength design method should be adopted for RCC members and yield line theory should be adopted for design of two-way

RCC slabs.

High strength deformed bars should be used as main reinforcement in RCC structures except for slabs of small span where mild-still bars should be used.

Use of richer mix of concrete for members carrying predominantly compressive loads will lead to economy. In large projects, it is desirable to go in for controlled concrete. Precast prestressed beams may be used in RCC framed structures where it is feasible and found economical.

Steel structures should be adopted only where other types of construction is technically not feasible.

Design aids in the form of charts, monograms, etc., for the latest methods of design should be published by NBO/ISI in consultation with S.E.R.C. and made available to all construction agencies and private designers. NBO should organise more workshops in various parts of the country for acquainting the engineers with the new design methods.

Pending revision of the relevant codes, ISI should consider making some immediate modifications to the prescribed superimposed loads and load factors in the existing codes. Government should issue directives to the various Power House authorities to the effect that they should take special steps to be made available to construction Agencies Fly-ash of specified and uniform quality.

Measures should be taken to produce more quantity of Pozzolana cement using flyash. Ready-mixed concrete plants should be set up in large cities where flyash in building industry by publishing a detailed technical note.

Alternative specifications for principal items of building construction as given in Appendix B should be adopted with a view to reduce using of cement and steel.

Wherever the existing Departmental Rules do not provide for large scale manufacture/procurement of building materials like bricks, lime, *surkhi*, timber, etc., necessary amendments to the Rules and Procedures should be made. Longer periods of construction have to be allowed for in contracts where use of lime in place of cement for mortars and lean concrete is stipulated.

Important recommendations of the "Committee on Economy in Consumption of Steel in the Country" insofar they relate to building construction have been examined and endorsed.

The production of high strength deformed bars in the country should be increased.

Precast floor/roof compounds may be used wherever found economical.

To get the maximum advantage by use of precast units, building plans should be based on standardised units and with modular co-ordination.

Indian Standards Institution should prepare Codes of Practice for performance standards of various types of precast units.

The minimum size of kitchen specified in the National Building Code should be reduced from 5.5 sq m. For bathroom, the minimum area should be reduced from 1.8 sq m to 1.5 sq m with a width not less than 1.1 m wherever the bye-laws of local bodies are different from provisions of the National Building Code (subject to amendment as proposed above) in respect of minimum room sizes, wall thickness, floor heights and plumbing systems, suitable amendments should be made immediately.

State Governments may consider the desirability of enacting a Law empowering the State Government to notify that provisions of the Model Building Bye-laws as may be prepared, shall be applicable to all or any Municipalities for forthwith and to that extent the existing Bye-laws shall stand superseded.

Technical provisions should not form part of Corporation/ Municipal Act. Such provisions should form part of the Bye-laws/ Schedules so that these could be amended whenever necessary without procedural delays.

No amendment is required in the National Building Code for making greater use of local materials.

Building Bye-laws of local bodies should provide for construction of buildings with semi-permanent specifications in specified areas in towns and cities.

For increasing the production and improving the quality of bricks the Committee recommends that:

(a) The brick industry should be recognised as an organised industry.
(b) Urgent consideration should be given for the problems of supply and movement of quality coal for this industry.
(c) In Urban areas, local town planning authorities should set apart and allocate adequate areas of land for brick kilns.
(d) Land should be leased out on long terms basis.

(e) State Governments should set up pilot projects with the help of N.B.O. for training and demonstration in production of improved quality of bricks.

(f) If there is need, production of bricks may be supplemented through public enterprises.

For increasing the production and improving the quality of lime, the Committee recommends that:

(a) Government should allocate sufficient quantity of coal of proper quality for this industry.

(b) N.B.O. should set-up training-cum-demonstration plants at various places in the country.

(c) Large construction agencies like P.W.Ds., Housing Boards, Development authorities, etc., should establish lime manufacturing plants of their own to supplement the supply from open market.

(d) Government may consider advancing loans through HUDCO or such other financial institutions to private entrepreneurs for setting up modernised lime manufacturing plants.

The Committee recommends that:

(a) Construction agencies should conduct proper tests on *surkhi* produced from grinding of brickbats before using the same as a Pozzolana in lime morter.

(b) The technique of manufacture of Reactive *Surkhi* from burnt clay should be popularised through setting up of pilot-cum-demonstration plants with the help of N.B.O.

(c) Large construction agencies like P.W.Ds., Housing Boards, Development authorities, etc., should make arrangements for manufacture of Reactive *Surkhi* with the technical know-how of N.B.O.

The Committee recommends that large construction agencies should, in their future schemes, provide for joinery using secondary species of timber and should obtain their requirements of joinery from wood-working plants already existing in the country. If need arises, more such plants could be set-up later in the public sector. In places where it is economical to use stone slabs in place of RCC and

Construction Agencies have large-scale programme of such construction, they should make advance arrangements for procurement of this material.

The Ministry of Works and Housing should set up a unit under a technical officer in the Ministry of monitoring the progress of implementation of the various recommendations. State Governments should also set-up similar units. Construction Agencies should have suitable set-up for ensuring effective implementation of the recommendations contained in this Report.

Civil supply offices controlling issue of cement for private construction should be assisted by technical officers who could lay down norms for consumption of cement for various types of buildings in different areas.

State Governments should associate technical officers having adequate experience and knowledge of brick technology with task of regulatory control on manufacture of bricks.

Ministry of Works and Housing should give wide publicity of this report and make arrangements for supply of copies of the Report to all concerned.

12

COMMITTEE OF EXPERTS ON NATIONAL DOCUMENTATION CENTRE ON MASS COMMUNICATION, 1974 — REPORT[1]

Chairman Shri S. Dayal

Members Shri T.S. Rajagopalan; Shri Girja Kumar; Shri D.S. Mehta; Shri R. Tripathi; Shri K. Sarwar Lateef resigned and replaced by Shri A.K. Kidwai

M. Secy. Shri S.N. Sadhu

Appointment

A scheme to set-up a National Documentation Centre on Mass Communication (NDCMC) during the Fifth Five Year Plan was approved, in principle, by the Ministry of Information and Broadcasting and the Planning Commission. A token grant of Rs. 20,000 was sanctioned for the scheme, out of which a sum of Rs. 10,000 was made available in 1974-75 for preparing a project report on the establishment of NDCMC.

In pursuance of the proposal, an *ad hoc* Committee of Experts consisting of Mass Communicators and documentalists was constituted by the Information and Broadcasting Ministry vide Letter No. G. 29011/4/72 Adm. dated July 15, 1974.

Terms of Reference

1. To define objectives, functions and scope of the proposed centre;

2. To draw up a detailed project report for establishing the National Documentation Centre on Mass Communication in a phased manner during the Fifth Plan period, including the following

1. New Delhi, Ministry of Information and Broadcasting, 1975, 133c p.

aspects:

(a) Staffing and budget requirements;
(b) Physical facilities and equipment;
(c) Building up of library collection;
(d) Organisation of Library and Documentation Services;

3. To survey and assess the information resources and potential available in the country and the information requirements of all types of persons engaged in Mass Communication studies at all levels with a view to provide a basis for planning an integrated National System of Information for Mass Communication;

4. To suggest measures of liaison and collaboration in the field of Mass Communication documentation with Government and other reputed information agencies in India and abroad;

5. To suggest measures for obtaining necessary assistance and equipment from National and International Agencies for establishing the National Documentation Centre on Mass Communication;

6. To determine the administrative character of the Proposed Centre and suggest the composition of membership of its Governing Advisory bodies;

7. To study the pattern of the membership of the Centre whereby government and other organisations may be able to enrol themselves as institutional members for obtaining the facilities in the centre for their sponsored scholars;

8. To assist in the development of documentation techniques and resources of State government and non-government agencies engaged in Mass Communication activities;

9. To establish Data Bank on Mass Communication as a part of the proposed centre; and

10. To examine the procedure and methods for document collection, storage, handling, retrieval and dissemination so that information on Mass Communication available within the country and abroad is at the disposal of media operators, administrators, planners, research scholars and others who are interested in it.

Contents

Documentation Services; Role of Documentation Services in Mass Communication; Design for Establishment of NDCMC; Library Resources and Services; Documentation Work and Services; Data Centres Services; Reprography Unit; Printing Unit; Personnel and Equipment; Collaboration with International Organisations; Summary of Conclusions and Recommendations; Table from 1 to 14; Appendices from 1 to 8.

Recommendations

The conclusions and recommendations should be read against the background material in the report and interpreted in the light of observations in the paragraphs to which the recommendations relate.

Conclusions

1. Mass Communication media have made significant progress during the last twenty seven years of Independence. All the major media of Communication, i.e., press, radio, TV, film, advertising, publication, field publicity, etc., are used to provide entertainment and information to the people and motivate them for the venture of economic development. (Para 2)

2. The process of information transfer chain requires that mass communication information, which is widely scattered among the available sources, may be documented to serve the needs of media users. Such documentation would, in turn, become a new and integrated source of information. (Para 3.1)

3. At present there is no service which indexes exclusively periodicals published in mass communication. The number of periodicals published in the field of mass communication indicates that an estimated 20,000 items on this subject appear every year. (Para 3.3.3)

4. India has established or is in the process of establishing national centres of information in science technology, medicine, agriculture, defence sciences, nuclear sciences, patents, small industries, social sciences, etc. Some of the already established centres, such as INSDOC, ISI, etc., are well known nationally and internationally for the progress they have achieved, in their respective fields. (Paras 4.1.2 to 4.1.2.8)

5. Documentation and information services are looked upon as vital support not only for research and development activities and

academic pursuits but also for management, decision-making, planning and policy formulation and for social, political, economic and developmental activities. (Para 4.2)

6. Mass Communication studies are multidisciplinary in character. The mass communicators are interested in all the fields, though specialisation in specific fields is not uncommon. The information services to be offered to mass communicators have therefore to embrace diverse subject fields. (Para 5.2.1)

7. The users of information in mass communication may belong to different specialities, such as, research teaching, management, planning, field work, journalism, film production, advertising, publishing and public relations. The information requirements of these different categories of users are naturally varied in subject, purpose, content and level. There is a genuine need to provide them access to information they require as quickly as possible. (Para 5.2.2)

8. The volume and complexity of literature in mass communication is such that an individual worker can no longer hope to know all that has been published in this field. He is in need of a service to know exhaustively, expeditiously and pin-pointedly what is being published in his field of interest. But for the service, he will be lost in the flood of literature, unable to locate information of his interest and he will have very little time left for actual reading and professional work. (Para 5.2.3)

9. The operators of mass media, administrators, planners and others required information on various aspects of mass media, which is inadequate. They are now ill-served and are thereby seriously handicapped in performing their duties efficiently. (Para 5.3)

10. Various committees which examined the question of organisation of mass communication services have recommended that the Research and Reference Division should play an increasing role in providing documentation services. (Paras 5.3.1 to 5.3.5)

11. The multi-disciplinary character, volume and complexity of mass communication literature and different requirements of users, pose problems in having access to information because of inadequacy of existing library and documentation facilities. The various Committees appointed by the Government have also emphasised the need for provision of good library and documentation facilities. The survey conducted by this Committee (Para 5.4) for assessing the information requirements and potential available in the country also reveals the inadequacy of existing resources and facilities and points to the need

for provision of efficient documentation and information services on a national scale. (Para 5.5)

Recommendations

1. The broad objectives of the National Documentation Centre on Mass Communication (NDCMC) would be to collect, analyse, interpret and disseminate information relating to mass communication studies and problems. The mass communication dispersed all over the country and engaged in diverse aspects of mass communication work would have access to the required information as economically and expeditiously as possible. (Para 6.1)

2. The scope of the NDCMC may include the whole gamut of mass communication subjects such as press, radio TV, Film, advertising, drama, etc. The Centre would draw on diverse disciplines having a bearing on mass communication and would engage itself in data collection and data service. It may also collect posters, exhibits, models and other communication aids. (Para 6.2)

3. The committee would perform the following functions: –

1. Collect and retain all publications relating to mass communication;
2. Maintain a depository of all Indian literature on mass communication, both published and unpublished;
3. Inform mass communicators and others of current literature of value by bringing out documentation lists;
4. Offer documentation services, including translation and reprography services;
5. Serve as a channel through which the work done in India on mass communication is made known and available to all those interested;
6. Answer specific enquiries on the basis of information sources available in the Centre;
7. Maintain a referral centre for directing the users to existing information sources and services;
8. Prepare annotated bibliographies on various aspects of mass communication;
9. Compile and bring out national union catalogue of holdings of mass communication literature;
10. Index and abstract articles, keep clippings, microfilms and

documents on subjects that have a direct or indirect bearing on mass communication; and

11. Establish and maintain international co-operation with documentation and information centres on mass communication.

4. The NDCMC would be established and administered by the Ministry of Information and Broadcasting. In addition to exercising complete authority for the management of the Centre, the Ministry of I&B would also ensure financial resources and facilities for the development of the NDCMC.

It is suggested that the ultimate objective should be to make the NDCMC an autonomous institution. (Para 6.4)

5. The responsibility for administering the NDCMC would be entrusted to the Research and Reference Division of the Ministry of Information and Broadcasting in the informative years. In the later years, the pattern of its administration would be decided by the Ministry of Information and Broadcasting according to the rules applicable to other Government sponsored autonomous national institutions. (Para 6.4.1)

6. Information, documentation, and library services being undertaken by the Indian Institute of Mass Communication for its own requirements should be dovetailed to the over all programme of the NDCMC, so that there is no overlapping in services. (Para 6.4.2)

7. The Director of the Research and Reference Division would be the executive head of the NDCMC with powers for taking decisions on all matters connected with the functioning of the Centre.

Since the Director, R&R Division will be over all incharge of the NDCMC, his status should be that of other Media Heads of I&B Ministry.

The Deputy Director (Documentation) would be the technical head with responsibility for technical management and routine administration of the Centre. (Para 6.4.3)

8. An Advisory Committee consisting of experts in documentation and representatives of mass media units and of users' institutions may be constituted to advise and frame policies on all matters connected with the functioning of the NDCMC. The Director, R&RD and the Deputy Director (Documentation) would be its Chairman and Secretary, respectively. (Para 6.4.4)

9. The work of the NDCMC would be organised according to

four main sections viz (i) Library; (ii) Documentation Section; (iii) Data Centre; and (iv) Reprography and Printing Section. (Para 6.4.5)

10. The Administrative Section of the Research and Reference Division will look after the administration and accounts of the NDCMC. The present staff will have to be strengthened simultaneously to cope with increased work. (Para 6.4.6)

11. Pending the decision of the Ministry of Information and Broadcasting on this project report, the Committee recommends that posts of one Documentation Officer, two Documentation Assistants, one LDC/Typist and one Daftry from among the proposed staff, may be sanctioned and filled immediately for undertaking the spade work required for the Centre.

12. The Library of Research and Reference Division is to be regarded as an integral part of the NDCMC. In its future development, the rate of acquisition in the field of mass communication may be stepped up. The Library will provide (i) consultation service; (ii) loan service; (iii) inter-library loan service; (iv) reference service and (v) acquisition of documents. It will bring out regularly "Monthly List of Additions" and once in a year "List of Periodicals Currently Received". (Para 7)

13. A systematic routine has to be established for processing current information appearing in newly received information sources. Suitable criteria have to be determined as to the kind of information to be selected for processing. The selection of information requires careful judgement. (Para 8.1.2)

14. Index Cards containing standard bibliographical description of the information sources have to be prepared for each selected item of information. Care has to be taken to render the bibliographical descriptions in uniform manner. (Para 8.1.3)

15. The depth schedules for classifying micro-literature in mass communication studies have not yet been developed. Therefore, there would be many practical problems in using a classification scheme for organising information. The NDCMC is advised to take steps to develop classification schedule in various fields of mass communication in collaboration with organisations such as the Documentation Research and Training Centre, Bangalore. The adoption of alphabetical subject indexing system is recommended for the present. (Para 8.1.4)

16. The index entries prepared for all the selected information may first be made use of for various services to be offered. After that

they may be eventually merged into a perpetually cumulated file, known as the Central Information File. (Para 8.1.5)

17. The NDCMC may plan to offer the following anticipatory/ responsive services. The services are described in detail in the project report: –

(i) Current Awareness Service
(ii) Selective Dissemination of Information Service
(iii) Abstracting Service
(iv) Information Service for the Top Administrators
(v) Bibliography Service
(vi) Foreign Broadcasts on Mass Communication
(vii) Trend Report on Special Topics
(viii) Newspaper Clipping Service
(ix) Reference Information Service
(x) Document Procurement Service
(xi) Translation Service
(xii) News Brief
(xiii) Technical Digest
(xiv) Mass Communication Standards
(xv) Abstract of Doctoral Theses
(xvi) Future Events in Mass Communication
(xvii) Digest of Internatinal Conventions
(xviii) Referral Service
(xix) National Union Catalogue
(xx) Legislation in Mass Communication
(xxi) Who's Who of Mass Communicators
(xxii) Honours Conferred on Mass Communicators
(xxiii) Market Information
(xiv) Cultural Agreements

These services will be taken in phases, spread over a period of five years. In Table No. 2 of the Report a time scheme for taking up the services and professional staff required are given. (Para 8.2)

18. A suitable methodology should be devised to collect data directly from the various sources generating the data. There should be also a mechanism for updating the data from various published secondary sources. Assessment of users requirements should be made to enable a proper selection of data to be put into the system. For the present, conventional techniques should be used for data col-

lection. (Para 9.3 to 9.5)

19. It is recommended that the Reprography Unit should be set up in the third year of the Fifth Five Year Plan. (Para 10)

20. It is proposed that printing unit should be set up in the fifth year when the services of the NDCMC would be in full swing. (Para 11)

21. Early steps may be taken to create posts for various units of the NDCMC according to the recommendations made in the project report. Appointments to the posts may be made in a phased manner, as suggested in the report. (Details are given in Table Nos. 1 to 6 of the Report.) Number of posts with designations and grades for Documentation Unit are given below for ready reference:

Designation	*No. of Posts*	*Grade*
1. Deputy Director (Documentation)	1	1500-1800
2. Documentation Officer	2	650-1200
3. Documentation Assistant	10	550-900

(Paras 12.1 to 12.3.4)

22. The present strength of the library staff need to be augmented in accordance with the recommendations made in the report. Two posts of Library Assistants in the grade of 380-640 should be created in the Library. (Para 12.3.5)

23. It is estimated that 4 typist/LDCs one daftry and 4 peons would be required for Documentation and Library Unit. Appointments to the posts may be made in a phased manner as shown in (Table 4). (Para 12.3.6)

24. The question of providing translation service may be taken up at a later stage. For the present, no provision of staff for translation service has, therefore, been made. (Para 12.3.7)

25. Staff for Reprography Unit and Printing Unit should be appointed during third and fifth year respectively. Details are given in (Table 5 and 6). (Paras 12.3.8 to 12.3.10)

26. It is suggested that ways and means should be found to make the required space available either in Shastri Bhavan or adjacent to it. It is estimated that nearly 5000 sq.ft. space will be required for NDCMC. (Para 12.4.1)

27. A sum of Rs. 53,000 would be required in five years for purchase of furniture equipment in a phased manner for Library and Documentation Unit (Table 7). (Para 12.5.1)

28. A sum of Rs. 3,08,190 (capital expenditure Rs. 2,62,190 and recurring expenditure Rs. 46,000) would be required for setting up Reprography Unit (Table 8). (Para 12.5.2)

29. A sum of Rs. 3,29,175 (capital expenditure Rs. 2,54,175 and recurring expenditure Rs. 75,000) would be spent for setting up printing unit (Table 9). (Para 12.5.3)

30. A total sum of Rs. 3,52,000 would be spent over a period of five years for books, periodicals, reports and newspapers on mass communication. An account of document collection on mass communication is given in (Table 12). The details of expenditure are given in (Table 10). (Para 12.6)

31. For the development of NDCMC, a sum of Rs. 14,46,300 as recurring and a sum of Rs. 5,69,365 as capital expenditure would be the investment during the first five years (Table 14). (Para 12.7.3)

32. The NDCMC right from its inception should establish liaison with International Information System on Research in Documentation (ISORID) and other international organisations of similar character. (Para 13.1)

33. The NDCMC should take steps to seek assistance from UNESCO, UNDP and such other international sources for development of the Centre. (Para 13.4)

13

THE EXPERT COMMITTEE ON THE ENVIRONMENTAL IMPACT OF MATHURA REFINERY, 1974 – REPORT[1]

Chairman Dr. S. Varadarajan

Members Shri M. Kurien; Shri T.S. Nayar; Shri J.M. Dave; Dr. B.B. Sunderesan; Dr. Ashok Khosla; Shri Thomas Mathew; Shri H.K. Mulchandani; Dr. A.K. Mukherjee; Dr. B. Padmanabha Murthy; Dr. S.D. Shukla; Shri A.B. Malik; Shri Desh Raj Singh; Shri R. Sengupta

Subsequently a representative from Archaeological Survey of India was also nominated as a member.

M. Secy. Shri R.N. Bhatnagar; Shri S.K. Nayak

Appointment

The Government of India announced its decision to set-up a large oil refinery in the Mathura region to meet the growing petroleum products demand of the North-West region. This decision was based on techno-economic studies which has established the need to locate the refinery at Mathura for the following principal considerations:

(i) Mathura is located centrally within the demand area; and
(ii) It has both BG and MG lines and also is on National Highway No. 2.

Subsequent to this decision, some apprehensions were raised

---

1. Ministry of Petroleum Chemicals and Fertilisers Department of Petroleum, Government of India, New Delhi, 1978, 93 p.

about the possible adverse effects on the monuments in the Agra-Mathura region as a result of gaseous effluents to be discharged from the refinery. Since this was a matter of great concern, the then Minister of Petroleum and Chemicals, Shri D.K. Barooah, immediately took a meeting with the senior officers of Ministry of Petroleum and Chemicals, National Committee on Environmental Planning and Coordination, Planning Commission, Bhabha Atomic Research Centre and IOC in September 1973. The consensus of opinion during the meeting was that technological processes were available for containing pollutants in gaseous effluents to desirable limits as required from the point of view of preservation of monuments. The Hon'ble Minister had then directed IOC to take necessary precautionary measures to ensure that the effluents discharged in the atmosphere from the refinery will not have any adverse effect on the monuments at Mathura and Agra.

It was agreed that no effort should be spared for protecting the monuments, particularly, the Taj Mahal. Subsequently, the Government of India constituted an Expert Committee vide Government of India, Ministry of Petroleum and Chemicals Memo No. IS-46011/10/73-OR-I dated July 16, 1974, to advise the project authorities on the measures to be taken for keeping the pollution effect to the absolute minimum (Annexure I). The Committee was not only to guide Mathura Refinery Project in Planning and implementing effective pollution measures, but also to advise the Ministry on the pollution aspects of other ancillary and downstream units.

The Government vide Ministry of Petroleum's letter No. IS-36012/4/76-OR-I dated 4th April 1977 asked the Committee to also cover the aspect of effect of pollutants on the birds in the Bharatpur Sanctuary. Copy of the letter is given at Annexure II.

This Report of the Committee covers, in brief, the activities of the Committee so far and its findings and recommendations.

Terms of References

(i) To advise the project authorities, on the measures to be taken for keeping the pollution effect by the absolute minimum.

(ii) To advise Ministry on the pollution aspects of other ancillary and down stream.

Contents

Introduction; Activities of the Committee; Observations by the Committee, Conclusions; Recommendations; Annexures I to XII.

Conclusions

Based on the data made available to the Committee as well as the results of the studies and investigations undertaken, the following conclusions are made:

There is substantial level of pollution of sulphur dioxide and particulate matter in the Agra region. The possible sources are all coal users consisting of two Power Plants, a number of small industries mainly foundries (approximately 250) and a Railway Shunting Yard. As far as suspended particulate matters are concerned, because of use of coal, contribution will be substantial. Even though the total amount of emission of sulphur dioxide from these sources may be small, on account of their proximity to the monuments, their contribution to the air quality of the zone will be considerably high.

IOC has estimated that total emission of sulphur dioxide from the refinery would be limited to one tonne per hour and these estimates have been confirmed by the representative of the Ministry of Petroleum. Since basically low sulphur fuel will be used in the furnaces and modern instruments are available for proper measurement of emissions, it would be possible to ensure that the actual emission is limited to one tonne per hour. IOC have also assured that modern technology will be used for electrostatic precipitators of the power plant so that particulate emission from the stack is effectively controlled.

Based on the dispersal studies made by IMD and the investigations conducted by Tecneco and *NEERI* it has been estimated that the contribution from the refinery to the long term concentration of sulphur dioxide at Agra would be of the order of one to two micrograms per cubic metre compared to the existing level of 15 to 20 micrograms per cubic metre. Short term (one hour) peak concentration of the order of 65 micrograms per cubic metre could be expected under worst meteorological conditions in winter and the frequency for such occurrences are 2 to 4 per cent for Agra region and one per cent for Bharatpur region.

Adequate facilities are being provided for treatment of water effluents to meet the required specifications laid down by the Indian Standard Institution and the U.P. Government. Arrangement will be made for ensuring proper dilution of the treated effluents on occasions when enough water is not available in the river for dilution. Adequate expertise and proven technology is available indigenously for such treatment plants. IOC are operating similar plants in their existing refineries satisfactorily.

So far as the effect on the Bharatpur Bird Sanctuary is concerned, it has been established that there is no likelihood of any adverse effect either on the birds or the plant life at Bharatpur on account of the refinery.

Effective steps need to be taken quickly to reduce the existing level of pollution in Agra.

It will be necessary to ensure that the actual long term contribution to the sulphur dioxide levels at Agra as a result of the refinery is not more than two micrograms per cubic metre.

Winter refers to the 90 days period from the beginning of December to end of February. When the temperature profile in the atmosphere is such that it prevents a parcel of air to rise above a certain height, the atmosphere is said to be stable. Usually, stable condition mean that a rising parcel of air can rise up to a height of 100 to 500 metres, but its further ascent is prevented by an adverse temperature profile. The adverse temperature gradient is referred to as an "inversion" in meteorological literature. Meteorological data indicate that the frequency of wind direction towards Agra during the winter months varies from 14 to 28 per cent. Out of this percentage, the frequency of conditions which prevents the dispersal of pollutants due to stable conditions is approximately 2 to 4 per cent for Agra. This implies that the possibility of joint conditions of favourable northwesterly winds towards Agra, and stable atmospheric conditions in winter, is likely to be small.

Recommendations

Although primarily the Committee has been formed to advise the project authorities on the measures to be taken for keeping the pollution effect to the absolute minimum, conscious of the great responsibility entrusted to the Committee and its deep concern for the preservation of the priceless monuments at Agra and particularly the Taj Mahal, the Committee considers it of utmost importance that the following recommendations be considered by the Government for urgent and expeditious implementation in order to reduce substantially the existing pollution levels at Agra and to forestall creation of any future sources of pollution.

Efforts should be made immediately to minimize the existing pollution from sources close to the monuments in the Agra zone. The U.P. State Electricity Board had given indications that the old thermal power station (nominal 10 MW capacity) near the Agra Fort would be dismantled as soon as the grid for power supply to Agra is ready and the other power station (10 MW capacity) at Itmat-Ud-Daulah which is in good condition will be shut down and used only as a stand-by in emergencies. Closing down of these two power plants is expected to make a significant reduction in the existing levels of sulphur dioxide and particulate matter at Agra. It is recommended that early steps are to be taken to close down these two power plants.

Railways may be advised to replace the present coal-based locomotives with diesel-based locomotives at the marshalling yard at Agra. Since the marshalling yard is very close to the Agra Fort, this measure is expected to reduce the sulphur dioxide and particulate matter levels significantly.

Steps may be taken to ensure that no new industry including small industries or other units which can cause pollution are located north-west of the Taj Mahal.

Efforts may be made to relocate the existing small industries, particularly the foundaries, in an area south east of Agra beyond the Taj Mahal so that emissions from these industries will not be in the direction of the monuments.

Similar considerations may apply to large industries such as Fertilizer and Petrochemicals. Such industries which are likely to cause environmental pollution may not be located in the neighbourhood of the refinery. The Committee further recommends that no large industry in the Agra region and its neighbourhood be established without conducting appropriate detailed studies to assess the environmental effect of such industries on the monuments. Location should be so chosen as to exclude any increase in environmental pollution in the area.

The Committee wishes to record its deep concern regarding the existing level of pollution in Agra. It recommends that an appropriate authority be created which could monitor emissions by industries as well as the air quality at Agra on a continuous basis. This authority should be vested with powers to direct industries causing pollution to limit the level of emission and specify such measures as are necessary to reduce the emission whenever the pollutant level at the monuments exceeds acceptable limits. The Committee particularly desires that the recommendations made in regard to reduction of existing pollution levels at Agra should be converted to a time-bound programme and should be implemented with utmost speed.

The Committee recognises that there is urgent need for continuous study and investigations to ensure that the monuments at Agra are not exposed to further threats from the pollutants or from any cause. Therefore, it recommends that such studies should be periodically conducted with a view to determine whether any deterioration has occurred and if so, scientifically analyse the causes for the same to enable taking suitable measures for prevention of such deterioration. Since the Archaeological Survey of India are in charge of preservation of the monuments it is logical that they should be entrusted with the responsibility for getting such continuous studies made. For this purpose, ASI may have adequately staffed cell which can carry out studies and additionally utilise the services of other organisations such as National Environmental Engineering Research Institute, India Meteorological Department, National Physical Laboratory, Bhabha Atomic Research Centre, National Aeronautical Laboratory, etc., for determining the status of the monuments and also the effects of pollutants thereon. Adequate funds should be made available to ASI for these investigations.

The Committee also recommends that studies should be undertaken by competent agencies to explore the possibility of protecting the monuments by measures such as provisions of a green belt around Agra in the region between Mathura and Agra.

Even though assurances have been obtained from IOC that adequate precautions would be taken to contain the pollution on account of using coal in the power plant, the Committee is of the opinion that till such time this problem is studied in depth and suitable technologies have been found to be satisfactorily in use elsewhere, the use of coal in the refinery power plant should be deferred.

In order to ensure that the emissions from the refinery and their dispersion towards Agra are in accordance with estimates made and assurances given, a minimum of 3 monitoring stations beyond 10 km from the refinery in the direction of Agra at suitable intervals may be established. These should be operated well before the Commissioning of the refinery and operated continuously thereafter. The agency proposed earlier under para 5.7 shall audit these measurements.

The Committee recommends that the Government should establish facilities and expertise in organisation such as India Meteorological Department, National Environmental Engineering Research Institute, Bhabha Atomic Research Centre, Environmental Division of Dept. of Science and Technology, National Aeronautical Laboratory, Physical Research Laboratory and Raman Research Institute for developing dispersion models suitable for conditions as are actually obtainable in different parts of the country. This is essential for studies as the one entrusted to this Committee.

ANNEXURE I

No.I S-46011/10/73-OR.I
Government of India
Ministry of Petroleum and Chemicals
(Department of Petroleum)

New Delhi, the 16th July, 1974

Memorandum

Subject: Environmental Impact of Mathura Refinery – Appointment of an Expert Committee to advise on

A petroleum refinery with a capacity of 6 Million Tonnes is being set-up by the Indian Oil Corporation near Mathura in Uttar Pradesh. The environmental impact of Mathura Refinery and other ancillary and down stream units particularly the possibilities of gaseous effluents affecting the Taj Mahal and other historical monuments in Agra and Mathura has been engaging the attention of the Government for sometime. The Project authorities have been taking some steps to incorporate anti-pollution measures in the refinery. To advise the Project authorities on the measures to be taken for keeping the pollution effect by the absolute minimum, it has been decided to set-up an Expert Committee consisting of the following experts:

1. Dr. S. Varadarajan, Chairman, IPCL – Chairman
2. Shri M. Kurien, Adviser (R), Ministry of Petroleum & Chemicals – Member
3. Representative of the National Environmental Engg. Research Instt., Nagpur – Member
4. Representative from the Office of the Environmental Planning and Coordination, Deptt. of S&T, New Delhi – Member
5. Representative from the Indian Institute of Petroleum, Dehra Dun – Member
6. Representative from the Meteorological Department, Ministry of Tourism & Civil Aviation – Member
7. Representative of the Government of Uttar Pradesh – Member

8. Managing Director, Indian Oil Corpn. Ltd. (R&P Div), New Delhi – Member Secretary

Representatives of other concerned organisations such as Department of Archaeology, Indian Standards Institution, etc., will be invited to the Committee as and when considered necessary.

The Expert Committee will review the steps being taken by the Project authorities for prevention of the pollution and advise them of the additional measures to be taken. The Committee will also take into account the considerable progress made in different parts of the world in devising technical solutions to the pollution problems of refineries and particularly to air pollution and examine whether these solutions are proven and can be incorporated in Mathura Refinery. The Committee will not only guide Mathura Refinery Management in planning and implementing effective pollution control measures but will also advise Ministry on the pollution aspects of other ancillary and down stream units.

The Committee will meet as often as necessary and will work on a continuing basis. All secretariat assistance required by the Committee will be rendered by the Indian Oil Corporation. No remuneration, etc., will be payable to the members of the Committee TA/DA, etc., of the Members of attending the meetings of the Committee will be borne by their respective organisations.

The Committee will also keep the Government informed of their deliberations from time to time.

ANNEXURE II

Baseline Air Quality Survey at Agra
First Quarterly Report
(19 November 1975 to 29 February 1976)

Introduction

On the recommendations of the Expert Committee to advise on the environmental impact of Mathura Refinery, the National Environmental Engineering Research Institute (NEERI), Nagpur was awarded the work of conducting air quality survey around the national monuments at Agra by the Indian Oil Corporation. The object of the study was to set-up a baseline of pollution around national monuments at Agra before the proposed refinery at Mathura is established. As per the Expert Committee's opinion it was felt necessary to conduct air quality study for a period of 12 to 15 months which will cover at least two winter seasons so that observations would be of more confirmative nature. A work programme and financial proposal by NEERI was submitted to the Indian Oil Corporation and in order not to miss the first available winter of 1975 the sampling work was immediately started on 19th November 1975 at the Taj Mahal and subsequently at four other sites for the survey.

Air quality survey programme has been satisfactorily progressing since its inception with the kind cooperation of the Indian Oil Corporation, the Archaeological Survey of India, the District Magistrate of Agra and the Nagar Mahapalika. A small laboratory cell has been established in the Officers Hostel Building located in the Circuit House premises. A space for laboratory was made available with the kind cooperation and help of the Commissioner of Agra region and the District Magistrate. This accommodation is ideally suited for the survey work.

The Office of the Superintending Archaeologist, Northern Circle, Agra, have been extending their all time cooperation in locating air monitoring stations at different monument sites, permitting entries in the monuments and in the security of the air sampling instruments left at these places. Nagar Mahapalika authorities have kindly permitted to locate the monitoring station on the Mahapalika building. This is the first quarterly report of the work done by NEERI covering the period from November 1975 to February 1976.

2. Air Monitoring Sampling Stations

In Agra, the most important monument is Taj Mahal. The other ones being Red Fort, Sikendra and Itmat-ud-Daulah where study on air quality data is a must. It was also felt necessary that general city air pollution level should be obtained for comparison purpose. This means five stations are the minimum required for the survey. Therefore, five air sampling stations are fixed at the following sites:

	Sampling site	Date of sampling and frequency
I	Taj Mahal	Every alternate days started from 19 Nov. 1975
II	Agra Fort (Red Fort)	Every fourth day started from 22 Nov. 1975
III	Itmat-ud-Daulah	Every fourth day started from 2 Dec. 1975.
IV	Sikendra	Every fourth day started from middle of Dec. 1975.
V	Nagar Mahapalika	Every fourth day started from middle of Dec. 1975

The above air sampling stations were located taking into consideration the monumental importance. The city station at Nagar Mahapalika is the additional one to get the general air quality pattern of the city as it represents typical commercial and residential area.

3. Pollution Parameters

As per the work done in other countries, the common pollutants that affect the monumental construction materials like marble, sand stone and plaster are sulphur dioxide and particulate soot as primary pollutants to cause damaging effects. These are also index of average pollution carried by fossil fuel like coal, oil, etc., and other industrial activities. NO_2 is also a common pollutant of secondary importance as it gives an index of high temperature combustion for other photochemical activity. Therefore, sulphur dioxide, suspended particulate matter, NO_x (as NO_2) and sulphation rate were selected as pollution parameters.

Wind data with respect to direction and speed are also collected. This is a vital tool to interpret the pollution data of the air pollution survey. Though the airport at Agra records the climatological data, it was felt necessary to collect micro-meteorological data near Taj

Mahal site by setting independent meteorological station at the Officers Hostel building in the Circuit House premises.

4. Sampling Programme

Air sampling programme is designed as follows: At Taj Mahal the frequency of sampling is on every alternate day and therefore each day of the week is covered twice in a month. At other places seven sampling days per station are fixed for every month as shown in Table 1. These seven days cover all the seven days of the week (i.e., Monday, Tuesday – Saturday and Sunday). A sampling day comprises 24 hours period and normally the sampling gets started by about 10 hours in the morning and continues till the next day up to 10 hours. This completes the sampling of the day. On that basis efforts are being made to follow up the sampling frequency as described in Section 2 as above.

The tentative schedule of sampling is shown in Table 1:

TABLE 1: A Schedule of Sampling at Monitoring Stations

1st week							2nd week						
M	T	W	TH	F	S	Sn	M	T	W	Th	F	S	Sn
a	b	a		a	b	a		a	b	a		a	b
e	d		c	e	d		c	e	d		c	e	d

3rd week							4th week						
M	T	W	TH	F	S	Sn	M	T	W	Th	F	S	Sn
a		a	b	a		a	b	a		a	b	a	
	c	e	d		c	e	d		c	e	d		c

a — Taj Mahal;
b — Agra Fort;
c — Itmat-ud-Daulah;
d — Sikendra;
e — City centre.

Gaseous samples are collected normally on 2 hours basis for 24 hours continuously. This gives twelve samples per site per sampling day. Suspended particulate matter is collected on single 24 hrs. basis. Sulphation rate is measured by exposing lead peroxide candle for 30 days on a calendar month basis.

5. Observations

This report limits its observations only for a period starting from middle of November 1975 till the end of February 1976. This period can be classified as winter period and the observations made can be attributed to the winter conditions at Agra. Presence of sulphur dioxide and particulate matter are the main features of the observations made on air quality survey. Other parameters, namely, sulphation rate and NO_x are found to be considerably low during this survey period. These are discussed below.

5.1 *General Pattern of* SO_2 *Levels*

Figure 2 shows the general pattern of SO_2 levels. Taj Mahal, Red Fort and Itmat-Ud-Daulah show comparatively higher levels than the other two monitoring sites, namely, Sikendra and Nagar Mahapalika. November, December and January data show similar pattern of SO_2 level whereas February data indicates the receding trends. Three bars for each station show three different features of SO_2 level for that particular month. An open bar in the figure represents a maximum single 2-hour value recorded in that month. This value signifies the possibility of pollution reaching the monitoring site from the neighbouring or a distant sources. This high value is only for a short interval of time (2 hours). The middle bar with slanting line-represents the calculated 24-hours maximum average value observed on a particular day in a month. The third bar with dark blue column represents the calculated means value of sulphur dioxide for 24-hours on monthly basis.

The 24 mean value for sulphur dioxide is almost near about 20 micrograms/M^3 at most of the stations except at the Red Fort. The Red Fort value reaches the level of 40 micrograms/M^3. At Sikendra the SO_2 level is minimum in comparison to the other stations. The Taj Mahal monitoring site stand second in the order of SO_2 level other Red Fort, Itmat-ud-Daulah comes in third position. Table 2 gives the evaluation summary of sulphur dioxide levels at different stations. The last column of the table depicting 2 hours maximum value recorded during the survey shows the instance of pollution level up to the mark of about 100 to 200 micrograms/M^3. This is, however, for a short interval of time say, 2 hours. Such situation can be repeated in a month more than once. This confirms that there is a significant source of pollution in the neighbourhood. The values recorded though for a short interval are at the Red Fort and the Taj Mahal which are vulnerable to the effect of pollution.

5.2 *Diurnal Pattern of Sulphur Dioxide Level*

Figure 3 represents the variation in sulphur dioxide level for different periods of the day.

The normal trend in the diurnal variation is a depression in the level during the afternoon hours, say from 12.00 to 16.00 hrs. The pollution seems to get started rising during evening hours and maintain throughout the night and after the sun gets brighter and hotter the pollution starts receding. This can be explained by calm condition in the morning and right and windy ones in the afternoon. Also ground level diurnal inversion prevents dispersal of pollutants at night.

Figure 3 gives the illustration of the diurnal pattern for Taj Mahal, Red Fort, Itmat-ud-Daulah. Sulphur dioxide level at Taj Mahal could be soon ranging between 20 and 30 micrograms/M^3 with a depression of its level below 10 micrograms/M^3 during afternoon hours. At the Red Fort sulphur dioxide levels are slightly higher than those at Taj Mahal. The values ranging between 30 and 35 with a depression of 14 micrograms/M^3, in the afternoon. Similarly, levels at Itmat-ud-Daulah were also seen in the range of 30 to 40 micrograms/M^3 with a slight depression during night (15 to 20 micrograms/M^3). Itmat-ud-Daulah also records only 10 micrograms/M^3 level at the afternoon period.

Since Nagar Mahapalika and Sikendra monitoring sites were having almost negligible variations these sites have not been illustrated in the figures.

TABLE 2: Diurnal Variation in SO_2 Levels at Agra (Micrograms/M^3—4-hr. average)

Station	Month	Time of the Day						No. of days	24 hr.* avge.	24hr.* max.	2hr.* max.
		04-08	08-12	12-16	16-20	20-24	00-04				
Taj Mahal	Nov. 1975	19	18	8	23	30	28	5	22	35	77
	Dec. 1975**	25	26	11	29	31	24	14	24	50	122
	Jan. 1976**	22	26	7	17	26	18	10	17	58	160
	Feb. 1976	19	21	6	11	14	20	10	15	32	102
Red Fort	Nov. 1975	44	54	13	35	43	38	4	38	62	140
	Dec. 1975**	39	46	17	43	49	31	8	39	93	188
	Jan. 1976**	20	12	10	15	22	39	6	24	50	188
	Feb. 1976	36	14	11	11	14	18	5	17	21	58
Sikendra	Dec. 1975	11	15	6	8	13	10	3	10	16	22
	Jan. 1976	11	10	6	10	16	28	4	12	18	56
	Feb. 1976	6	6	6	6	8	10	5	7	10	30
Itmat-ud-Daulah											
	Dec. 1975**	17	33	12	46	32	20	8	26	64	134
	Jan. 1976**	16	26	10	35	36	18	6	24	43	110
	Feb. 1976	16	18	6	24	23	10	7	17	25	78
Nagar-Mahapalika											
	Dec. 1975	15	19	6	19	31	22	2	20	30	64
	Jan. 1976	13	13	7	19	29	15	6	16	27	74
	Feb. 1976	10	10	7	16	21	19	7	14	27	70

* Refer to Figure 2.
** See also Figure 3.

5.3 *Sulphation Rate Measurements*

Sulphation rate measurement though started from the month of December, the values of December and January could not be obtained due to technical difficulties. February values are reported in Table 3.

TABLE 3: **Sulphation Rate Measurement at Agra**

Name of the Station	Sulphation rate in February 1976
Taj Mahal	0.33
Red Fort	0.54
Sikendra	0.49
Itmat-ud-Daulah	0.67
Nagar Mahapalika	0.37

Sulphation rate measurements will be continued regularly till the end of the survey and the values will be more conclusive after the collection of one year data.

5.4 *NO_x Levels*

Normally the levels for NO_x (as NO_2) were measured at all the different stations and are found to be very close to the lowest detectable levels. Most of the time the values for NO_x are found in traces and therefore could be said negligible. In order to collect more volume of air the sampling programme for NO_x was prolonged from 2 hours to 4 hours in a single impinger and the values are almost all the same magnitude, i.e., under traces about 20 micrograms/M^3 or below.

5.5 *Suspended Particulate Matter in the Air at Agra*

Twenty-four hour samples for the suspended particulate matter record the particulate levels in the air ranging from 450 micrograms/M^3 in November and December whereas 250 micrograms/M^3 in January and February (Figure 4) all the monitoring sites have recorded similar trend of particulates with a little variation depending on the local activities.

Particulate matter at all the monitoring stations except Sikendra are identical. Red Fort site being slightly higher than other because of neighbourhood activities of the power station and transport.

Sikendra site which is identified as control station in relation to sulphur dioxide levels also holds goods in this respect. The exceptionally high value during the month of February (at Sikendra) was due to dust storm on one particular day of sampling. Normally, the average value at Sikendra is about 150 micrograms/M^3. The general pattern of suspended particulate level has been illustrated in Figure 4.

5.6 *Wind Pattern*

Winds are recorded from the Officers Hostel Building at the Circuit House compound. Exposure of the wind instrument observed to be ideal and could be a representative for the Taj Mahal and Red Fort area.

Monthly wind roses are drawn from December 1975 and January-February 1976 (Figure 5) . Special feature of the wind for the winter season (December to February) seems to be with prevailing calm conditions. About 25 to 30 per cent time the winds are calm. However, weak winds with a velocity ranges of 0 to 5 km/hr was also recorded during December and January. February winds seems to have been little more active and the winds were rising occasionally in the velocity range of 6 to 10 km/hr.

5.7 *Directional Pattern of the Wind*

Calm conditions prevail most of the time in December and occasionally south-westerly winds were recorded. In January the magnitude of the wind speed remain unchanged. However, the direction pattern was observed north-westerly as that of January with little more active winds in the movement. This explains the different levels of pollutants at Red Fort, Taj Mahal and Itmat-ud-Daulah during December-January.

5.8 *Temperature and Humidity*

The temperature during three months survey was about with maximum 78°F and minimum 55.F° and humidity about 40 per cent during the day time and 80 to 90 per cent in the night.

6. General Remarks

The data presented in this report is a factual data without conclusive interpretation. More data covering various aspects of meteorology, pollution, etc., are required for conclusive interpretation in future. The survey is being continued on those lines. However this will be discussed in the final report after completing the studies of the whole year.

ANNEXURE VIII

Report on the Dispersal of Pollutants from a Refinery Stack

by

P.K. Das, R.K. Dutta and B.M. Chhabra

of

India Meteorological Department, Lodi Road, New Delhi-110003

Abstract

There is proposal to establish a refinery near Mathura during the late Fifth Plan or early Sixth Plan. Mathura is about 40 km from Agra, where one of the major tourist attractions in India – the Taj Mahal is located. The designers of refinery are, as a consequence, concerned about whether the quantum of sulphur dioxide released from the refinery stacks would damage the Taj Mahal.

To meet this requirement, we have computed the concentration of sulphur dioxide at different distances downstream from refinery attack assuming Gaussian distribution of the pollutants. Delhi wind data have been used for the computations, the same have been discussed here. In particular, we present quantitative estimate of the impact of errors in vertical diffusion coefficients, the plume rise and meteorological data. A comparison has been made of concentration values obtained with a limited number of Agra winds with the estimates based on Delhi wind data. Computations have also been for the refinery in Madras, so that the model could be tested against field data in the vicinity of the Madras Refinery. We also show the use of power-law to define vertical wind profile. It reduces the concentration estimates without it by a factor of approximately 1/2.

Summary and Conclusions

It must be emphasised that the present study is handicapped by lack of field data under Indian conditions. We have used formulations for the diffusion coefficients, and the power law for wind profiles, which are used in extra-tropical latitudes. It is not clear how far these values would be applicable in India, without further field experiments. Despite this limitation, the main conclusions of the study may be summarised as follows:

(i) The vertical diffusion coefficient (6z) could be changed by a factor of 4 by 20 per cent error in 'a', 'k' the coefficients used by McElroy (loc. cit) to express the dependence of 6z on downwind distance.

(ii) If the ratio 6z/h exceeds 1.0, then the error in concentration estimates, purely on account of errors in 6z or h, would be small. On the other hand, for very small values of this ratio ($\leq$ 0.5), a small error in 6z or h could create very large error in concentration values. An examination of typical values suggest that errors in 6z, could generate an average error of about 50 per cent in our estimates of concentration.

(iii) If the wind profile is expressed by a power law, then (a) the estimates of peak concentration, and (b) the concentration 40 km downwind would be reduced approximately by a factor of 1/2. Some doubt exists, however, on the appropriate value of the exponent to be used in the power law. A value of $n = 0.5$ was used in the present study. The use of this wind profile suggests a maximum long term concentration of 28/μg/M^3 in January at 2 km from the stack. At a distance 40 km downwind, the maximum concentration is 0.44 in January for a 80m stack.

(iv) More reliable Dines Anemograph data are needed at the site of the refinery to improve our calculations which are based on Delhi wind observations. To overcome this, a meteorological observatory has been established at the site of Mathura Refinery and another will be located near Taj Mahal at Agra.

(v) Long term concentrations of sulphur dioxide from the refinery in Madras have been computed and presented in Appendix IV. They could be used to test the results of this mathematical model.

(vi) The present computations assume a single source. An assessment of the effect of multiple stacks will improve the results.

(vii) To avoid acute injury to vegetation, the risk of pulmonary diseases in human beings and corrosion of building material, the permissible level of sulphur-dioxide would be approximately, 1000/μg/M^3 for short term (1 hour) and 10-20/μg/M^3 for long term (annual concentration).

ANNEXURE IX

Summary of the First and Second Reports on the Studies for the Preservation of Monuments from Mathura Refinery Air Pollution Made by M/s Tecneco.

Messrs Tecneco of Italy were entrusted by IOC to undertake studies for:

(i) Determination of typical meteorological conditions in the Mathura-Agra region and calculation of long term ground level concentrations of effluents (particularly SO_2) at Agra on account of emission from the Mathura Refinery.

(ii) Determination of the existing level of pollutants in the Agra zone.

(iii) The present status of preservation of monuments and studies for determining permissible concentration of effluents from the point of view of preservation of monuments.

M/s. Tecneco have submitted the 'First and Second Report' covering the studies at (i) above. A brief summary of this report is given hereinafter.

The report is based on the following data given by IOC:

(1) Direction and wind speed at all times of the day from 1965 to 1974.

(2) Maximum and minimum temp. and humidity.

(3) Degree of cloudiness and global solar radiation.

(4) Radiosonde data of New Delhi for the period 1965-1974.

(5) Average monthly rainfall in mm for last 10 years.

(6) Map showing zone Agra, Mathura and location of Refinery and monuments.

(7) Emission data for each chimney for each operating conditions and height and diameter of chimney.

Based on the studies using the above data, the Report covers the following aspects:

The month with highest speed is June and lowest is November. The frequency of 36 km/hr speed is highest in the month of June (1.2%).

Wind Steadiness

Only for West-North-West direction the wind steadiness data at New Delhi have been studied. Steadiness more than six hours occurs only for wind speed more than 28 km/hr. The most frequent wind speed is 4 km/hr for the steadiness of 2 hours.

Atmospheric Stability (Based on cloudiness, solar radiation and wind data)

The frequency of unstable and stable conditions is higher compared to that of neutral conditions. In Winter and Post-Monsoon period strongly stable conditions are more frequent while in Pre-Monsoon and monsoon periods unstable conditions are more frequent.

Joint Steadiness of Wind Speed

Highest value of frequency is for steadiness till 2 hours only.

Ground level Concentration of SO_2 discharged by Refinery.

Dispersion Model used to calculate the short term ground level concentration SO_2 is Gaussian Plume Model. SO_2 concentration from each single source are considered additive. SO_2 is considered chemically and physically inert, i.e., physical and chemical removal process of SO_2 are not considered. The model assumes stationary meteorological conditions with respect to wind speed, direction and atmospheric stability.

Meteorological conditions used for calculating short term SO_2 concentrations.

(i) Wind Direction	Mathura to Agra within West-North West Sector.
(ii) Wind speed	6 to 36 km/hr
(iii) Air Temperature	34.50°C (Corresponding to maximum value of average monthly temperature at Agra.

Assumptions Made

(i) Flat Terrain.

(ii) Wind speed less than 6 km/hr is excluded (The distance of 40 km from Agra to Refinery implies that wind speed below 6km/hr will not effect monuments and it requires several hours to reach the monument zones. As per data, available from 1965 to 1974).

(iii) Meteorological parameters measured at New Delhi are representative of Mathura and Agra.

(iv) Vertical profiles of winds and temperature are assumed constant for short term calculations.

(v) Wind steadiness: (which of course is not very true).

Short Term Concentration of SO_2

Short term concentrations between Refinery and Agra as well as near the monuments have been calculated for various meteorological conditions. A summary of the frequency of these values is given below:

Frequency of short term ground level concentrations of SO_2

Concentration SO_2 micrograms/M^3	Around Taj		Between Refinery & Agra	
	Monsoon	Post-Monsoon	Monsoon	Post-Monsoon
Undefined	14.88	26.13	14.88	26.13
100	83.75	72.84	79.25	66.49
100	1.37	1.03	5.87	7.38
Total	100.00	100.00	100.00	100.00

It should be noted that according to Tecneco, based on their experience, calculated short term value of SO_2 concentrations are about 10 to 25 times higher than actual measured ones. This is essentially due to the assumption that wind speeds and directions will remain unchanged for long periods whereas actual practice steadiness of wind even in stable conditions is limited to 2 hours in the Mathura case.

Long-term Ground-level Concentrations of SO_2

Calculations have been done to obtain daily and seasonal average concentrations. These are given in the following tables:

Maximum daily average long term ground level concentration of SO_2

	Near Taj Mahal
Month	Maximum daily average Micrograms/M^3
Jan.	6.75
Feb.	3.80
Mar.	5.90
Apr.	2.50
May	3.50
June	2.25
Jul.	1.00
Aug.	0.80
Sept.	2.00
Oct.	2.25
Nov.	5.75
Dec.	7.00

Seasonal long term ground level concentrations of SO_2

Season	Near Taj	Maximum Concentration Micrograms/M^3	Distance from the Refinery (km) at which max. concentration occurs
Pre-monsoon	1.5	2.5	20
Monsoon	0.5	6	2
Post-Monsoon	2	6	1.5
Winter	3	7	1.5

ANNEXURE XI

Summary of the Third and Final Report Made by M/s. Tecneco on the Studies for the Preservation of Monuments in Agra from Mathura Refinery Air Pollution

1.Introduction

1.1 M/s Tecneco of Italy were entrusted by IOC to undertake studies for:

(a) Determination of typical meteorological conditions in the Mathura-Agra region and calculation of long-term ground level concentrations of effluents (particularly SO_2) at Agra on account of emission from the Mathura Refinery.

(b) Determination of the existing level of pollutants in the Agra zone.

(c) The present status of preservation of monuments and studies for determining permissible concentration of effluents from the point of view of preservation of monuments.

1.2 M/s. Tecneco had already submitted their First and Second Report covering the studies at (a) above. Summary of these two reports were circulated to Members on 30-12-1976. Their third and final report covering the studies (b) and (c) above has also been received.

1.3 M/s. Tecneco's third report includes following chapters:

(i) Introduction
(ii) Collection of Samples: Criteria and Methods.
(iii) Petrographic, Chemical and Physical Analyses.
(iv) Biological Analyses.
(v) Discussion of the Results of the Chemical, Physical and Biological Analyses.
(vi) Determination of Meteorological Parameters and Air Quality in the Monument Zone.
(vii) Conclusions.
(viii) Appendix I – Glossary of Biological Terms.
(ix) Appendix II – Deterioration of Stone Monuments: Chemicals,

Physical, Mechanical and Biological Causes; Effects of Atmospheric Pollution.

(x) Bibliography.

1.4 The report also gives various Tables, Drawings, Figures and Photographs as per the details given below:

Chapter	Tables	Drawings	Figures	Photos
2	2	3	—	4
3	12	2	8	103
4	10	—	—	9
6	29	17	—	—
9	3	—	—	—

2. Summary of the Report

2.1 Present Status of Preservation of Monuments (Chapter 1 of the report) gives a brief introduction of the work carried out by M/s Tecneco. This third and final report completes the studies carried out by M/s. Tecneco for the preservation of monuments in Agra from Mathura Refinery Air Pollution. To carry out the studies M/s. Tecneco had secured the help of Scientists and Specialists from some of the Research Organisations in Italy and particularly Institute Centrale del Restauro in Rome. This is probably the first time that such types of studies are carried out and as such no previous reference was available to correlate concentration of pollutants and the degree of degradation of the stone monuments. The studies, therefore, were carried out using the basic knowledge available.

2.2 *Collection of Samples (Chapter 2 of the Report)*

2.2.1 In order to establish the present status of preservation of the monuments, M/s. Tecneco had collected stone and dust samples from the monuments. Two on the site inspections were made to select the monuments to be examined in Agra zone and to decide upon the samples required to be taken to each of the selected monuments. The first examination was made at the end of 1974 and the second in January 1976 just before the collection of the samples. As substantial uniformity was observed in Agra monuments, both from the point of view of quality of the building material and that of the State of conservation of the surface of the material, it was decided to limit the study to the three monuments namely, Taj Mahal, Agra Fort and Akbar Tomb.

2.2.2 Basically these monuments are constructed of only two types of stones, white marble coming from Makrana quarry and red sand stone coming from Tantpur and Paharpur quarries. During the inspections the following forms of alterations were noticed:

For Marble

(i) More or less abundant deposit of yellow grey dust on the surface where rain cannot reach the stone. This dust can be easily removed by a brush.
(ii) A thin black hard layer or small black spots covering some projecting parts mostly on the north side, near the floor and on the upper parts where rain can easily reach.
(ii) Some cracks on the slabs along the greyish veins, from where a visible algae growth is penetrating inside.

For Sandstone

(i) A heavy exfoliation of stone along the sedimentation planes.
(ii) In some places a white efflorescence is present on the detaching layers.
(iii) In some places large and black entrusted layers cover the surfaces.
(iv) In some places insects and weeds are present.

2.2.3 Mode of collection of samples. – Samples were collected to study in more details the following forms of alterations: –

– Earth dust (present on marble)
– Black spots (present on marble)
– Black spots (present on sand stone)
– White efflorescence (present on sand stone)

Samples were taken using sterile scalpel (spots and efflorescence) and with a sterile brush (dust). The material collected from every type of alteration from each monument was put in a sterile tube, closed with a rubber stopper wrapped in a sheet of aluminium and kept in a refrigerator (about 4°C) up to the time they were transported to Rome in portable refrigerated cases. The collection of samples was done during the period from 6th to 16th Jan., 1976. Some pieces of marble and sand stone detached from the three monuments during the previous maintenance work were given by the Archaeological Survey of India to be analysed and compared with the corresponding quarry stones.

2.3 *Petrographic, Chemical and Physical Analyses carried out on the Samples*

To establish the actual State of conservation of monuments two types of studies were made on the samples collected. One was of chemical and physical nature and the other of biological, Chapter 3 of the report discussed the studies carried out with Petrographic, Chemical and Physical Analyses – following methods were used:

2.3.1 *Petrographic study* – This was done to determine the lathe types and their characteristics. Phenomena of aging and of alterations in the building materials depend not only on external conditions but on their mineralogical composition and internal structure. For this reason microscopic and mineralogical microscopic observations were carried out on thin sections of the samples. Macroscopic observations were not possible for many of the monument samples because of their small sizes. The report discusses the observation made and also give some paragraphs showing textures of the stones. (Summary of the findings is given in paras 2.5.1, 2.5.2 and 2.5.3).

2.3.2 *Porosimetric Characteristic* – A knowledge of the Porosimetrical characteristics of the stone material, i.e., the volume of the Pores and their distribution in relation to the section, is important for classifying the stone according to its internal structure. The mechanical properties and the durability of the material depend upon the pore structure. A knowledge of the structural modification caused to lapiseous material as a result of aging is also a help in the study of the causes of alteration and their mechanism. The measurement of the absorption of water is carried out to have an indication of the capacity of the stone to absorb water.

The Report gives details on the techniques and methods used for carrying out these studies. The results obtained are given in tabular forms and also in graphical forms. (Summary of the findings is given in paras 2.5.1, 2.5.2 and 2.5.3).

2.3.3 Superficial strata of the stone were subjected to the following tests for investigating the presence of soluble salts and mechanism of their action;

(a) X-ray diffraction; Thus technique helped in furnishing additional information on mineral constituents.
(b) Chemical analyses – qualitative and quantitative.
(c) Morphological examination by electronic scanning microscope, metallographic and mineralogic microscopes.

The Report discusses in detail the various observations made and also describes the techniques and methods employed for the analyses. (Summary of the findings is given in paras 2.5.1, 2.5.2. and 2.5.3).

2.4 *Biological Analyses: (Chapter 4 of the Report)*

2.4.1 The biological research was guided by the following objectives:

(a) A direct survey of the biological profile of each monument;
(b) The study of specific biological deteriorations; and
(c) An indirect evaluation of the State of conservation by determination of the microbic charge of all types of alterations.

This objective (a) was carried out in situ with the verification of generic alterations and the presence or absence of alterations of biological origin.

The objective (b), which was carried out with laboratory tests, includes the survey of specific phenomena of bio-deterioration, their recognition, their morphological classification and the characterisation of the dominant biological agent.

For the third objective (c) using specific liquid and solid cultures, isolation was effected in the laboratory of those microbic groups which are considered on account of their metabolic characteristics, to play a part in the alteration of monuments. The report gives details of each of the tests and discussed the findings. (Summary of the findings is given under para 2.5.4)

2.5 *Findings of the Chemical, Physical and Biological Analyses: (Chapter 5 of the Report)*

2.5.1 The different types of analyses carried out on the samples from monuments and quarries showed considerable agreement. Materials used in these monuments are same and state of conservation is comparable. From the quantitative difference of soluble salts in the marble samples it can be presumed that there is slightly more attack at Agra Fort than that at Taj Mahal. Attack on Akbar's Tomb can be considered as the least.

2.5.2 *Observation on Marble* – Marble is essentially constituted of calcite and dolomite. It is structurally compact and unaltered. It is quite resistant to climatic factors of aging as it is not porous and has low absorption of water. The superficial layers were analysed by X-ray diffraction, enemically, by electronic microscopy, and by X-ray nucroprobes. It was evident that major cause of alteration is biological as the presence of soluble salts found, percentage of sulphates and chlorides were large. In some samples from the zones where rain water does not reach, presence of some gypsum was observed. Accumulation of gypsum presents danger for good conservation. Dust samples collected from the marble showed presence of soluble salts. This also presents potential danger.

2.5.3 *Observation on Sand Stone* – Sand Stone used in the monuments is basically of one type only. It is essentially constituted of quartz and alkaline foldspar. The layer structure is such that flaking takes place according to the planes parallel to that of sedimentation. Flaking is a major form of alteration. The quarry stones have porosity comparable with that of other stones of similar type but absorb more water. This may be the reason for lesser resistance of the material to the atmospheric agents. Structural variations due to process of aging are (a) decrease in porosity and (b) increase in pores of smaller diameters. This is normally due to formation of clay materials as confirmed by the diffractometric present, alteration is mainly due to biological action and corrosion is limited to the surface. In this zone soluble salts are practically absent except for sulphates which are present in near about same amount, as observed in stone samples with white efflorescence. On samples with white efflorescence the degradation of superficial structure is due to presence of soluble salts, mainly chlorides and nitrates of sodium and potassium. Biological alteration is practically absent.

2.5.4 *Biological Investigation* – Even though these investigations were limited to only one set of samples of stones and that too limited to as obtainable during one season, they furnished interesting information.

2.5.4.1 *Black Spots* – Monuments examined were in a similar and sufficiently uniform State of conservation from a microbiological point of view. Both types of stones were similarly altered by black spots. This type of alteration is attributed to multiplication of microscopic algae which are also accompanied by decomposing microorganisms or at least using their organic and inorganic remains (sulphur bacteria-predominantly oxidising type, ammonifying and heterotrophic bacteria, fungi and actonomy cotes). Algae responsible for black spots (both on marble and sand stone) are generally blue green algae, i.e., cynophiceae. This indicates the presence of humidity, a little mould and of saline nutrients (bird excrement). Since this type of algae have pigments such as phycobmn, they can survive even in low light conditions. This explains their presence in all the cardinal points and also in zones in shadow. The major portion of the algae determined is of covering and corrosive type because of action of their constituents like exalic and muramic acids. Some form (e.g.) cocoals can cause disintegration and pertorations on the stone. Other forms (chroococcus, ciooccapsa lyngbya) are able to fix atmospheric nitrogen to produce nitrogen compounds, these compounds are used by nitro bacteria thus causing further corrosion attack. This type of attack, however, is not noticed at this stage.

It was observed that cynophiceae algae was present in great number. Sulphur bacteria was present in very small number, less than patelegic, heterotrophic and ammonifying bacteria, actinomycetes and microscopic fungi. All these were present in small amount indicating their development is in stages due to the algae.

2.5.4.2 *White Efflorescence on Sand Stone* – White efflorescene, which causes accumulation of salts and is quite damaging to stone, has a microbic charge consisting of nitrosifying, ammonifying, sulphur-oxidising heterotrophic bacteria and fungi. These are however, present in very insignificant amount. This much amount is normally found in every surface exposed to air.

2.5.4.3 *Earth Dust from Marble* – Reddish grey or brown or yellowish dust recovered from the surface of marble, contained not only salts but also a number of micro-organisms both heterotrophic bacteria, actinomycetes, fungi and chemosynthetic autotrophic (sulphur oxidising and reducing). The origin can be attributed from the surrounding earth.

2.6 *Air Quality in Monument Zone and Meteorological Parameters (Chapter 6 of the Report)*

2.6.1 For determining the existing level of pollutants in the Agra Zone M/s Tecneco had installed some instruments in Agra. One continuous Analyser for SO_2 was installed near Taj Mahal and one sampler giving 24 hours average SO_2 concentration was located at the same place. Continuous SO_2 Analyser was installed for determining the maximum values while sampler was installed to have a reliable daily average values. It has been found that for most part of the survey graphs, the values were very near to zero. From continuous analyser readings, hourly average readings and daily average readings were computed. Hourly average readings were related with wind speed and Direction results. Hourly concentrations have been higher than 150 micrograms/M^3 for 4 times and higher than 200 micrograms/M^3 for 2 times only. All these situations occur during calm conditions when wind velocities are low. Daily average concentration results are less than 60 micrograms/M^3. The daily average concentration vary invariably and do not form any particular pattern.

2.6.2 M/s Tecneco had positioned some huts at different locations in the monuments. Filters treated with K_2CO_2 were suspended in these huts for the measurement of acidic compounds in the atmosphere. After exposing these filters to a period of about 2 weeks they were regularly sent to Italy for further analyses.

K_2CO_3 filters exposed to Agra atmosphere were tested for sulphur, nitrates and chlorides. The chlorides were found negligible. Average values for sulphur and nitrates for 3 monuments are as under:

Monuments	Milligrams of NO_3Cm^2 day	Miligrams of 'S'/Cm^2 day
Agra Fort	0.039	0.17
Taj Mahal	0.028	0.12
Akbar's Tomb	0.027	0.06

The average figures given above for Sulphur compounds can generally be related to Sulphur dioxide as it is the major pollutant normally present in the atmosphere.

2.6.3 *Meteorological Parameters*

(i) *Air Temperature inside and outside monuments* – Values measured outside Taj and outside Akbar's Tomb are similar. Area covered thus shows homogeneity as regards air temperature.

Outside temperature variations over a day range above 10°C and at some points of the order of 20-22°C. Maximum value was observed in the beginning of June, i.e., 43°C. Minimum value was observed in Jan., i.e., 5°C.

(ii) *Surface temperature of monuments* – In order to estimate the possibility of condensation phenomenon, the surface temperature of the stones and temperature of air at 1/2 metre distance from stone were measured. The dew point was calculated considering humidity records.

Only in 0.38 per cent of cases examined condensing conditions were present. These conditions occurred more frequently at Taj.

(iii) *Wind Speed and Direction* – The continuous measurement of wind speed and direction was carried out at Taj. These readings were converted to obtain the hourly average speeds and direction from which the frequency of each direction and speed was calculated.

There is considerable agreement between Delhi results (as reported in Reports 1 and 2) and Agra results for the months of Jan., Feb. and March.

For the months April, May, June and July the wind data for Delhi and Agra differ. The difference is difficult to explain.

The lowest level of wind speed at Agra as recorded is 2 km/hr and at Delhi it is 1 km/hr. This is attributed to the difference in the sensitivity of the instruments.

Chapter 7 of the Report giving conclusions is reproduced hereunder:

2.7 *Conclusions*

As a reference parameter of the State of atmospheric pollution in the Agra Zone, the concentration of SO_2 in the atmosphere has been taken into consideration. This is above all because SO_2 is the atmospheric pollutant emitted by the Mathura Refinery in the highest concentration and which can reach Agra, even if the levels of concentrations result very low on the basis of the theoretical calculations carried out in "First and Second Report". The surveys of this parameter, carried out at the Taj Mahal from January to July 1976, led to the conclusion that the Agra zone has a very low index of atmospheric pollution.

In fact the daily level of concentration of SO_2 measured is usually only a few micrograms/M^3. Only on some days does it reach values of 10-20 micrograms/M^3 and in very exceptional cases higher values (60 micrograms/M^3).

During the whole period, there is a total average of about 6 micrograms/M^3.

The primary standards of the Environmental Protection Agency U.S.A. for the quality of the air concerning sulphur oxides (sulphur dioxide) are:

- 80 micrograms/M^3 as an annual average
- 365 micrograms/M^3 an average over 24 hours not to be exceeded more than once in a year.

Various nations in Europe have established as a target a maximum monthly concentration of 150 micrograms/M^3 and a maximum annual concentration of 100 micrograms/M^3.

The World Health Organisation recommends as a target, for SO_2 and suspended particulates measured in conjunction:

- SO_2 annual average 60 micrograms/M^3 98 per cent of observation below 200 micrograms/M^3.
- Suspended particulates annual average 40 micrograms/M^3.

Over the last years, average annual levels of SO_2 have been observed as follows:

	(micrograms/M^3)
Copenhagen	60
Stockholm	70
Amsterdam	80
Liege	130
Brussels	170

Paris	110
London city	250
London, greater	150
Milan	600
Venice, industrial area	130
Venice, city	70
New York - Manhattan	110
New York - Richmond	50
Los Angeles	70
Toronto, city	170
Toronto, residential	30

With monthly average included among some tens of micrograms/ M^3 and:

Copenhagen	120
Stockholm	130
Amsterdam	130
Liege	250
Brussels	300
Paris	250
London, city	400
Milan	1400
Venice, city	150
Venice, industrial area	200
New York - Manhattan	130
New York - Richmond	70

SO_2 has been taken as a parameter to evaluate the increase in atmospheric pollution in the Agra zone caused by the Mathura Refinery. This is because, as has been previously pointed out, SO_2 is the alone polluting substance emitted by the Refinery which can reach Agra and even if it does, only in very small concentrations.

The concentrations of SO_2 emitted by the Refinery which can reach Agra have been estimated using a mathematical model of Gaussian type, taking into consideration the anemological data of New Delhi relative to the ten-years period 1965-1974 and the emission characteristics supplied by the Indian Oil Corporation.

In consideration of the great distance between Mathura and Agra, the calculated values should be considered even more valid the longer the period to which they refer. This means that the most valid are the annual averages, less valid the seasonal averages and even less significative the short term averages.

The average annual theoretical concentrations of SO_2 in Agra caused by the Mathura Refinery result as being very much reduced; i.e., 1.5-2 micrograms/M^3: analogously, the seasonal averages, which go from 0.5-1 micrograms/M^3 (monsoon period) to 3 micrograms/M^3 (winter). Therefore, it can be affirmed that the atmospheric pollution caused by the Refinery does not constitute, except for very improbable high levels of concentrations due to exceptionally bad meteorological conditions, a modifying element of the atmospheric situation of Agra because of its extremely low levels of concentration which it could add to the already existing low levels. Petrographic and minerological analyses, X-Ray diffractometry, chemical analyses, macroscopic analyses with X-rays, morphological examinations with optical and electronic scanning microscopes and biological analyses were carried out on samples of marble and sandstone taken from Agra Fort, Akbar's Tomb, the Taj Mahal and from the quarries and on dust samples taken from the three monuments so as to be able to define their state of conservation. On the basis of the results obtained, the following can be affirmed:

Marble – on the basis of the results obtained, it can be affirmed that the state of conservation of the marble is still good. The optical microscopic and electronic scanning macroscopic examination as well as the biological analyses reveal that the prevailing form of alteration is due to the superficial corrosion by algae, which for the most part of the cases is not than some tons of microns on the material.

On the other hand, in the earth dust samples and in the TM filter (put at a few tons of meters from the ground) the presence of chlorides, sulphates and nitrates was found.

The chemical and diffractometric analyses show the presence of insignificant quantities of soluble salts and the porosimetric measurements show that in the worst case, the internal structure of the material compared to marble from the quarry only an initial alteratiõn. In the marble samples taken from near those in which dust samples were taken, these salts were in lesser quantities than in the dust and such as not yet to have caused any remarkable alteration. However, it is evident that presence represents a potential danger for the good conservation of the marble.

Sandstone – The sandstone doesn't appear in a good condition mainly because the nature of the material (chemical-mineralogical composition, structure and porosity).

Over and above the alterations of biological origin, mainly due to the algae which have an analogous action as that already explained on the marble, there is also peeling and scaling due to the strata structure of the stone.

This caling forms the most obvious and common alteration. The variation in porosity of the stone of the monuments, compared to the quarry stone, shows a more obvious aging phenomenon than in the case of marble. Some areas of the sandstone present serious forms of alterations caused by the presence of white efflorescence formed by soluble salts (mainly chlorides and nitrates) the origin of which can be connected with atmospheric pollution phenomena. The presence of these soluble salts induce, in the porous structure of the stone, a series of phenomena connected with processes as dissolution – crystallisation and hydration – dehydration which cause considerable degradation, taking in account the structure and texture of the stone.

The determination of the surface temperatures of the monuments together with the air temperatures and relative humidity has demonstrated that, at least during the period being considered, the probability that condensation phenomena on the stones occur is rather small.

This situation means that the attack of atmospheric SO_2 on the stones is more difficult.

On the other hand, it should be considered that the deterioration phenomena are not linear but exponential.

This means that the more a stone is altered, the more it will be sensitive to the action of any alteration agent.

From this point of view, the bad conservation of standstone makes this stone more sensitive to the action of any degradation agent including atmospheric pollution.

Another consideration concerns the accumulation phenomena consisting in the fact that eventual chemical attacks on a stone, even if low in absolute values, induce an irreversible modification on the stone itself which is added to the others, even if slight, which preceded it and which will follow.

However, it is evident, that if such modifications are slight in absolute values, they become secondary compared to those more important induced by other alteration agents.

Excluding some fragments of stone taken from substitutions

carried out during maintenance work, all the other marble and sandstone samples are taken from the surface of the various deteriorated zones of the three monuments.

As far as the marble is concerned, on the whole the alterations are limited to only a few zones.

On the contrary, the alterations of the sandstone are present nearly everywhere.

Therefore, in conclusion, the marble results as being well conserved in all three monuments and its state of aging can be considered initial while the sandstone is generally in a bad condition.

Since the concentration levels of pollutants taken into consideration are very low, it can be taken for granted that the atmospheric pollution actually present in the Agra zone does not constitute a prevailing cause of alteration such as to notably increase the natural aging of the stone.

The levels of SO_2 concentrations in the Agra Zone due to the refinery (from 1.5 to 2 micrograms/M^3 as an annual average) form an objective increase of present levels; however, the concentration levels at Agra Zone, increasing from 6 micrograms/M^3 to 7.5-8 micrograms/M^3 as an annual average will remain as very low absolute values.*

For this reason, although keeping in mind the previous considerations on the State of conservation of the stones and on the accumulation effect, it can be considered that the foreseen pollution levels will not form one of the main causes of deterioration of the monuments. It is necessary to remember that the annual increase of SO_2 of 1.5-2 micrograms/M^3 is the result of theoretical calculations which, although carried out with due care, have necessarily large margins of uncertainty connected to the schematization taken for the meteorological parameters.

As already referred in our comments on page 15 of our First and Second Report it should be noted that in their calculations SO_2 is considered chemically and physically inert. This means that physical or chemical removal processes of SO_2 are not taken into considera-

---

* *Note*: It was already said in chap. 6. the value 6 micrograms/M^3 really represent the average during the 6 months of measurement, from 12th July, 1976. But we can consider that the annual average concentration should not be higher than 6 micrograms/M^3 because during the other 6 months, in which the measurements were not made, there are three months affected by monsoons.

tion. This assumption does not affect very much the short term concentrations while overestimates the long term concentrations.

The model assumes a stationary meteorological condition, that is speed and direction of wind and atmospheric stability are considered constant during the transport of pollutants.

2.8 *Glossary of Biological Terms*

Appendix I gives Glossary of Principal Biological terms used.

2.9 *Deterioration of Stone Monuments*

In Appendix II. M/s Tecneco have described in detail the various aspects of the deterioration of stone monuments and the factors, causing the deterioration, such as chemical, physical, mechanical and biological and also the effects of atmospheric pollution based on available published literature.

ANNEXURE XII

Bharatpur Bird Sanctuary Correspondence Exchange

Copy of:

Letters from Member-Secretary No. MRG/6/6 Dated 18th April 1977 and 12th June 1977 to Messers Nature Conservancy Council, The Royal Society for Protection of Birds and the Wild Fowl Trust, All of U.K.

As you are perhaps aware, construction work on a large oil refinery of a capacity of processing six million metric tonnes of crude per annum has commenced at a place near Mathura, which is situated at about 150 km South East of New Delhi. The Refinery will have the normal process units, storage tanks, despatch facilities and would also include a power plant. It is expected to be commissioned by early 1980.

As a measure of limiting emission of pollutants from the refinery, a decision has been taken to use only low sulphur fuels so that the total emission of sulphur dioxide from the refinery would not be more than one tonne per hour. This was primarily from point of view of conservation of monuments such as the Taj Mahal and the Agra Fort.

Subsequent to the decision to locate the refinery at Mathura some apprehensions have been raised about its possible adverse effects on the Bird Sanctuary situated at Bharatpur, approximately 30 km south west of the refinery. This Sanctuary used to be the famed duck shooting preserve of the rulers of the former State of Bharatpur. It consists of a natural depression, sparsely covered with medium sized trees and shrubs. It is one of the best breeding places of water birds. They assemble in large numbers during the month of July and August and breeding takes place until October, when the young birds are usually big enough to fly away. Prominent among these birds are the open bill, painted stork, spoonbill and grey heron, egrets, darter or snakebird and white ibis.

We understand that you have considerable data on the effects of plants such as the refinery on birds. We would, therefore, like to have your guidance on the steps to be taken to assess the effect of the

Mathura Refinery on birds and the measures to be taken to ensure that there would be no adverse effect. We shall be grateful for your advice on the line of action that we could take for this purpose.

Should you desire for further details we can furnish the same after hearing from you.

Thanking you in anticipation of an early reply.

Copy of:

Reply received from Messers the Royal Society for the Protection of Birds Dated 20th May, 1977.

I am replying to your letter of 18th April seeking information about the effects of refineries on birds. It is difficult to comment with absolute confidence without more detailed information but it appears likely that the effect of the refinery on the birds will not be significant.

As the refinery is located some 20 km from the sanctuary we assume that there is no likelihood of effects arising from disturbance or from disposal of effluents into water courses and the only potential impact would arise from sulphur dioxide emissions and these are not known to effect birds. However, some plants are susceptible and there could, as a result, be a change in vegetation with consequent effects on the birds' food supply and habitat. This seems unlikely but if you wish to pursue it further, I would recommend that you contact Dr. Humphery Bowen of the Department of Chemistry at the University of Reading, Berkshire, England. I imagine that he would need to know the main plant species involved before being able to comment.

If after further consultation you feel that it is possible that there would be an effect from the refinery, it would be desirable to set-up a biological monitoring programme so that once it is in operation any serious changes can be identified, correctly attributed to their cause and appropriate remedial action taken. This might involve undertaking seasonal counts of selected bird species and relating their natural fluctuations on their overall populations levels, but it is more likely that the programme would be based on monitoring changes in the numbers and distribution of lower organisms or plants within the sanctuary area.

I am sorry that our advice cannot be more precise, but this is impossible without more detailed information; I hope that it will be of some help.

Copy of:

Letter received from Messers Nature Conservancy Council, dated 24th June, 1977.

I apologise for the delay in replying to your letter of 18th April but the problem of the possible effects of pollution from the proposed Mathura Oil Refinery on the Bharatpur Bird Sanctuary has necessitated consultation with advisers both within and outside our organisation. The problem is best considered under several headings as follows:

Sulphur

It is pleasing to learn of the decision to limit emissions of pollutants from the projected refinery by using only low sulphur fuels to conserve the Taj Mahal and the Agra Fort. With reference to the Bharatpur Sanctuary and nature conservation interest in general some plants, notably lichens, are very susceptible to injurious effects of gaseous sulphur. However, a case can be made out for sulphur as benefit to water birds. Sulphur dioxide emissions benefit to water birds. Sulphur dioxide emissions are an acidic sulphur contribution to the environment but when neutralized act as a significant fertilizer. This tends to increase the protein contents of aquatic and emergent plants as well as increasing plankton and bottom invertebrate levels in what otherwise might be relatively infertile waters. Providing this process is not overdone, and so lead to over-enrichment, the presence of some additional sulphur would not seem to be deleterious to the Bharatpur Sanctuary. The relationship between water-fowl density and sulphur abundance is illustrated by reference to the situation at the Canadian Shield of Ontaric. In general only a sparse water bird population is supported but there are two areas of the shield, downwind from the smelters at Sudbury and Wawa, that support populations of duck that are comparable to high breeding duck densities elsewhere. A similar situation of benefit to water birds exists at Lake Myvatn is Iceland which has sulphur not springs and geysers.

Other Pollutants

Other pollutants will occur either as gaseous emissions or are water borne. There will be a substantial emission of hydrocarbons, phenols and other poisons but although their pollution effect should not pose a problem it is dependent on local factors at present unknown to me. These possible influential but unknown factors will include:

(a) The physical geography of the area including the effect of shadow of hills and prevailing wind. From this type of information it should be possible to construct isobars of expected pollution fallout at ground level.

(b) Information on processing, such as the fields of origin of oil and therefore the type of crude being processed and its wax content, together with the height of the stack releasing the gaseous emission, would be further relevant factors in the matter.

(c) If the process was water cooled rather than air-cooled the source of water obtained for the process, and in particular its release, would again be matters for attention. The effluent quality would be a problem if its release contaminated waters feeding the Bharatpur Sanctuary. It is certain that accidents will occur through human error or plant failure and any consequential pollution of water courses will undoubtedly cause concern.

Controls

I need hardly say that adherence of the strictest code of conduct, control and supervision in all activities aimed at keeping gaseous emission, only waste and general pollution down to a minimum will be the best safeguards.

Summary

From the evidence available to me it is thought unlikely that the Bharatpur Sanctuary will be at risk from the proposed refinery. The possible addition of sulphur may in fact be advantageous to the birds. The main danger is likely to arise from accident and in particular from pollution of the water sources of the Sanctuary.

I am sending under separate cover three booklets which may be of general interest to you. They are Pollution Research and the Research Council (1977) Combustion-General Pollution (1976) and Effects of Airborne Sulphur Compounds on Forests and Freshwater (1976).

If there is any further help or information you may need please do not hesitate to contact me.

I am copying this letter and enclosures to the Scientific Counsellor to the Indian High Commission, London, and the letter to the London Office of International Tanker Owners Pollution Federation Ltd. who have both been in touch with us on the matter.

Copy of:

Reply Received from Messers The Wild Fowl Trust Dated 30th June, 1977.

Thank you for your letter of 13th June seeking advice regarding the likely effect of emission of sulphur dioxide from the Mathura Refinery on the Bird Sanctuary at Bharatpur.

We have already been consulted by our Nature Conservancy Council on this question and we have passed all the relevant data we have to them. I have checked that the NCC have recently despatched their reply to you and therefore I will not seek to duplicate it.

May I say how impressed we are with the environmental concern shown by your Corporation. If you feel there are any further points on which we can assist, when you have examined the NCC reply, do not hesitate to let us know.

Copy of Letter No. MRG/6/6 Dated 12th September 1977 from Member-Secretary to Dr. Salim Ali, President, Bombay Natural History Society, Bombay.

Permit me to draw your kind attention to the discussion with Dr. S. Varadarajan, Chairman of the Expert Committee on Environmental Impact of Mathura Refinery, during your visit to Delhi on 11th August. During the discussions you had kindly agreed to give us details of some of the bird sanctuaries abroad and the organisations responsible for their maintenance so that we could get in touch with them and find out about the precautions being taken for preservation of the sanctuaries. We had also requested you to give us an introductory letter to the officer in charge of the Bharatpur Sanctuary so that we could contact him and obtain various details of the sanctuary. May I request you kindly to furnish us this information at your earliest convenience?

I would also take this opportunity to express our sincere thanks for the keen interest you have shown in our activities.

Trusting that this will find you in good health and with kind regards.

P.S. I am sending herewith a brief note on the clarifications/information that was brought out during your discussion with the Chairman in respect of the anti-pollution measures that are being taken at Mathura Refinery, which, I trust, you will find useful.

Encl: As above.

Copy of Annexure:

Clarifications/Information Brought out During the Discussion with Dr. S. Varadarajan, Chairman, Expert Committee on Environmental Impact of Mathura Refinery on 11th August, 1977.

1. There is sufficient technological development and know-how available to ensure that the effluents discharged by the refinery to the atmosphere are within the limits stated by IOC, viz., SO_2 being less than one tonne per hour. Equipments are available and would be installed for monitoring discharge of wind pattern is such that it is away from Bharatpur effluents as well as for measuring the fair quality at various distances from the Refinery. The general most of the time and therefore the carry over to SO_2 to this area will be negligible.

2. The Indian Standards Institution is considering a draft Standard for the air quality. As per this the annual long-term concentration of sulphur dioxide permitted for urban areas is of the order of 40 micrograms/M^3 as compared to 60 micrograms/M^3 as specified by W.H.O. It should, however, be noted that in industrially developed countries, although the limit has been specified as 60 micrograms/M^3, the actual concentration of sulphur dioxide is much higher as illustrated in the table given below:

Copenhagen	60
Stockholm	70
Amsturdam	80
Liege	130
Brussels	170
Paris	110
London, city	250
London, greater	150
Milan	600
Venice, city	70
Venice, Industrial Area	130
New York-Manahattan	110
New York-Richmond	50
Los Angeles	70
Toronto, city	170
Toronto, residential	30

The actual concentration of sulphur dioxide at Agra and Bharatpur, even after taking into account the contribution from the refinery, is far lower than the figure of concentration being attempted at in the other countries.

3. As mentioned by both the Nature Conservancy Council (UK) and the Royal Society for the Protection of Birds (UK) the effect of sulphur dioxide on birds will be nil. However, it has been stated that water effluents could effect the plant life and consequently effect the bird sanctuary. The water effluents from the refinery would be treated to meet the stringent specifications laid down by the Indian Standards Institution for discharge of treated effluents into inland waters which are being used for domestic consumption after usual municipal treatment. In any case, the effluent from the refinery will be discharged into the Yamuna river downstream of Brahmanand ghat and, therefore, there is no likelihood of the same reaching Bharatpur Sanctuary. Nonetheless, a detailed study of the water courses around the refinery and Bharatpur will be made to ensure that there is no likelihood of the refinery's treated effluents reaching Bharatpur under any circumstances.

Copy of the Reply Received from Dr. Salim Ali, President, Bombay Natural History, Bombay – Dated 14th September, 1977.

Thank you for your letter dated 12th September and the note on my recent discussion with the Chairman, Expert Committee on Environmental Impact of Mathura Refinery, on the Bird Sanctuary at Bharatpur. The best people to inform you about the steps taken in the U.K. to keep the waters of bird sanctuaries free from industrial wastes and chemical pollutants would be the Nature Conservancy Council and the Royal Society for the Protection of Birds, with whom you are already in touch. I am sure they would be only too glad to furnish all the relevant information. Another source for information and advice in this matter would be: Station Biologique La Tour du Valat, Le Sambue, 13200 Arles, France, if you will give the Director (Dr. Morgan) all the details of our problem. Mentioning my name would perhaps help.

Meanwhile it is good to be assured that it is unlikely for the effluent from the refinery to reach the Bharatpur Sanctuary. All the same, I feel it essential that the water in the Sanctuary should be kept under sustained monitoring, so that any untoward happening from this source is detected in good time. With the cooperation of your Department, we would like to set-up a hydrobiological monitoring station in the Sanctuary, for which a site has been already gifted to us by the ex-Maharaja. Would it be possible for one of your experts to meet myself and Shri N.D. Jayal, Joint Secretary, Ministry of Agriculture (Forests & Wildlife) in Bharatpur on 7th October when we are there? Perhaps it would be a good idea if we could meet together with the Officer-in-Charge and brief him and discuss the various details required by you. If you think this would help. I suggest that you contact Shri Jayal and fix up details about the visit with him.

With kind regards to yourself and Dr. Varadarajan.

14

STUDY GROUP TO FRAME GUIDELINES FOR FOLLOW-UP OF BANK CREDIT, 1974 – REPORT[1]

Chairman Shri Prakash Tandon

Members Shri S.K. Bhattacharyya; Shri P.P. Dhir; Shri A. Ghosh; Shri T.S. Kannan; Shri R.C. Maheshwari; Shri P.B. Medhora; Shri P.K. Nanda; Shri N.C.B. Nath; Shri S. Padmanabhan; Shri N. Rajan; Shri Sampat P. Singh; Shri Y.V. Sivaramakrishnayya; Shri P.J. Fernandes replaced by Shri N. Rajan, Dr. N.C.B. Nath

M. Secy. Shri A.K. Bhuchar

Appointment

Till nationalisation of the major Commercial Banks in July 1969, the main contenders for bank credit were large and medium scale private industry and internal and external trade. Very little credit went to small industry, the self-employed and agriculture, or to the public sector, apart from the assistance given by a few banks. There has never been and there still is no tradition of bank lending for personal consumption.

Nationalisation of the major commercial banks, following upon social control, called for a new policy, both for deposit mobilisation through accelerated branch expansion and for equitable disbursal of credit. The banking system was asked to adopt a new approach as a credit agency, based on development and potential rather than on security only, to assist the weaker sectors of society and later to lend to the public sector also. Significant sectors of the economy, which were once outside the scope of bank lending, have now been brought within its ambit. While assistance to the new credit users has gone up

---

1. Bombay, Reserve Bank of India, 1975, 136, 3, 9, 10, 2, 4, 7, 5, 5, 3, 7, 17 p.

substantially since nationalisation, the bulk of bank credit continues to go to organised industry, although its share as a percentage of total credit has now somewhat diminished.

Indian industry has not always made the best use of resources. Traditionally cheap labour, cheap money and a sheltered market have not been conducive to efficient resource employment. Few borrowers planned their credit needs and, until recently, few banks planned their resource mobilisation and credit disbursal.

A world-wide flare up of prices and stagnation in our agricultural and industrial production recently, fuelled an unprecedented rise in prices and, in turn, led to a rise in demand for credit. The unprecedented inflation has been, in fact, a phenomenon of the past two to three years. Alongside, monetary policy raised liquidity requirements of banks. Pressure on bank resources thus developed over the recent years.

To fit in with prevailing economic compulsions, the Reserve Bank has used selective credit controls, differential interest rates and varying liquidity requirements as part of monetary policy.

In 1973, when demand for credit rose steeply at a time when production was not rising, the Reserve Bank imposed certain credit restraints. Later in 1974, when inflation touched the unprecedented level of 31 per cent, a package of measures aimed at curbing it was introduced. Both steps, along with other fiscal measures, proved effective.

Along with these steps, it was felt that the time was opportune to bring about other reforms in the bank credit system, so that it could be geared to fulfil a developmental role in the economy in the coming years.

It was against this background that the Reserve Bank constituted the Study Group to frame guidelines for follow-up of bank credit in July 1974.

Terms of Reference

(i) To suggest guidelines for commercial banks to follow-up and supervise credit from the point of view of ensuring proper and use of funds and keeping a watch on the safety of the advances and to suggest the type of operational data and other information that may be obtained by banks periodically from such borrowers and by the Reserve Bank of India from the lending banks;

(ii) To make recommendations for obtaining periodical forecasts from borrowers of (a) business/production plans, and (b) credit needs;

(iii) To make suggestions for prescribing inventory norms for different industries both in the private and public sectors and indicate the broad criteria for deviating from these norms;

(iv) To suggest criteria regarding satisfactory capital structure and sound financial basis in relation to borrowings;

(v) To make recommendations regarding the sources for financing the minimum working capital requirements;

(vi) To make recommendations as to whether the existing pattern of financing working capital requirements by cash credit/overdraft system, etc., requires to be modified, if so, to suggest suitable modifications; and

(vii) To make recommendations on any other related matter as the Group may consider germane to the subject of enquiry or any other allied matter which may be specifically referred to it by the Reserve Bank of India.

Recommendations

Till nationalisation of the major commercial banks in July 1969, the main contenders for bank credit were large and medium scale private industry and internal and external trade. Nationalisation called for a new policy and the banking system was asked to adopt a new approach as a credit agency, based on development and potential rather than on security only, to assist the weaker sectors of the society, and later to lend to the public sector also. (Paras 1.1 and 1.2)

In the early years, bank lending in India was mostly directed to financing of movement of agricultural produce from the grower to the trader. Advances were sanctioned against the security of stocks charged to the banks. With the growth of industrialisation, the same system of bank lending continued with minor changes, the general pattern of lending to industry being security-cum-guarantee advances. The security-oriented system tended to favour borrowers with strong financial resources, irrespective of their economic function. This system aided concentration of economic power. (Paras 3.1 to 3.3)

Since nationalisation, there has been a new sense of direction in bank lending and indeed advances to new claimants of credit, and especially to small industry and agriculture have since gone up. The public sector too has emerged as an important user of credit in recent years. Another new source of demand is the growing awareness of the need to achieve an equitable geographical development of industry, and in its wake the distribution of credit. (Paras 3.6 to 3.8)

In the last six or seven years, industrial production has risen at a slow pace but the call on bank credit, essentially for maintaining inventories even at the same level, has gone up with increasing prices. If the growth process is resumed – as indeed it has begun to do – then perforce the volume of inventory required to maintain a higher level of production will increase and correspondingly the demand for bank credit. Banks will thus have to operate in a context in which demand for bank credit for growth requirements will be large. (Para 3.10)

The problem of potential imbalance in demand for and supply of funds is assentuated by the manner in which banks extend credit under the present cash credit system of lending. Under this system, the level of advances in a bank is determined not by how much a banker can lend at a particular point of time but by the borrower's decision to borrow at that time. This makes credit planning difficult in banks. Also, cash credit advances are repayable on demand only in name. To the extent that outstandings in the cash credit account never fell below certain level during the course of a year, there is an element of what is called a 'hard core' borrowing which is in reality a quasi-permanent lock up of bank funds in the borrower's business. (Paras 3.12 to 3.20).

In the light of the foregoing, time is now opportune to review the existing system and effect changes in such a way that under the new system the borrower would plan his credit needs and the banker also would be able to plan, having known the borrower's requirements. (Paras 3.22 and 3.23)

A borrower needs funds for the operation, mainly to carry current assets required for the purpose. Inventory and receivables comprise the bulk of the current assets. There is no uniformity in approach among banks in assessing working capital requirements, especially with regard to inventories. If bank credit is to be viewed as a tool of resource allocation in the economy, one cannot get away from the problem of defining reasonable levels of inventories (including safety stock) and receivables in cash industry and hence the need for norms for these current assets. (Paras 4.1, 4.2 and 4.7)

In the new context, the main function of a banker as a lender is to supplement the borrower's resources to carry an acceptable level of current assets. The implications are two-fold; one, the level of current assets must be reasonable and based on norms; two, a part of the fund requirements for carrying current assets must be found from long terms funds comprising owned funds and term borrowings including other non-current liabilities. (Para 4.8)

Norms have been suggested for 15 major industries, taking into account, inter alia, company finance studies made by the Reserve Bank, process period in the different industries, discussions with the industry experts and feed-bank received on the Interim Report. The norms proposed represent the maximum levels for holding inventory and receivables in each industry. If, however, a borrower has managed with less in the past, he should continue to do so. (Paras 5.7 and 5.8)

In view of the special characteristics of the heavy engineering industry, particularly the large tie-up of funds in current assets, the banking system may find it difficult to cope with the industry's demand for funds in its entirety. The working capital requirements of the heavy engineering sector should, therefore, be assessed taking into account the alternative ways of financing the needs and the extent to which banks may meet them may be determined, case by case, on merits. (Paras 5.9 to 5.11)

Norms cannot be absolute or rigid. Deviations from norms may be visualised under certain circumstances, e.g., bunched receipt of raw materials, power cuts, strikes, transport delays, etc. However, delayed payments by Government agencies and sometimes by large units in the private sector cannot be treated as circumstances warranting deviations and the matter should be tackled at the sources rather than throwing upon the banking system the burden of providing additional credit. The Reserve Bank should discuss the matter with Government agencies and the Bureau of Public Enterprises; Government and public enterprises should set an example in prompt payments. (Paras 5.12 and 5.13)

Concessions under the criteria for deviating from norms should not be expected as a matter of course but must be fully justified. Deviations should be for known specific circumstances and situations (which should be recorded) and allowed for agreed periods which should be relatively short; and there should be a return to norms when condition revert to normal. (Paras 5.14 and 5.15)

Norms should apply to all industrial borrowers, including small scale industries, with aggregate limits from the banking system in excess of Rs. 10 lakhs and extended to smaller borrowers progressively as early as possible. (Para 5.16)

In the case of industries not covered by norms at present, the purpose and spirit behind the norms should be kept in view when extending credit facilities. (Para 5.17)

The list of industries covered by norms should be extended with experience. Norms should be kept under constant review. (Paras 5.18 and 5.21)

The principles should be uniform for all like industries, both in the private and public sectors. Thus, public sector industry should conform to the same norms as are applicable to comparable private industry, though in special cases, norms may have to be relaxed, but after a study in depth. (Paras 5.19 and 12.23)

All credit limits, whether enhancement is sought for therein or not, should be considered in the light of the norms and where the levels of inventory and receivables are excessive, they should be reduced bringing down also the dues to the bank and/or other creditors. (Para 5.20)

The process of adjustment of inventories and receivables should be completed in about two months, other things being equal. In the event of default, as a first step, the bank should charge a higher rate of interest. But even charging of a higher rate of interest should not give a permanent immunity to the customer from conforming to norms and some further action should be considered. (Para 5.20)

The working capital gap, viz., the borrower's requirement of finance to carry current assets (based on norms) other than those financed out of his other current liabilities, could be bridged partly from his own funds and long term borrowings and partly by bank borrowings. (Para 6.2)

The maximum permissible level of bank borrowings could be worked out in three ways. In the 1st Method, the borrower will have to contribute a minimum of 25 per cent of the working capital gap from long term funds, i.e., owned funds and term borrowings; this will give a minimum current ratio of 1 : 1. In the 2nd Method, the borrower will have to provide a minimum of 25 per cent of total current assets from long term funds; this will give a current ratio of at least 1.3:1. In the 3rd Method, the borrower's contribution from long term funds will be to the extent of the entire core current assets, as defined, and a minimum of 25 per cent of the balance current assets, thus strengthening the current ratio further. (Paras 6.3 to 6.8)

The classification of current assets and current liabilities for computing the permissible level of bank finance should be made as per the usually accepted approach of bankers. (Para 6.9)

The 3rd Method will provide the largest multiplier of bank finance; however, to avoid hardship to borrowers, a beginning may be made with the 1st Method, placing all borrowers in this method within a period of about one year, and the ideal of the 3rd Method may be reached in stages. The liberal approach under the 1st Method has been suggested as the first step, particularly to facilitate financial structuring of new companies, setting up projects in backward areas and also for flexibility in restructuring of existing companies with a weak financial base. (Paras 6.10 and 6.12)

The aim should be to move forward and borrowers in the third or second category should not revert to the second or first category respectively by increasing their dependence on bank borrowing. Also, when credit needs increase, the borrower should not slip back from a higher to a lower category. (Para 6.12)

Banks will work out the position of existing customers and any excess over the finance, to which a borrower would be eligible under the new formula, will have to be reduced progressively, by transferring the excess to a term loan, amortised over a suitable period. (Para 6.13)

The concept of bank credit forming only a portion of the working capital gap could also be used as an instrument for influencing the directional flow of credit, according to the priorities for industries indicated by the authorities concerned from time to time by varying the scales of finance. Also, when a manufacturer has reached a stable level of production for a reasonable number of years, there is no reason why bank finance should continue to be made available to him on the same scale, because if a portion of the finance made available to him could be withdrawn, such funds would be available for promotion of new economic activity. (Para 6.14)

In future, while funding new projects, the term lending institutions may provide for margins on the basis of the recommended proposals and the bank which is to finance the working capital requirements should be associated at this stage in determining the working capital and margin requirements. In the case of old units, where a part of the present cash credit borrowing is transferred to a term loan, to bring the borrowings in line with the recommended proposals, the funded debt and equity relationship may not immediately conform to the norms of the term lending institutions. In these cases, borrowers may have to be given time to bring the position to normal, but the total outside liabilities to owned funds relationship will have to be acceptable to the banks. (Paras 6.15 and 6.16)

A request for additional credit on a regular basis from a borrower who already has an excess borrowing under any of the three methods may be considered provided the borrower brings in matching contribution required under the relevant method of lending. In very exceptional cases, however, if the cash generating capacity of the borrower is sufficiently good, banks may grant a term loan for the purpose to a reasonable extent for a short period acceptable to the bank. If, however, the additional fund need is for a short duration for specific transactions/contracts, the bank may consider giving additional credit for such needs without insisting on matching contribution, on the clear understanding that the borrower would return to the stage as in the relevant method of lending within the stipulated period. Borrowers having excess borrowing in relation to inventory norms will not be eligible for additional limits on a regular basis until such time as the current assets are brought down to the required levels. (Paras 6.17 and 6.18)

The annual credit limit may be bifurcated into a loan, which would comprise the minimum level of borrowing throughout the year, and a demand cash credit, which would take care of the fluctuating requirements, both to be reviewed annually. There should, however, be no rigidity in the matter of bifurcation of the overall credit limit between loan and cash credit. (Paras 6.22, 6.23 and 7.1)

In the case of industries with a very high degree of seasonality, assessment of bank finance may have to be done on the basis of monthly cash budgets. (Para 6.24)

The demand cash credit should be charged a slightly higher interest rate than the loan component. This approach will give the borrower an incentive for good planning. The term loan representing the excess borrowing to be amortised should also be at a slightly higher rate than the cash credit rate. (Para 6.25)

In order to ensure that customers do not use the new cash credit facility in an unplanned manner, the financing should be placed on a quarterly budgeting – reporting system for operational purposes, as in the suggested forms. (Paras 6.26 and 6.27)

The borrowers expressed concern about the secrecy and sensitiveness of the information proposed to be called for from them. Banks are expected to take due notice of their apprehension. (Para 6.29)

Apart from loan and cash credit, a part of the total credit requirement, within the overall eligibility could also be provided by way of bill limits to finance seller's receivables. It is desirable that, as far as possible, receivables should be financed by way of bills rather than cash credit against book debts. As regards the question whether purchases may be financed by ways of cash credit or bills, each bank may take its own decision in consultation with the borrower, keeping in view the size of his operations, the individual transaction and the administrative set up obtaining in the bank. (Paras 6.30 and 6.31)

The proposed system of lending and the style of credit may be extended to all borrowers having credit limits in excess of Rs. 10 lakhs from the banking system, while the information system may be introduced, to start with, in respect of borrowers with limits of Rs. 1 crore and above the entire banking system and then extended progressively to others. (Para 6.32)

The mechanics of lending suggested covers examination of the borrower's total operational plan as also his past and current financial position. The borrower should, therefore, furnish to the banker an operating statement and funds flow statement for the whole year (i.e., the next year) as also projected balance sheet as at the end of the next year, along with the application for advance or renewal, for fixation of the overall credit limit. (Para 7.1)

The working capital gap will be computed, the extent of bank finance will be arrived at and the overall credit limit will be fixed, on the basis indicated in Chapter 6. (Para 7.1)

Actual drawings within the sanctioned limit will be determined by the customer's inflow and outflow of funds as reflected in the quarterly funds flow statement and the permissible level of drawing will be the level as at the end of the previous quarter plus or minus the deficit or surplus shown in the funds flow statement. (Para 7.1)

Within the overall permissible level of drawing, the day-to-day operations in the account will be regulated on the basis of drawing power (subjected to the margins stipulated by the banker against the different components of inventory and receivables), as per the monthly stock statements, which will continue to be submitted. (Para 7.1)

Variances are bound to arise in any budget or plan; variances to the extent of say ±10 per cent should be permissible, and beyond this, the banker and customer should discuss the reasons. (Para 7.1)

The recommendations regarding inventory/receivables norms and the mechanics of lending are to be viewed as a package; it is an integrated scheme and the borrower is expected to subject himself to the entire discipline envisaged. (Para 7.3)

A bank has to follow up and supervise the use of credit to verify first, whether the assumptions of lending in regard to borrower's operations continue to hold good and second, whether the end-use is according to the purpose for which the credit was given. (Para 8.1)

If the banker is to get away from security-oriented lending to production-related credit with security serving a subsidiary but necessary role, he will have to be in close touch with the borrower's operations. Since projected funds flow statement would form the basis for determining the line of credit, a banker would be justified in laying down a condition that any material change, say around 10 per cent of the figure projected earlier, would require his prior approval. Thus, the banker may stipulate certain minimum terms and conditions relating to matters having a material impact on the funds flow of the borrower. (Paras 8.4. to 8.6)

From the quarterly forms, the banker will verify whether the operational results conform to earlier expectations and whether there is any divergence reading as red signals; however, variance of, say around 10 per cent, may be treated as normal. (Para 8.8)

In addition to the quarterly data, the larger borrowers should submit a half-yearly proforma balance sheet and profit and loss account within two months of the end of the half-year. (Para 8.9)

In the new system, it is in the borrower's own interest that audited balance sheets are produced as early as possible, say, in three months, and he should take positive steps in this direction. (Para 8.10)

After the close of each year, detailed credit analysis should be done as in respect of new advances, when the banker will re-examine the terms and conditions and make necessary changes. (Para 8.11)

Stock statements will continue to be submitted but they need to be improved. The basis of valuation in the stock statements and the balance sheet should be uniform. The stocks should be reconciled in the stock statements, showing the opening and closing stocks, quantity-wise and value-wise. (Paras 8.12 and 8.13)

Stock inspection poses problems particularly in large industries. In such cases, there is no alternative to depending on financial follow-up. Where a banker feels, for special reasons, that a detailed stock verification is called for, a regular stock audit may have to be arranged with the assistance of outside consultants. (Para 8.16)

Managerial competence is an important factor in the efficiency of operations, reflected in profitability and working capital and financial management. Banker should keep in mind that appraisal of management may be essential particularly as we place a new emphasis on viability and development rather than on security alone. (Para 8.17)

To facilitate inter-firm and industry-wise comparisons for assessing efficiency, it would be of advantage if companies in the same industry could be grouped under three or four categories, say, according to size of sales and the group-wise financial ratios compiled by the Reserve Bank for furnishing to banks. (Para 8.18)

Industry organisations should also collect data from their members and publish whole-industry balance sheets, profit and loss accounts and relevant ratios. (Para 8.19)

In making inter-firm comparisons, besides examining financial and operating ratios, certain productivity ratios may also be examined to determine labour efficiency, capital efficiency and fixed assets efficiency. (Para 8.20)

For the purpose of better control, there should be a system of borrower classification in each bank. This will facilitate easy identification of the borrowers whose affairs require to be watched with more than ordinary care and will also provide a rational base for purposes of fixing rates of interest for the respective borrowers. (Para 8.22)

The only feasible manner in which the banker can satisfy himself in regard to end-use of funds would be to ensure, by calling for appropriate operational data and figures relating to financial position at periodical intervals, that the borrower's current ratio and the respective shares of bank finance and borrower's long term funds in meeting his working capital gap do not change adversely; if the position in this regard does not change adversely, the conclusion would be that bank finance has gone towards build-up of current assets. (Para 8.26)

Apart from the current ratio, the bank will look to the debt-equity ratio, which may be looked at as funded debt-equity relationship or total outside liabilities-equity relationship. It is not practicable to legislate absolute standards for these ratios. Where the debt-equity ratios of a borrower are worse than the median for his industry, the banker would endeavour to persuade the borrower to strengthen his equity as early as possible and the latter should pursue to reach the median on the basis of the data up-dated by the Reserve Bank. (Paras 9.1 to 9.9)

The change-over recommended should be effected with a minimum of inconvenience to the banker and the customer. Borrowers suggested that banks should reduce tiers and take quicker decisions. This is a matter for each bank to examine in relation to its own administrative systems and procedures and take appropriate action. There should be total commitment of the top management in each bank to the new approach. Extensive training facilities in credit appraisal should be provided for bank staff at all levels, with particular emphasis on the suggested information system and handling of inventory and receivables norms. (Paras 10.1 to 10.5)

A customer can no longer take a stand that having given security, there is no necessity for him to give any data to banks. There are rights and obligations on both sides. The banker as the lender is entitled to information which he deems nécessary for his appraisal and follow-up and also has a duty in turn towards the borrower to appreciate his difficult situations. On the same basis, the customer should also develop an accountability to his banker. (Paras 11.2 to 11.4)

While financing trade, banks should keep in view, inter alia, the extent of owned funds of the borrower in relation to the credit limits granted, the annual turnover, possible diversion to other units or uses and how much is being ploughed back from profits into the business. They should avoid financing of goods which have already been obtained on credit. (Para 12.2)

It will be useful if Government authorities like the Textile Commissioner or Jute Commissioner consult the Reserve Bank before prescribing stock levels for the industries concerned to the extent these may cut across the relative norms for inventory holding. (Para 12.4)

In view of the need for efficient transportation and availability of wagons, railways should assume some liability for undue delays as a part of their own discipline, as they do for damages in transit at railway risk. (Para 12.5)

The canalising agencies and public sector producers may review, from time to time, their distribution procedures so as to prevent unproductive lock-up of bank funds. (Paras 12.6 and 12.7)

Government and the public sectors are the biggest buyers in the country and tardy payments by them will only increase the level of receivables and, consequently, the need for bank credit. Government departments have already been following the accepted commercial practices in respect of their purchases from foreign suppliers but not in respect of their internal purchases. It will be useful if the Reserve Bank could initiate discussions on this matter. Further, Government should, pending streamlining its procedures, agree to pay interest on established delayed payments. (Para 12.8)

The possibility of switching over from credit sales to cash sales, wherever possible, both in the private and the public sectors, should be examined, or at least credit period allowed by sellers should be progressively reduced, in order to shorten the transaction cycle and enable bank funds to achieve a larger multiplier. (Para 12.9)

In the case of consortium advances or where a borrower is financed by more than one bank, the concerned banks should evolve a procedure to ensure a uniform handling of the account in conformity with the inventory and receivables norms and the financial discipline suggested. (Para 12.10)

If a borrower refuses to comply with the new requirements, there will be no alternative to the banker but to take first a holding action by raising the rate of interest until such time as the requirements are fulfilled; but if this fails, the banker will have no option but to stop operations in the account. (Paras 12.11 and 12.12)

Once danger signals are thrown up in the case of a borrower and signs of difficulty emerge, speedy action is called for on the part of the banker and timely and firm handling are of essence. In such cases, the banker may intervene even in management, if that is necessary, in the interests of all concerned and the public. To diagnose the ailment, the banker can go to a consultant and can then arrange for action, including a financial or structural reorganisation. (Paras 12.13 to 12.17)

The Indian Banks' Association has an important role to play in a study of the environment and particularly the impact of regulations and enactments on the working of banks. (Para 12.18)

Expertise has to be built up in the banking system in organising industry-wise studies, on an on-going basis, which should serve as a frame of reference for decision-making in regard to individual cases. (Para 12.19)

Instead of every bank attempting to make detailed studies of all the major industries it would be beneficial if some selected banks concentrate on one or two industries each, for which they may be best fitted to study; the results of their study could be made available to the other banks as also the Reserve Bank. (Para 12.20)

It is opportune to examine whether the limits for the credit authorisation requirements of the Reserve Bank should not be raised, in view of the altered value of the rupee since the introduction of the Credit Authorisation Scheme and the qualitative improvement in the lending skills of commercial banks. (Para 12.22)

Inventory/receivables norms should be given effect to immediately, while action should be initiated to implement the new approach to lending within the time-bound schedule as proposed in Chapter 6. (Para 13.2)

Steps should be taken simultaneously to introduce the suggested information system for all industrial borrowers with limits aggregating Rs. 1 crore and above from the banking system and the process completed within six months. (Para 13.3)

Banks should utilise this transitory period of six months for conducting training sessions for their operating officials. (Para 13.3)

Special courses should be organised by the National Institute of Bank Management and the Bankers Training College for training the banks' operating officials. These institutions may also help banks in training the trainers, preparing operational manuals, and in bringing about changes in their systems and procedures. (Para 13.4)

Each bank should conduct banker – borrower seminars to create an understanding between the operating officials in the respective banks and their customers. (Para 13.5)

After six months, a bankers' seminar may be convened in the Bankers Training College where operating officials can find solutions to any operational problems that might have been thrown up in the interim. (Para 13.5)

The prime contribution of the Committee of Direction appointed by the Reserve Bank will be to take forward the work of the Study Group to a continuing function of a dialogue with industry and banks to ensure smooth running of the new system and to take care of the need for any revision. (Para 13.6)

15

REVIEW COMMITTEE ON UNIVERSITY GRANTS COMMISSION, 1974 – REPORT[1]

Chairman	Shri V.S. Jha
Members	Shri R.C. Mehrotra; Dr. B. Datta (replaced by Shri G.C. Pande)
M. Secy.	Shri S.N. Pandita

Appointment

In pursuance of the recommendation made by the Public Accounts Committee of Parliament in its 114th Report, Government of India was pleased to appoint this Committee on August 31, 1974, to review the functioning of the University Grant Commission.

Terms of Reference

To review the functioning of the University Grants Commission, with particular reference to coordination and determination of standards of higher education, and make recommendations conducive to more effective discharge of its responsibilities.

Contents

Foreword; Introductory—A Survey; Coordination and Standards; Colleges and Standards; Grants; Research, Planning and Evaluation; Organisation and Structure; Constitutional and Legal Aspects; Concluding Remarks; Appendices from A to F; List of Persons Interviewed; Composition of University Grants Commission, New Delhi (as in January 1977); Composition of University Grants Committee,

1. New Delhi, Ministry of Education and Social Welfare, 1977, 165 p.

United Kingdom (as in June 1975); Statistical Tables (I to XIX); Staff of the UGC Review Committee; Selected Bibliography.

Recommendations

Introductory – A Survey

The retreat of Central Government under pressure from States and universities from the stand it had taken in the draft Universities (Regulation of Standards) Bill, 1951 and acceptance of radically diluted UGC Act, 1956, was a crucial event in the history of higher education in India. The result was a *laissez faire* in the growth of universities and colleges whose proliferation left the UGC in the position of a hopeless spectator. The number of universities grew from 33 in 1956 to 111 in 1975; the number of colleges rose from 1004 in 1956 to 4388 in 1975; the number of teachers shot up from about 36,000 to over 1.5 lakh in the same period and yet the teacher-pupil ratio worsened from 1.18 to 1.20. An open-door policy was followed with scant regard for available facilities like buildings, equipment, libraries and adequately qualified staff. In an atmosphere in which any advice or caution could be constructed as an infringement of the autonomy of the States, the UGC appeared to have been overwhelmed and it rarely tested the little initiative which it might have exercised. It did not even perform any clearing-house function, it was supposed to under the Act, on matters concerning higher education. It went on satisfying demands as far as it could. It would be unfair to put the entire blame on the UGC for not daring to go against the powerful trend which had full political support. Even the Planning Commission, a powerful organ of government responsible for economic and social planning—a concurrent subject which could and should include educational planning, could do little to attempt a methodical planning of higher education in the country. Its targets of increase in university and college enrolment in arts, science and commerce subjects from 1.69 to 2.66 million from 1968-69 to 1973-74 were nearly reached in 1970-71 itself. In fact, the "targets" were not related to any definition or purposes of this sector of education. The Planning Commission found it difficult to relate enrolment in higher education to manpower forecasts. Its emphasis on consolidation and improvement (rather than expansion) of higher education and rational location of institutions of optimal size when unheeded and universities and colleges continued to multiply fast-19 new universities and over a thousand new colleges coming into existence between 1969-70 and 1973-74. Its concern for better utilisation of funds for betterment of standards remained unshared. Even the Planning Commission perhaps saw little point in pleading for restraint. The not-so-unequivocal suggestion of the Education Commission (1964-66) in respect of cautious enrolment policy was unacceptable to the Parliamentary Committee on Education which did not agree to "the Commission's proposal that a system secondary and undergraduate stages" adding further that, "we believe that every effort should be made to provide admission to institutions of higher education to all eligible students who desire to study further." This tantamounts to an open-door policy without any concern for standards and costs. There is visible change in the nation's mood since the promulgation of emergency and sobered appreciation of realities which attend unlimited growth without commensurate inputs. This is reflected in the constitutional amendment placing education on the Concurrent List, as had also been recommended by us in our interim report of 4th May, 1976. This enabling measure opens up possibilities of rationalisation, planning and control with due regard to national priorities.

Coordination and Standards

1. A high-level coordinating body with heads of different organisations dealing with higher education and research like UGC, NCST, CSIR, AEC, ICSSR, ICHR, ICAR, ICMR and AICTE as well as senior representatives of the ministries of education, health and agriculture and the Planning Commission as its members, may be established to deal with matters of policy regarding coordination of activities and sharing of resources between areas of teaching and research involving universities falling within the purview of the UGC, higher educational institutions outside the purview of the UGC and non-university research organisations. This policy-making body should have a small standing committee which should from time to time review the implementation of its decisions and take other follow-up action.

2. In each State there should be a coordinating body, headed by the chancellor, consisting of all vice-chancellors of universities, selected college principles, independent academicians and represen-

tatives of the State government as well as of the UGC to effect co-ordination among higher educational institutions at the State level within the over-all national policy.

3. The Commission should be given the authority to have plans prepared and implemented for exchange of teachers, pooling of library and laboratory facilities, and coordination of research in universities.

4. It should be provided through proper legislative action that no university or college will be established unless the UGC concurs that it finds the need for a new institution justified and is satisfied that there is proper planning and adequate provision of resources for the purpose.

5. The UGC should lay down guidelines in respect of enrolment policy which should be followed by universities and colleges.

6. For the guidance of State Governments and institutions concerned, the Commission should evolve norms of work-load for university and college teachers which should be applicable at all levels. These norms should take into account the requirements of staff for class-room lectures, tutorials, internal assessment, conduct and guidance of research and other activities.

7. The UGC should with the help of academicians, draw a frame-work of remedial courses for students from weaker sections of society to enable them to get admission to universities and colleges on a level of equality.

8. The UGC's emphasis on research aptitude and training of candidates for posts of lecturers in universities and colleges is a move in the right direction. However, in view of the rigidity with which the qualifications prescribed by UGC are sometimes applied, it would be desirable to make candidates with first class career up to master's level eligible for selection as lecturers on the condition that they obtain within a period of five years a research degree or give evidence of research work of equally high standard, failing which their tenure would be liable to be terminated.

9. A national examination should be organised jointly by the UGC, UPSC and AIU for post-graduates in different subjects and candidates who are declared successful in this examination should be given weightage for selection to the posts of lectures and for research fellowships.

10. The Commission should maintain panels of experts in different subjects to able to advise universities and colleges. The Chan-

cellors of universities should select their nominees on the selection committees out of the panel of experts maintained by the UGC.

11. UGC should concern itself with the methods of appointment and tenure of professors of universities. It should maintain a panel of suitable persons for professorships in different subjects to be able to commend such names should a university want them.

12. The Commission should help the universities to organise initial training of teachers in universities and colleges. It should have a proper follow-up and evaluation of in-service training programmes which it is conducting.

13. In view of the adoption of Hindi and regional languages as media of instruction by various higher educational institutions, a detailed plan of action for training teachers to teach through the new media as well as for preparation of books and teaching material should be drawn up and implemented expeditiously.

14. The President of India should be the visitor of all universities and all acts and statutes as well as appointment of vice-chancellors should be subject to his prior approval. He should have the authority to issue, on the advice of the UGC, such directions to universities as may be considered necessary in matters relating to coordination and standards.

College and Standards

1. New colleges should be set-up only after a joint survey by the affiliating university, the UGC and the State government concerned regarding their need, location, courses of study, staff, limits of intake and other relevant factors. An adequate minimum financial support must be available before a college is started.

2. Once a college comes into existence with the Commission's approval, it should be eligible for assistance for measures to achieve coordination and standards right from the beginning. Conditions regarding eligibility of existing colleges to be entitled to UGC's assistance under Section 2(f) should not be rigid and newer colleges and those in remote areas should be given special consideration.

3. The UGC should, with the help of academicians, undertake continuous assessment of the standards of colleges and provide necessary guidance and help to them. It should be empowered to close down a non-viable college which only duplicates facilities already available in the same area or to reorganise it as an institution

for providing vocational courses to suit the needs of the region.

4. Affiliation of colleges must vest only with a university and be given on academic grounds alone and no extraneous pressures should be allowed to come into play. No new college should be given affiliation by a university without UGC's prior approval.

5. A reasonably uniform and sound system of grant-in-aid to affiliated colleges all over the country should be evolved from time to time by UGC which should be followed by the governments concerned so that colleges are run with adequate resources. The Commission should also lay down guidelines and procedures so that the managing committees function in the best interests of colleges.

6. The Commission should provide guidance to existing colleges so that within a specified time, with necessary help, they improve their functioning and conform to required academic and administrative standards. The procedures should contain a provision that a college will be liable to be derecognised if it does not show the required improvement.

7. The Commission should take initiative in selecting autonomous colleges and, with the cooperation of the State governments, help them to function as such.

8. Priority attention should be given by the UGC to restructuring courses, particularly in rural colleges, to make them relevant to rural needs and provide guidance and help to universities to evolve new courses for the special needs of different regions.

9. Faculty improvement programmes as well as programmes for improvement of teaching in colleges must be carefully planned with the participation of colleges, teachers and system of regular follow-up and feed-back evolved.

10. Two principals or teachers of colleges should be appointed members of the UGC.

11. The Commission needs to be given more funds to improve colleges which are back-bone of university education-having 85 per cent students and 83 per cent teachers in them.

Grants

1. To enable it to cope up with its role in respect of coordination and improvement of standards of universities, the University Grants Commission must be provided much larger funds than it has been so far.

2. The grants should be related to the financial position and needs of each university or college and aim at promoting as well as sustaining centres of excellence and developing the general standards in other institutions.

3. The Commission should take an over-all view of the financial position of universities and build up sound statistical information regarding different sources of income and different items of expenditure of universities and colleges. Such information together with data about per student cost in different institutions in terms of courses of study should be important considerations in the matter of allocation of grants.

4. Maintenance grants to central universities and their affiliated colleges should be separately budgeted, separately operated upon and dealt with in a separate post on maintenance activities as distinct from development activities.

5. On various items matching grants should be paid on the same basis to central as well as State universities by the UGC. However, in the case of colleges, particularly those in remote areas and poorer regions, the matching pattern needs to be further amended to the advantage of the institutions.

6. Consequent to education becoming a concurrent subject, rules and procedures should be laid down to ensure that the State governments make provision for their matching share in respect of all the schemes of the Commission for improvement of higher educational institutions. Also the UGC should be able to ensure that infrastructural facilities are fully provided by the sponsoring authority before an institution is established.

7. The UGC Act needs to be suitably amended to empower the Commission to advance loans for construction of such buildings by the higher educational institutions as would given them some returns, e.g., hostels and residences. The Commission needs to be provided revolving funds for starting a loan scheme of this type. The loans should preferably be interest free and recoverable in easy instalments.

8. The UGC should expedite laying down standard lay-outs and other specifications of all educational buildings.

9. Centres of excellence like the centres of advanced study, which are intended to serve as Pacesetters, need to be maintained by the UGC on a regular basis.

10. The Commission should also consider giving 100 per cent

assistance for improvement programmes for post-graduate and research studies.

11. The UGC should act as an advisory agency for procurement of sophisticated equipment for higher educational institutions, thus saving time of individual institutions and also ensuring uniformity in quality.

12. The procedures regarding release of instalment of grants need to be examined thoroughly and such a system evolved as would be conducive to efficient functioning of academic activities on a long-term basis.

13. Utilisation of grants needs to be checked up more thoroughly than merely through persuasion or by calling utilisation certificates. Small teams should make actual physical verification of such utilisation on a sample basis.

14. A system needs to be evolved with the co-operation of State governments so that the State PWD inspects academic buildings and issues necessary certificates without delay.

Research, Planning and Evaluation

1. A suitable organisation should be set-up as a limb of the UGC, with adequate freedom in functioning, and it should continually be engaged in studies and research on various aspects of higher education. The Science Research Council or other units already set-up or proposed to be set-up by the Commission should be merged with it.

2. The UGC, through this organisation, should conduct studies and various aspects of higher education like higher education costs and how to reduce them, rural higher education and how to make it relevant to socio-economic needs of the vast rural areas, enrolment and admission policy in higher education, courses of study and examination reform, innovation in teaching methods, educational material and technology, development of languages and production of books. It should perform clearing-house functions on behalf of the UGC. It should have a sound statistical unit as well as units concerned with higher educational planning and evaluation of higher educational institutions in general and monitoring of UGC's improvement programmes in particular.

3. Research departments of universities as well as individual academicians should be involved in conducting research projects.

Research activity should be linked with training programmes for higher educational planners and administrators.

4. Higher education planning should be the responsibility of the University Grants Commission which should work in close collaboration with the Planning Commission and with research bodies and other agencies dealing with specialised sectors of education not falling within the purview of the Commission. In order to have closer connection with the Planning Commission, Secretary, Planning Commission, should be an ex-officio member of the UGC. Similarly, the UGC and the university system should have closer links with the NCST and there should be larger representation of academicians on the latter body.

5. Educational planning in its very nature has to cover a generation and objectives as well as strategies have to be evolved in perspective. The UGC should prepare long term perspective plans for higher education and develop models suited to national needs. The plans for different five year periods should be drawn in the context of the perspective plan. The task of preparing plan proposals for the Commission's consideration should be entrusted to the proposed organisation for research, planning and evaluation.

6. Commitments by the Planning Commission in regard to outlays for higher education should be firm and made well in advance to enable proper planning of programmes for a plan period.

7. Education is in major part a "non-plan" activity and the non-plan sector of higher education calls for constant review and modification in the light of overall strategy for educational development. The UGC should be given the authority to oversee and modify non-plan programmes of higher education in the States. This should be possible as a result of education having been brought on the Concurrent List.

8. A system needs to be devised to ensure that adequate provision is made for all programmes when after a plan period they are covered under non-plan budget of a university. In the allocations made by the Finance Commission to the States the provisions corresponding to committed expenditure on higher education should not be diverted to other sectors.

9. Manpower requirements should guide framing of educational programmes even in non-professional higher education sectors and for the determination of an enrolment policy. Control of numbers in general higher education needs to be exercised to ensure

proper standards in universities and colleges.

10. The UGC in close cooperation with the Association of Indian Universities and other academic as well as professional bodies should undertake accreditation and grading of university departments and colleges and evolve a proper system of accreditation. The Commission be given the power to recommend to government derecognition of a degree of a university on grounds of lack of standards, as the Indian Medical Council is empowered in respect of Medical colleges.

11. There should be a system of evaluation of Ph.D. theses, of examinations, of class teaching in higher educational institutions through teams of academicians.

12. A system should also be evolved for assessment by the universities and colleges of the performance of teachers on an annual basis. This annual assessment should be taken into account in making periodic evaluation of teachers for suitable reward to outstanding persons. There should also be a system of disincentives against poor performance.

13. The working of the visiting committees needs to be improved and a larger number of academicians of attainment and integrity involved in the task of assessment and evaluation of institutions.

14. All the programmes aimed at improvement of teaching and the faculty in university departments and colleges should be monitored regularly.

Organisation and Structure

1. The number of members of the Commission should be increased from the present 12 (including Chairman and Vice chairman) to 18, by adding six members as follows: –

a) two college teachers (including principals) one of whom may, as far as possible, be from a women's college.
b) one person from the field of secondary education.
c) one expert in the field of rural higher education.
d) one expert in the field of non-formal education.
e) Secretary, Planning Commission, as an ex-officio member.

2. The choice of members should be so made that broad dis-

ciplines as well as universities in different parts of the country and expression in the Commission.

3. The Commission should organize annual conferences of education ministers, vice-chancellors, selected college principals and State education authorities in different parts of the country. Also some meetings of the Commission itself should be held at places other than Delhi every year.

4. The Commission's office should have two main divisions to deal with (a) educational planning and policy and (b) administration and grants.

5. The planning and policy division should be headed by an academician of standing who possesses expertise in planning, and should have four senior academicians belonging to different broad disciplines who should be in-charge of research and evaluation in their respective fields and be allotted areas for establishing regular contact with universities and colleges.

6. The head of the planning and policy division, who will also be the head of the research, planning and evaluation organisation referred to in Chapter V, should without being a member of the Commission, be of a status comparable to that of the vice-chairman and act as an expert adviser to the Commission and its chairman.

7. Senior academicians should be appointed, on a tenure basis on deputation from the academic field. Their terms of deputation should be generous and facilities of accommodation and opportunities for research work assured. Other academic staff in the Commission's office should also be appointed on deputation from educational institutions.

8. The secretary should head the administration division and be answerable to the chairman. The post should be filled on a tenure basis preferably by an administrator with experience of education or an academician with administrative experience.

9. Arrangement should be made for in-service training of various categories of staff.

10. The UGC should evolve its own procedure suitable for the efficient functioning of an organisation dealing with academic policies and programmes.

11. Staff requirement would need to be rationalised in the context of proposed organisational structure. Recruitment rules would also need to be reviewed.

12. The Commission should involve larger number of

academicians in the work of its Committees and give them facilities like accommodation for short stay, for efficient functioning.

13. The Annual Report of the Commission should not only give "true and full account of its activities during the previous year", as laid down in the Act, but also present to Parliament its assessment of problems and perspectives of higher education and of the state of coordination and standards in universities.

14. The UGC should evolve system of periodic review of its working and organisation at least once every ten years.

Constitution and Legal Aspects

1. Legal provisions be made as suggested from (a) to (e) in Para 7.3 of the Report.

2. Provision be also made for the implementation of suggestions made in (a) to (g) in para 7.4 of the Report.

3. Rules and regulations be framed by the UGC expeditiously. It should also be examined how the intention of our second interim recommendation can be achieved through suitable provision in rules or regulations, as suggested in para 7.2 of the Report.

Concluding Remarks

1. We commenced this report by recalling the vision of the founding fathers of our Constitution who had realized the necessity of coordination and maintenance of standards in university education and provide for making these areas a matter of national responsibility. We have referred to the serious thinking on the part of our leaders about the creation of an instrument for discharging this responsibility of the Central Government, which resulted in the establishment of an autonomous statutory body, the University Grants Commission.

2. We have taken note of the valuable work done by the UGC, as well as of the factors which have tended to inhibit its effective functioning during the two decades of its existence. We have attempted to spell out the major implications of coordination and determination of standards and the manner in which these objectives can be achieved. We have jointly and unanimously adopted the conclusions reached.

We have been profoundly impressed by the fact that a large body of responsible men and women involved in university education, whom we met, stressed the urgency of treating higher education as a matter of national concern and keeping it above all considerations of regional interests and party politics. We strongly endorse this view for, the hope of mankind lies in the emancipating role of education.

16

STUDY GROUP ON NON-BANKING COMPANIES, 1974 – REPORT[1]

Chairman Shri James S. Raj

Members Shri K.B. Chore; Shri V.G. Hegde; Shri A. Hasib; Shri D.M. Sukthankar; Shri R.N. Bansal; Shri V. Subramanian (replaced Shri D.D. Bhargava).

M. Secy. Shri B.N. Chikarmane.

Appointment

The Banking Commission constituted by the Government of India to review, *inter alia*, "the role of various classes of non-banking financial intermediaries, to enquire into their structure and methods of operation and to recommend measures for their orderly growth" made certain recommendations in this regard in its report submitted to the Government in January 1972. These recommendations were examined by the Reserve Bank of India. In the light of the views expressed by the Reserve Bank thereon, the Government of India decided that the relative provisions of the Reserve Bank of India Act, 1934 and the directions issued thereunder to non-banking companies may be reviewed to plus loopholes, if any, which were being taken advantage of, particularly by private limited companies.

With a view to examining this matter in all its aspects, the Reserve Bank of India, by an order Ref. No. DNBC 29/DG(S)-74 dated June 12, 1974 and Ref. No. DNBC 31/DG(S)-74 dated September 4 1974, constituted the present Study Group on Non-Banking Companies.

Terms of Reference

The terms of reference of the Study Group were as follows:

(i) To examine the relative provisions of the Reserve Bank of

---

1. Bombay, Reserve Bank of India, 1975, 151 p.

India Act, 1934, the Non-Banking Financial Companies (Reserve Bank) Directions, 1966, and the Miscellaneous Non-Banking Companies (Reserve Bank) Directions, 1973, with a view to assessing their adequacy in regulating the conduct of business by the non-banking companies covered by the said directions in the context of the monetary and credit policies laid down by the Reserve Bank from time to time; to suggest measures for further tightening up the provisions so as to ensure that the activities of such companies, insofar as they pertain to the acceptance of deposits, investments, lending operations, etc., subserve the national interest and serve more effectively as an adjunct to the regulation of the monetary and credit policies of the country besides affording a degree of protection to the depositors' monies.

(ii) To examine and make recommendations for regulating the conduct of the business of non-banking companies governed by the above sets of directions generally, and in particular, in regard to –

(a) the norms which may be adopted in respect of the capital structure and debt-equity ratio that may be maintained by the various classes of non-banking companies (NBCs) covered by the said directions;
(b) the extent to which and the periods for which such companies may borrow by way of deposits/unsecured loans and the distinctions, if any, to be made between public and private limited companies for this purpose;
(c) the maintenance of cash reserves and/or a percentage of their deposit liabilities in the form of liquid assets by such companies;
(d) the norms which may be adopted in respect of the rates of interest payable by such companies on their borrowings by way of deposits/unsecured loans and also those which may be charged on loans and advances made by them;
(e) the extent to which any of the activities carried on by these companies through their subsidiaries can or should be controlled;
(f) the need for the imposition of a ceiling on risk assets to be acquired or loans to be granted by the companies;
(g) the restrictions, if any, on the grant of loans to directors and their friends and relations and companies in which they are interested;

(h) the manner in which the loopholes, if any, in the existing directions taken advantage of by private limited companies in the context of certain concessions enjoyed by such companies under the provisions of the Companies Act, 1956, could be plugged; and

(i) the need to empower the Bank to apply for compulsory winding up of non-banking financial companies under certain circumstances.

To make recommendations on any other related topic which the Study Group may consider germane to the subject-matter of the enquiry.

Contents

Introductory; Approach to the Problem – Quantitative and Qualitative Aspects; Evolution of the Regulations Governing Acceptance of Deposits by NBCs; Non-Banking Non-Financial Companies; Non-Banking Financial Companies; Miscellaneous Non-Banking Companies; Administrative Arrangements; Summary of Major Conclusions and Recommendations; Appendices from I to IX.

Recommendations

While giving a summary of our conclusions and recommendations, it is not proposed to restate the full context in which they are made as the analysis and the arguments on which they are based have been fully explained in the preceding chapters. Chapter-wise recommendations are as follows:

Approach to the Problem — Quantitative and Qualitative Aspects

There is evidence to show that the dependence of non-financial companies on deposits has tended to increase, and at the same time, the liquidity of these companies in relations to the amount of deposits accepted by them has tended to decline.

Deposits with NBCs have grown in spite of the fact that there are certain advantages attached to commercial bank deposits which are not available in the other case. The basic reason for the growth of deposits of NBCs is that these companies pay interest rates higher than those paid by commercial banks.

The more recent spurt in deposits with NBCs is due to combination of factors such as the very rapid rise in prices and the consequent decline in the purchasing power of money, aggressive advertising campaign, both by companies and brokers, anti-inflationary measures undertaken by the Government and the Reserve Bank, particularly since the middle of 1974 and the restrictions placed on the declarations of dividends. Although the magnitude of deposits with NBCs in relation to the total bank deposits and other savings media is still limited, there is enough evidence of the acceleration in the growth of these deposits.

While the total level of savings is unlikely to increase on account of the deposits flowing to NBCs, the pattern of savings would undergo a change. There will also be a shift in the ownership of bank deposits from the household sector to the corporate sector. It is likely that over a period the level of deposits of the banking system may remain almost unchanged or may be reduced negligibly by the amount of cash in hand that these companies might wish to keep. The growing volume of deposits with these companies affects the operation of monetary and credit policy to the extent that it involves loss of direct control on the use of these funds. The current situation, therefore, calls for a negotiation but not prohibition of the acceptance of deposits by NBCs. Nevertheless, the long run objective should be to bring about a progressive reduction in the quantum of deposits with non-banking non-financial companies.

A selective approach will have to be taken in regard to the regulation of the activities of NBFCs since these institutions very greatly in the nature of their operations. In making recommendations on regulating the acceptance of deposits by NBCs, a distinction has to be made between non-banking non-financial companies and NBFCs. The reason is that the latter are para banks whose activities consist of accepting deposits for the purpose of making loans and advances, unlike the manufacturing and trading companies which normally accept deposits for use in their own business.

In regulating deposits with NBCs, it should be ensured that while their magnitude is kept within reasonable limits, they subserve the objectives of monetary and credit policy and that a larger degree of protection is afforded to the depositors' interests.

Non-Banking Non-Financial Companies

While arguments advanced for and against the necessity and justification for acceptance of deposits by non-financial companies have merits of their own, the consensus of opinion as put forward before the Group was that the present situation in which there has been a spurt in the soliciting of deposits from the public is an abnormal one brought about by a combination of temporary factors.

The broad approach to the problems posed by public deposits with non financial companies should be such that measures must be designed to ensure the efficacy of monetary and credit policy and to avoid disruption of the productive process, consistent with the need to safeguard, to the extent possible, the depositors' interests. At the same time, the ultimate objective should be to discourage the further growth of these deposits and to roll them back gradually so that they cease to be significant source of finance for industry and trade.

The Group is not in favour of giving insurance cover to deposits with NBCs on the lines of the cover offered by the Deposit Insurance Corporation in the case of deposits accepted by banks because the risks to be insured would differ widely as between companies and partly because it would be conceptually wrong to confer on unsecured company deposits the same protected status as has been conferred on bank deposits. A degree of risk is an inevitable concomitant of higher interest rates offered on company deposits.

The *status quo* in respect of the minimum period of deposits (i.e., six months) may be maintained while the maximum duration of deposits should not exceed three years.

The Group is neither in favour of prescribing any ceiling on the rates of interest offered by non-banking non-financial and financial companies on deposits received from the public nor on interest rates chargeable on advances by financial companies.

A lending bank should invariably take into account the quantum of deposits received by the borrowing company while sanctioning/ renewing credit facilities to it and also stipulate that the borrowing company should advise the bank about the quantum of deposits proposed to be raised by it.

Non-banking non-financial companies should be required to maintain in the form of liquid assets (excluding cash in hand), a sum which shall not be less than 10 per cent of their deposit liabilities maturing during the course of the year.

The deposits received from directors of all companies as well as from the shareholders of a private company should continue to be exempted so that there are no restrictions on these persons bringing in their own funds and increasing their stake in the business of the company.

The deposits of shareholders of private companies, both non-financial and financial, deemed to be public companies by virtue of Section 43A of the Companies Act, 1956, should be given the same treatment as those of shareholders of other private companies.

The Central Government may, by suitably amending the Companies Act, 1956, assume powers to grant extension of time comply with or exempt any company or class of companies from all or any of the provisions of the Companies (Acceptance of Deposits) Rules, 1975.

It would not be desirable to withdraw entirely the exemption of inter-company deposits currently available under the Rules. However, the relative provisions in the Rules may be amended to provide that the exemption would be admissible only where the recipient company is a new company, i.e., a company which has not gone into commercial production and it does not also accept any deposits on its own from the public. In other cases, for getting the benefit of exemption the recipient company may be required to obtain the prior approval of the Central Government.

There is no justification for doing away with the exemption in respect of security/dealership deposits which are accepted by manufacturing companies as a traditional business practices.

Convertible debentures/bonds may be exempted from the term 'deposit' under the Rules and the Directions.

The present criterion of relating the quantum of deposits to the net owned funds of a company is by far the most dependable since it is relatively stable in the course of the accounting year of a company and is also administratively feasible.

Notwithstanding the recent reduction of the ceiling in respect of unsecured loans guaranteed by directors, shareholders' deposits, etc., from 25 to 15 per cent of the net owned funds of a company, the Study Group feels that even the reduced ceiling is somewhat on the liberal side. Hence, the aforesaid ceiling of 15 per cent may be reduced by another five per cent with effect from January 1, 1977 and the balance of 10 per cent may also be completely withdrawn with effect from January 1, 1978.

The exemption from the ceiling restrictions available to companies — both non-financial and financial – in respect of deposits secured by the creation of mortgage, charge or pledge of any of their assets is fraught with dangerous consequences and hence, the exemption should be withdrawn.

Besides suggesting certain amendments to the provisions relating to advertisements issued by non-banking non-financial and financial companies, the Group has also recommended furnishing of certain additional particulars in the advertisements, application forms so that the prospective depositors could have a clearer picture of the State of affairs of a company over a period as also the legal implications arising out of keeping deposits with the company. If a private company, whether financial or non-financial, issues any advertisement soliciting deposits, it shall be deemed to be a public company for the purpose of sections 198, 220 (1), 372 and 373 of the Companies Act, 1956.

Non-Banking Financial Companies

While the magnitude of deposits with NBFCs as compared to the deposits with commercial banks may appear to be small, considering the absolute amount and the large number of depositors involved as well as the incidence of malpractices in these companies, effective regulation of their activities merits careful consideration. NBFCs should be subjected, by and large, to the same type of controls as banks under the Banking Regulation Act, 1949.

In order to decide upon the nature of regulation of NBFCs, the Group has made a distinction between financial companies which are run purely on commercial considerations such as hire-purchase finance, housing finance, investment, loan and miscellaneous financial companies on the one hand and companies which are run for the mutual benefit of the members, viz., companies conducting only conventional types of chits and mutual benefit financial companies (*nidhis*), on the other.

The extension of insurance cover to deposits with NBFCs is neither feasible nor desirable for the present but can be a long-term objective. Before the question of extending insurance cover to NBFCs is considered, weaker units are weeded out by amalgamation or otherwise and their working is generally put on sound footing.

The minimum period for acceptance of deposits by NBFCs may remain at six months at present. As regards the maximum period, it should be fixed at 3 years in the case of hire-purchase finance, investment, loan, and miscellaneous financial companies and 5 years in the case of housing finance companies. In the case of nidhis, the present position under the directions which do not lay down any minimum or maximum period for acceptance of deposits may be maintained.

Deposits of hire-purchase finance and loan companies should not exceed 10 times their net owned funds. As regards investment companies, the existing ceilings on their deposits should continue for the time being but the ceiling of 15 per cent of the net owned funds in respect of unsecured loans guaranteed by directors, shareholders' deposits, etc., may be reduced by 5 per cent with effect from January 1, 1977 and the balance of 10 per cent may also be completely withdrawn with effect from January 1, 1978. Miscellaneous financial companies may be identified as falling in one or the other of the above categories and the ceilings applicable to them should be determined accordingly.

The present exemption in the case of housing finance companies insofar as the ceilings on deposits are concerned may continue. As regards nidhis, moneys received from their members are excluded from the term 'deposit'; as such the ceilings on deposits are not applicable to them and the *status quo* may be maintained.

The group has suggested that every NBFC other than a nidhi which commences business after the proposed regulatory measures are brought into force shall have a paid-up capital of not less than Rs. 5 lakhs; if such company conducts business only at one place with a population of less than five lakhs, the paid-up capital shall not be less than Rs. 2 lakhs. As regards an existing company other than a nidhi, its net worth (i.e., paid-up capital plus free reserves less balance of accumulated loss and other intangible assets, if any, as appearing in its latest audited balance sheet) shall not be less than Rs. 2 lakhs if it conducts its business at only one place with a population of less than five lakhs; in any other case, its net worth shall not be less than Rs. 5 lakhs. NBFCs (including nidhis) should be required to transfer to the Reserve Fund a sum equivalent to not less than 20 per cent of their annual profits before declaring any dividend till such time as the amount in the Reserve Fund is less than the paid-up capital of the company.

NFBCs (including nidhis) shall, at all times, maintain liquid assets which shall not be less than 10 per cent of the deposits received by them and outstanding in their books. The Reserve Bank may be authorised to vary the liquid assets ratio of NBFCs in accordance with its monetary and credit policy.

Loans and advances by NBFCs to their directors and firms in which they are interested as partners, managers, etc., should be prohibited.

No NBFC, other than an investment company, but including a nidhi, should be allowed to form any subsidiary, except for the purpose of carrying on the same line of business as that of the holding company. An exception may be made in the case of hire-purchase finance companies.

For the effective regulation of NBFCs, the Reserve Bank should be vested with powers on the lines of certain provisions of the Banking Regulation Act, 1949.

It would be desirable to enact a separate comprehensive legislation in the place of Chapter III-B of the Reserve Bank of India Act, 1934, for giving effect to the recommendations. Pending enactment of such legislation, the existing provisions of Chapter III-B may be invoked for issuing directions in respect of such of the recommendations as could be implemented.

The Group is of the view that the Reserve Bank of India is the appropriate authority for regulating the activities of NBFCs.

Miscellaneous Non-Banking Companies

Prize chit/benefit/saving schemes, etc., benefit primarily the promoters and do not serve any social purpose. On the contrary, they are prejudicial to the public interest and also adversely affect the efficacy of fiscal and monetary policy. Such schemes, by whatever name called, should be totally banned in the larger interests of the public and suitable legislative measures should be taken for the purpose if the provisions of the existing enactments are considered inadequate.

As regards conventional chit funds, the Group, while forwarding its comments to the Reserve Bank on the Model Bill drafted by the latter at the instance of the Central Government, has made certain recommendations, the more important of which are the following:

(1) the Bill should be enacted as a Central Act by Parliament as this step, besides ensuring uniformity in the provisions applicable to chit fund institutions throughout the country, would also prevent such institutions from taking undue advantage

either of the absence of any law governing chit funds in any State or exploit the benefit of any lacuna or relaxation in any State Law by extending their activities to such States;

(2) the administration of the proposed legislation should be left to the State Government concerned which, in turn, may seek the advice of the Reserve Bank on policy matters;

(3) private limited companies as also unincorporated bodies the latter on a restricted scale, may continue to be allowed to run chits; and

(4) chit fund institutions may be prohibited from accepting deposits except as advance payments of subscriptions or deposits from the prized subscribers by way of security towards payments of their future instalments.

Administrative Arrangements

The Department of Non-Banking Companies of the Reserve Bank will have to work in close liaison with the Department of Company Affairs. For an effective implementation of the proposed regulatory measures, DNBC will require to be strengthened and reorganised. For this purpose, it will be necessary to decentralise its functions so that the impediments now faced under a centralised set-up are removed.

The additional responsibilities devolving on the Department of Company Affairs may be discharged within the existing administrative framework with such augmentation of staff as may be necessary at the regional levels to cope up with the increased work-load involved in the implementation of the provisions of section 58-A of the Companies Act, 1956 and the Rules made there under.

The Reserve Bank may consider making arrangements for undertaking research on a continuous basis on the working of NBFIs and related aspects in the Economic Department of the Bank.

17

SELECT COMMITTEE ON DELHI SALES TAX BILL, 1973 – REPORT[1]

Chairman Shri S.M. Siddayya

Members Shri Syed Ahmed Aga; Shri Shrikrishna Agrawal; Shri H.K.L. Bhagat; Shri Bhagirath Bhanwar; Shri Chakleshwar Singh; Shri Amarsinh Chaudhari; Shrimati Premalabai Dajisaheb Chavan; Shri Dalip Singh; Shri M. Deiveekan; Shri Shanker Narayan Singh Deo; Shri Biren Dutta; Shri C.C. Gohain; Shri N.E. Horo; Shri Chiranjib Jha; Shrimati Subhadra Joshi; Shri Sat Pal Kapur; Shri Vikram Mahajan; Shrimati Shakuntala Nayar; Shri Arvinda Bala Pajanor; Shri Sudhakar Pandey; Shri Birender Singh Rao; Shri P.V. Reddy; Shri Arjun Sethi; Dr. H.P. Sharma; Shri M.R. Sharma; Shri Ramavatar Shastri; Shri Somchand Solanki; Shri Amarnath Vidyalankar; Shri C. Subramaniam

Alterations Shri Chakleshwar Singh appointed w.e.f. 9.9.74 *vice* Shri Rudra Pratap Singh resigned; Shri Dalip Singh appointed w.e.f. 19.11.74 *vice* Shri Buta Singh resigned; Shri M. Deiveekan appointed w.e.f. 9.9.74 *vice* Shri R.P. Ulaganambi resigned; Shri Biren Dutt appointed w.e.f 9.9.74 *vice* Shri Madhuryya Halder resigned; Shri Sat Pal Kapur appointed w.e.f 19.11.74 *vice* Shri K.R. Ganesh resigned; Shri Sudhakar Pandey appointed w.e.f. 19.11.74 *vice* Shri Vishwanath Pratap Singh resigned; Shri C. Subramaniam appointed w.e.f 19.11.74 *vice* Shri Y.B. Chavan resigned.

Legislative Counsel

1. Shri S. Harihara Iyer – Joint Secretary and legislative counsel

---

1. Lok Sabha Secretariat, Government of India, New Delhi, 1975, 106 p.

2. Shri S. Ramaiah – Additional Legislative Counsel Representatives of the Ministry of Finance (Department of Revenue and Insurance)
   1. Shri K. Narasimhan – Additional Secretary
   2. Shri O.P. Mehra – Dy. Secretary
   3. Shri S.D. Ramaswamy – Under Secretary
   4. Shri Virendra Prakash – Commissioner, Sales Tax, Delhi.

Representatives of the Ministry of Home Affairs

1. Shri K.R. Prabhu – Additional Secretary
2. Shri D.S. Misra – Deputy Secretary

Secretariat

1. Shri P.K. Patnaik – Additional Secretary
2. Shri H.G. Paranjpe – Chief Financial Committee Officer
3. Shri J.R. Kapur – Chief Financial Committee Officer
4. Shri H.L. Malhotra – Senior Legislative Committee Officer

Appointment

The Bill was introduced in Lok Sabha on the 9th April, 1973. The motion for reference of the Bill to a Select Committee of the House was moved in Lok Sabha by Shri K. R. Ganesh, the then Minister of State in the Ministry of Finance on the 6th September, 1974 and was adopted.

Terms of Reference

The taxable Quantum to be raised and the Central Sales-tax Act should be amended.

Contents

Composition of the Select Committee; Report of the Select Committee; Minutes of Dissent, Bill as Reported by the Select Committee; Appendices from I to IV.

Recommendations

The observations of the Committee with regard to the principal changes proposed in the Bill are detailed in the succeeding paragraphs.

Clause 2 [*Explanation to Sub-clause* (1)]—The Committee are of the view that the Explanation to sub-clause (1) of clause 2 of the Bill is redundant in view of the provisions contained in section 4(2) of the Central Sales-tax Act, 1956.

The Explanation has been omitted accordingly.

Clause 3 —(i) *Sub-clause* (3).—The Committee feel that in the event of a dealer's turnover falling below the taxable quantum in any year, he may be allowed to apply for cancellation of his registration certificate after the expiry of one year following that year in which his turnover has failed to exceed the taxable quantum. The dealer should be liable to pay tax in respect of goods purchased by him prior to the cancellation of his certificate free of tax on the strength of such certificate.

Provison to sub-clause (3) has been inserted accordingly.

(ii) *Sub-clause* (7) —The Committee are of the view that the taxable quantum should be raised from Rs.15,000 to Rs. 30,000 in the case of manufacturers and from Rs. 15,000 to Rs. 1,00,000 in the case of other dealers. The Committee are also of the view that the turn over of all sales should be taken into account for the purposes of computing the taxable quantum of a dealer irrespective of whether such sales are taxable under the Bill or not. Sub-clause (7) has been amended accordingly.

An Explanation to the sub-clause has also been inserted to provide that all sales will be included for the purpose of computing the taxable quantum.

Clause 4—*Sub-clause* (1) —(i) The Committee are of the view that the rate of tax in respect of goods included in the First Schedule appended to the Bill might be raised from ten paise in the rupee of twelve paise in the rupee.

Sub-Clause (1)(a) has been amended accordingly.

(ii) The Committee feel that the levy of tax in respect of any food or drink served for consumption in a hotel or restaurant with which a cabaret, floor show or similar entertainment is provided therein should be at the rate of forty paise in the rupee.

New sub-clause (1) (c) has been inserted accordingly.

(iii) The Committee feel that in the case of taxable turnover in respect of any other goods, the tax at the rate of seven paise in the rupee might be levied.

Original sub-clause (1) (c) [New sub-clause 1(d)] has been amended accordingly.

(iv) Proviso to sub-clause (1) has been amended so as to permit amendment of the First or the Second schedule either retrospectively or prospectively and it has been provided that no such retrospective amendment would prejudicially affect the interests of any dealer.

(v) *Sub-clause* 2(a)(*i*) has been amended to be in the line with the provisions of clause 5 of the Bill.

(vi) *Sub-clause* 2(a)(*iv*) —The Committee feel that the goods which have been purchased by a dealer within a period of twelve months prior to the date of his registration should be deducted from his turnover, provided the goods have been sold by the dealer within a period of twelve months from the date of his registration and the claim for such deduction is included in the return to be furnished by the dealer in respect of such sale.

Sub-clause 2(a)(iv) has been substituted accordingly.

(vii) *Sub-clause* 2(a)*(v)(A)*.—Since newspapers are not goods for the purpose of levy of sales tax in Delhi, the Committee feel that it might be made clear that raw materials for the purpose of the printing of newspapers should not be entitled to get exemption from tax.

Sub-clause 2(a)*(v)*(*A*) has been amended accordingly.

(viii) *Sub-clause* 2(a)(*v*)*(C)* —The Committee feel that sales of only such containers or other materials as are used for the packing goods or class of goods specified in the certificate of registration of a dealer should be allowed tax free.

Sub-clause 2 (a)*(v)(C)* has been amended accordingly.

(ix) *Second and Third provisos to sub-clause* (2) —The changes made are of drafting nature.

Clause 5 — The Committee feel that the power of the Administrators to specify the point of sale at which any goods or class of goods should be taxed, be subject to such conditions, if any, as may be specified in the notification specifying the point of sale. The Committee also feel that where a point of sale (other than the last point on which the tax would be generally levied) is notified by the Administrator under this clause, the exemption on points of sale other than the point of sale so notified should be available on the production of prescribed declaration forms. The Administrator may, however, be empowered to exempt any goods or classes of goods or dealers or classes of dealers from the requirement of production of declaration forms subject to such restriction and conditions as may be specified in the notification to be issued in this behalf.

Clause 5 has been amended accordingly.

Clause 7 —The Committee feel that with the previous approval of the Central Government, the Administrator should have the power to amend the Third Schedule either retrospectively or prospectively and on such retrospective amendment should prejudicially affect the interests of any dealer.

Clause 7 has been amended accordingly.

Clause 9—(i) *Sub-clause* (2) —The Committee feel that the Administrator might be authorised to appoint Additional Commissioners of Sales tax and Sales Tax Officers, besides other persons, to assist the Commissioner in the execution of his functions under the Bill.

Sub-clause (2) has been amended accordingly.

(ii) *Sub-clause* (3).—The Committee are of the view that the jurisdiction of the various officers should be specified by the Commissioner instead of the Administrator, as provided for in the Bill.

Sub-clause (3) has been amended accordingly.

Clause 10 —The Committee are of the opinion that the powers to specify jurisdiction of officers under clause of 9(3) of the Bill and to sanction prosecution in clause 52(1) of the Bill should be exercised by the Commissioner only. The powers to conduct search and seizure should not be delegated to any person lower in rank to a Sales-tax Officer and those under sub-section (1) of clause 49 should not be delegated to any person other than an Additional Commissioner of Sales Tax. The other powers could be delegated to any person appointed to assist the Commissioner under clause 9(2) of the Bill.

Clause 10 has been amended accordingly.

Clause 11 —The Committee are of the view that it should be made clear that the proceedings under this Bill should mean any proceedings which might be pending on the date when an order is passed under this Bill or which might have been completed on or before such date and include proceedings which might be commenced after that date.

An Explanation to this clause has been added accordingly.

Clause 13 —The amendment made in this clause is consequent on the repeal of the Code of Criminal Procedure, 1898 and the re-enactment of the Code of Criminal Procedure, 1973, after the introduction of this Bill.

Clause 14 —(i) The Committee are of the view that a provision should be made in the Bill itself for prescribing a period within which a certificate of registration should be granted.

(ii) The Committee feel that it might be made clear that the goods or class of goods in respect of which a notification is issued under clause 5 specifying the point at which the goods will be taxed, will not be specified in the registration certificate to a dealer. Further, such goods or class of goods, if any, are specified in the registration certificate and a notification in respect of such goods is issued under the said Section 5 on any subsequent date, the certificate should be deemed to have been amended so as to omit the reference to such goods or classes of goods.

(iii) The Committee also feel that if the concerned authority is of the opinion that an application for registration is not in order, the same might be rejected within the prescribed period after recording the reasons therefor.

The clause has been amended accordingly.

Clause 16 —(i) *Sub-clause* (1) —The amendment made is consequent upon the amendment made in clause 3(7) of the Bill.

(ii) *Sub-clause* (2) —The Committee feel that the registering authority should specify the restrictions and conditions in the provisional certificate of registration to be granted to a dealer who intends to start a manufacturing business in Delhi.

Sub-clause (2) has been amended accordingly.

(iii) *New Sub-clause* (7) —The Committee feel that a person, who has been granted a provisional certificate of registration fails, without sufficient cause, to establish a manufacturing business within the period specified in the provisional certificate of registration or fails to comply with any of the restrictions or conditions subject to which the certificate was granted, should be liable to pay a penalty equivalent to one and a half times the amount of tax which a dealer might have paid had he not been so registered.

New sub-clause (7) has been inserted accordingly.

Clause 18 —(i) *Sub-clause* (1) —The Committee feel that the Commissioner should be empowered to demand, in appropriate cases, security for proper custody and use of declaration forms.

Sub-clause (1) has been amended accordingly.

(ii) *Sub-clause* (2) —The Committee are of the opinion that in the case of a new dealer coming up for registration under this Bill, quantum of security might be determined with respect to the amount of tax which may be or become payable by the applicant having regard to the nature and size of his business. As regards the security for proper custody and use of forms, it may be computed with reference to the amount of tax which might be saved by a dealer by the issue of such declaration forms, and, in other cases, the amount of security should not exceed the estimated tax payable on the taxable turnover of a dealer for the year in which security is demanded.

Sub-clause (2) has been amended accordingly.

Clause 19 —The amendment made is of a clarificatory nature.

Clause 20 [*Sub-clause* (3)(d)] —The Committee feel that a dealer could avoid cancellation of his registration certificate by filling some returns in a year while not submitting the others. The case of such a dealer would be covered by the residuary powers for cancellation of registration certificate as contained in re-numbered item (f) of the sub-clause.

Sub-clause (3)(d) has, therefore, been omitted.

(ii) *Sub-clause* (7) —This sub-clause has been substituted by a new sub-clause with a view to clarify that a person would be liable to pay tax in respect of the sales effected by him prior to the date of cancellation of his certificate of registration.

(iii) *New Sub-clause* (8) —The Committee are of the view that where it is found that a person registered as a dealer ought not to have been so registered, then such person should be liable to pay tax for the period he was registered, as if he were a dealer.

Sub-clause (8) has been inserted accordingly.

Clause 23 —(i) *Sub-clause* (6).—The Committee are of the view that, when a dealer liable to pay tax under the Bill has failed to get himself registered, the amount of penalty to be imposed on a dealer should not be more than twice the amount of the tax assessed.

Sub-clause (6) has been amended accordingly.

(ii) *Sub-clause* (7) —The amendment has been made with a view to reduce the period of assessment from eight years to six years in the case of a dealer who is liable to pay tax and who has failed to get himself registered.

Clause 24 —The amendments made in this clause are with a view to reduce the period of re-assessment of an escaped assessment from eight to six years.

The other amendment made is of a clarificatory nature.

Clause 25 —The amendments made are of clarification nature.

New Clause 26 —This clause has been inserted with a view to provide for the continuation of recovery proceedings, in respect of which any appeal or revision application or other proceedings are filed. Where the amount of tax or penalty is enhanced, fresh notice to the dealer should be issued only in respect of the amount by which such Government dues are enhanced. Where the amount of tax or penalty has been reduced, no fresh notice for the reduced amount would be necessary. The Commissioner, in such a case, would give intimation to the dealer and to the authority with whom such proceedings are pending about such reduction.

New Clause 27 —The Committee note that the Public Accounts Committee (1973-74) in their 116th Report has recommended the inclusion of a provision for levying interest for belated payments. The Committee, are, therefore, of the opinion that simple interest should be paid by the dealer at the rate of one per cent. If the default is for a period of one month and at the rate of one and a half per cent per month where the default is for more than a month, for so long as there is default in the payment of the tax. The interest may be deemed as tax payable under the Bill.

New clause 27 has been inserted accordingly.

Clause 28 *[Original clause* 26] —*New Sub-clause* (7) —The Committee feel that the Commissioner or any other person appointed to assist the Commissioner should be empowered to apply to a court for payment to him of any amount, belonging to a dealer, which is lying in the custody of the court, in order to discharge the liability in respect of tax and penalty due from such a dealer.

New Sub-clause (7) has been inserted accordingly.

Clause 30 [*Original clause* 28]—(i) *Sub-clause* (1) —The amendment is made of a clarificatory nature.

(ii) *Sub-clause* (3) —The Committee feel that the Commissioner may for sufficient cause allow a claim for refund being made after the expiry of the period of twelve months but not later than twelve months from such expiry.

Sub-clause (3) has been amended accordingly.

(iii) *Sub-clause* (4) —The Committee feel that in the case of delayed refunds due to person, the Commissioner should pay interest at the same rates as given in clause 27 above if refund is not made within ninety days from the date of his making the claim.

Sub-clause (4) has been amended accordingly.

(iv) *New Sub-clause* (5) —The Committee feel that where any question arises as to the period which is to be excluded for the purposes of calculation of interest, the decision of the Commissioner should be taken as final in such cases.

New Sub-clause (5) has been inserted accordingly.

(v) *Sub-clause* 8 [*Original Sub-clause* (7)] —In view of the provisions of Section 15(b) of the Central Sales Tax Act, 1956, sub-clause (2) has been amended to provide that the amount in respect of local sales tax paid on declared goods which are subsequently sold in the course of inter-State trade or commence should be reimbursed to the person who makes such sale in the course of inter-State trade or commerce.

Clause 31 [*Original clause* 29] —The Committee feel that it should be made clear that set off would be admissible if delay in granting the registration certificate to a dealer is beyond the period prescribed for grant of such registration certificate.

The clause has been amended accordingly.

Clause 32 [*Original clause* 30] —*New Sub-clause* (2).—(i) The Committee feel that the liability of the transferee of a business should not be limited to the value of the assets obtained by transfer.

Proviso to sub-clause (1) has been omitted accordingly.

(ii) The Committee feel that the transferee or the lessee in a business should be liable to pay tax on the sale of goods effected by him after the date of transfer of the business and the transferee or the lessee, where he is an existing dealer, should make an application for the amendment of the registration certificate.

New sub-clause (2) has been inserted accordingly.

Clause 35 *and* 36 [*Original clauses* 33 *and* 34] —The amendments made are of clarificatory nature.

Clause 38 [*Original clause* 36] —The Committee feel that the Commissioner may be empowered to direct any class of registered dealers to keep such accounts as may be specified by him in the notification.

New sub-clause (2) has been inserted accordingly.

Clause 39 [*Original clause* 37] —The Committee feel that the statutory requirement of issuing a bill/cash memorandum should be only in respect of sales where value of goods sold in any one transaction exceeds rupees ten. Further the Administrator should be empowered either to exempt any goods or class of goods or dealers or class of dealers from the requirement of issuing a bill/cash memorandum for sale of goods exceeding ten rupees in value in anyone transaction or specify in the notification that the bill/cash memorandum would be required to be issued if the sale of goods is of such amount exceeding ten rupees as is mentioned in the notification.

The clause has been amended accordingly.

Clause 41 [*Original clause* 39] —*Sub-clause* (7).—The amendment made in this sub-clause is consequent on the repeal of the Code of Criminal Procedure, 1898 and re-enactment of the Code of Criminal Procedure, 1973, after the Bill was introduced.

Clause 43 [*Original clause* 41] —(i) *Sub-clause* (1) —The Committee are of the opinion that any person (including a dealer) aggrieved by any order should have the right to prefer an appeal against such order.

Sub-clause (1) has been amended accordingly.

(ii) *Sub-clauses* (2) *and* (4) —The Committee feel that the Commissioner should also have the right to appeal to the Appellate Tribunal if he is aggrieved by the order of the first appellate authority. In such a case, the Commissioner is not required to pay the fee of fifty rupees which is required to be paid when the appeal is filed by any other person.

Sub-clause (2) and (4) have been amended accordingly.

(iii) *Sub-clause* (5) – The Committee feel that a provision might be made in the Bill itself that no appeal would be entertained by the appellate authority unless the amount admitted to be due has been paid by the Appellant.

Second proviso to sub-clause (5) has been inserted accordingly.

Clause 45 [*Original clause* 43] —*Sub-clause* (1) —This sub-clause has been amended with a view to bring it on the lines of an identical provision in the Income-tax Act, 1962.

The other amendment made is of consequential nature.

Clause 46 [*Original clause* 44] —The Committee feel that a final order under this clause should be made before the expiry of five years from the date of the order sought to be revised.

Proviso to this clause has been substituted accordingly.

Clause 48 [*Original clause* 46] —(i) *New sub-clause* (3).—This sub-clause has been inserted with a view to permit the authority passing any order to amend any order if the matter covered by such order is identical to the matter already decided in any proceeding by way of appeal or revision.

(ii) *New sub-clauses* (6) *and* (7) —The Committee feel that there should be a provision for review of orders passed by any authority or by the Appellate Tribunal and before any order in review is passed, any person likely to be affected adversely should be given reasonable opportunity of being heard.

New sub-clauses (6) and (7) have been inserted accordingly. Other amendments made are of verbal nature.

Clause 49 [Original clause 47] —The Committee feel that a period should be prescribed within which any disputed question should be determined by the Commissioner.

The clause has been amended accordingly.

Clause 50 [*Original clause* 48].

(i) *Sub-clauses (b), (c)* and *(d)* —The Committee feel that onus in respect of offences mentioned in sub-clauses (b), (c) and (d) of the clauses should be on the person within whose knowledge the facts relating thereto would be.

(ii) *Sub-clause (g)* —The Committee feel that the burden of proof should be on the person who makes any collection of tax otherwise in accordance with the provisions of the Bill and the rules made thereunder.

(iii) *Sub-clause (h)* —This sub-clause has been amended in the light of amendments made in clause 38 of the Bill.

(iv) *New sub-clause (o)* —The sub-clause creates a new offence where the owner or person in charge of a goods vehicle fails, neglects or refuse to comply with the requirements contained in clause 64 of the Bill.

(v) The Committee feel that imprisonment in respect of offences mentioned in this clause of the Bill should be rigorous and not simple and the quantum of daily fine in respect of a continuing offence should be raised to two hundred rupees and in respect of certain offences, if the court is satisfied that the offence has been committed wilfully, the offender should be punished with rigorous imprisonment for a term which might extend to six months and with fine, and when the offence is a continuing one, with a daily fine of three hundred rupees during the period of continuance of the offence.

(vi) The Committee also feel that a person who has applied for registration in accordance with the provisions of clause 14(2) or clause 17(2) should not be deemed to have committed an offence under sub-clause (b).

Sub-clause (2) has been inserted accordingly.

Clauses 52 *and* 53 [*Original clauses* 50 *and* 51].—The term "magistrate of the first class" has been substituted by the term "Metropolitan Magistrate". This amendment and the other amendment to this clause and the amendment to Clause 53 (original clause 51) are consequent on the repeal of the Code of Criminal Procedure, 1898 and the re-enactment of the Code of Criminal Procedure, 1973 after the introduction of the Bill.

Clause 54 [*Original clause* 52] —*Sub-clause* (1) —This sub-clause provides for compounding of offences for a sum not exceeding five thousand rupees or double the amount of tax which would have been payable by a person whichever is higher. The Committee feel that since the quantum of penalty in lieu of prosecution has been raised of two and a half times, the quantum of composition money should also be raised to a sum not exceeding three times the amount of tax which would have been payable it such person had complied with the provisions of the Bill.

Sub-clause (1) has been amended accordingly.

Clause 55 [*Original clause* 53] —*Sub-clause* (1) —Item (b) of sub-clause (1) has been omitted as a provision in this regard has been made in sub-clause (5) of clause 25 of the Bill.

The other amendments made are with a view to raise the quantum of penalty in lieu of prosecution for an offence relating to non-furnishing of return or non-payment of tax within due time, from a sum not exceeding one and a half times of a sum not exceeding twice the amount of such tax sought to be evaded and where no tax is payable by a person, the quantum of penalty in respect of the said offence should be raised from a sum not exceeding one thousand rupees to a sum not exceeding two thousand rupees.

Sub-clause (1) has been amended accordingly.

Clause 56 [*Original clause* 54] —The amendments made in this clause are on the lines made in clauses 54 and 55 of the Bill.

Clause 57 *[Original clause 55] sub-clause* (1) –The amendment made is on the lines made in clause 56 of the Bill.

The Committee recommends that there should be a provision in the Bill to penalise officers conniving or colluding with the tax evaders. The Government should also consider to include similar provisions in other taxation laws.

Clause 58 [*Original clause* 56] —The Committee are of the view that notices on all the adult members of the erstwhile Hindu undivided family shall be served in case the person who was the last manager of such family could not be found.

Clause 56 has been amended accordingly.

Clause 64 [*Original clause* 62] —(i) *Sub-Clause* (3) —The Committee feel that the owner or person in charge of a goods vehicle entering or leaving Delhi should file a declaration in the prescribed form which should be obtained from the prescribed authority. The Committee further feel that a penalty not exceeding two and a half times the tax or one thousand rupees, whichever is higher, should be imposed if the owner or person in charge of a goods vehicle fails to carry goods which are meant to be carried to a place outside Delhi to that place within the prescribed period without reasonable cause.

Sub-clause (3) has been amended accordingly.

(ii) *Sub-clause* (4) —The Committee feel that an officer empowered by the Administrator should be authorised to search the goods vehicle or part thereof and also to examine the contents therein.

Sub-Clause (4) has been amended accordingly.

(iii) *New sub-clause* (5) —The Committee feel that an officer empowered by the Administrator should have the power to detain the goods if such officer has reason to believe that the owner or person in charge of the goods vehicle is attempting to evade payment of tax. The goods so detained should not be allowed to be transported unless a security for an amount not exceeding one thousand rupees or the amount of tax payable if such goods were sold in Delhi, whichever is more, is furnished.

(iv) *New sub-clause* (6) —The Committee feel that where the security is not furnished within the prescribed period, the goods in question should be disposed off in such manner and subject to such conditions as may be prescribed.

Clause 65 [*Original clause* 63] —The Committee feel that the Commissioner should publish in the official Gazette such particulars as may be prescribed at intervals not exceeding three months of dealers whose registration certificates are cancelled under the provisions of the Bill.

Clause 63 has been substituted accordingly.

New clause 68 —The Committee feel that transfer of any assets by way of sale, mortgage, gift or exchange or any other mode during the pendency of any proceedings under the Bill should be void as against any claim in respect of any tax or any other sum payable under the Bill.

New clause has been inserted accordingly.

New clause 69 —The Committee feel that chapter XXXVI of the Code of Criminal Procedure, 1973 should not apply to any offence punishable under the Bill, or to any other offence which under the provisions of that Code might be tried along with such offence.

New Clause has been inserted accordingly.

New clause 70 —The Committee feel that it should be made clear that where any amount is recoverable as an arrear of land revenue under the provisions of the Bill, such recovery should be made in accordance with the provisions of the Delhi Land Reforms Act, 1954 if the recovery is to be made inside Delhi and of the Revenue Recovery Act, 1890 if the recovery is to be made in any inserted accordingly.

New clause has been inserted accordingly.

Clause 71 [*Original clause* 66] —The amendments made in this clause are of consequential nature.

New clause 75 —The Committee feel that a dealer who is liable to pay tax under the Bengal Finance (Sales Tax) Act, 1941, as in force in Delhi, but who is not liable to pay tax under the provisions of the Bill, should continue to be liable to pay tax on sales of goods purchased by him prior to the commencement of the Bill.

New clause has been inserted accordingly.

The First Schedule –

(i) *Entry* 2 —The Committee are of the opinion that "cycle combination" might be changed to "motor and cycle combinations". The Entry has been amended accordingly.

(ii) *Entries* 4 *and* 7 —The Committee recommend that the existing rate of tax on transistors and watches at ten per cent should continue.

(iii) *Entry* 15 —The amendment made by the substitution of this entry is of a clarificatory nature.

(iv) *Entry* 16 —The Committee are of the view that spoons are essential item of every household and should, therefore, be excluded from this entry. The Entry has been amended accordingly.

(v) *Entry* 18 —The Committee feel that the existing rate of tax at 7 per cent on cheaper variety of crockery should continue.

(vi) *Entry* 23 —The Committee recommend that the existing rate of tax on motor spirit and high speed diesel oil at the rate of 7 per cent should continue.

(vii) *Entry* 25 —The Committee are of the view that leather belts are mostly used by students and should, therefore, not be included in this entry. The Entry has been amended accordingly.

(viii) *Entry* 26 —The Committee feel that the existing rate of tax on wooden furniture should not exceed ten per cent.

(ix) *Entry* 31 —The Committee feel that the goods made out of plastic, celluloid, bakelite and other similar goods having the value not exceeding thirty rupees per piece might be excluded. The Entry has been amended accordingly.

The Second Schedule [Entry 1] —The Committee recommend that no tax should be levied on "charcoal". The Entry has been amended accordingly.

The Third Schedule –

(i) *Entry* 1 —The Committee feel that all forms of rice and cooked *dal* might also be included in this Entry. The Entry has been amended accordingly.

(ii) *Entry* 3—The Committee are of the opinion that bread (*double roti*) prepared either with power or without the aid of power should be free from tax. The Entry has been amended accordingly.

(iii) *Entry* 14 —Geometry boxes and instruments such as instruments used in mechanical drawing and biology used by students should not be taxed. The Entry has been amended accordingly.

(iv) *Entry* 15 —The words "and charcoal" have been inserted in this Entry for the reasons set out in paragraph 61 above.

(v) *Entry* 17 —The Committee are of the opinion that agricultural implements including chaffcutters and persian wheels and electric motor including monoblock pumping sets of 3 to 7-1/2 horse power are required by all farmers. These items should, therefore, be exempted from tax. The Entry has been substituted accordingly.

(vi) *Entry* 26 —The Committee are of the opinion that "prepared pans" should also be free from tax. The Entry has been amended accordingly.

(vii) *New Entries* 32 *to* 36 —The Committee recommend that the following items should also be included in the category of exempted goods:

1. "Handspun yarn.
2. *Achar* and *Murabba* except when sold in sealed containers.
3. Scientific goods including scientific glass goods, geometrical and drawing goods used in schools and colleges for teaching and for use by students.
4. Livestock including poultry.
5. Cotton paddings."

These items have, therefore, been inserted in the Third schedule.

Clause 1 and Enacting Formula —The amendments made are of a formal nature.

The Committee recommend that the Bill, as amended, be passed.

The Committee also recommend that—

(i) while fixing rates of tax the peculiar position of Delhi as a trade distributing Centre, should be kept in view;

(ii) with a view to check evasion of tax and also to facilitate collection, wherever possible, the tax should be levied at the first point;

(iii) the tax on silk and pure silk fabrics should be levied at the first point;

(iv) the tax on hosiery goods and umbrella cloth covers which is at present being charged at one per cent should continue to be so charged for the present;

(v) the tax on kerosene and matches should be levied at the first point and it should not in any case be more than three per cent on kerosene and four per cent on matches;

(vi) the tax on black lead and coloured pencils used by students should be levied at the first point and should not in any case be more than five per cent;

(vii) cycle, cycle-rickshaw and tri-cycle and the parts thereof which are at present being taxed at the general rate should continue to be so taxed; and

(viii) the concessional rate of tax allowed to *halwais* may be continued.

Minute of Dissent

The taxation policy of the Government should be such which should not hit the common man. But it is not so today. The present policy of the Government is hitting the poor people and sparing the rich to a great extent. This is also evident in the Delhi Sales Tax Bill, 1973 as reported by the Select Committee.

For checking evasion of tax and also facilitating collection, the principle of single point Sales Tax, i.e., at the first point should be adopted and implemented. This demand is raised from almost all the quarters. This system will also lessen the expenditure of the Government and will check corruption to a greater degree. The present system of Sales Tax is responsible for tax evasion and corruption. By adopting corrupt means, hundreds of crores of rupees are eaten up by the business community who are liable to pay sales and other taxes.

However, the Select Committee have attempted in this direction by recommending levy of first-point Sales Tax, wherever possible. This is a welcome step.

For the purpose of levying Sales Tax on coal, it has been included in the Second Schedule. It comes under the category of essential commodities. Coal is used by a large number of poor people for whom it is becoming difficult to meet their both ends. Coal is consumed mostly by the poor and middle class people who are badly hit by the rising prices. The price of coal is itself beyond the reach of the common man. The imposition of Sales Tax on coal further increase the price. So, in my opinion, coal should not be taxed and this should be included in the Third Schedule of the Bill as it is vitally linked with the life of the people as an article of mass consumption.

According to the Select Committee, the tax on kerosene and matches should be levied at the first point and it should not in any case be more than three per cent on kerosene and four per cent on matches. I violently disagree with this provision of the Bill.

It is well known that these two articles are used almost by all people. But, in comparison to the rich, these articles are used more by the poor and the middle strata of the population who constitute not less than 95 per cent. So, the imposition of Sales Tax on these two articles will hit them most. Nobody can appreciate this anti-people stand of the Government, who are professing by socialism day in and day out. So, these two articles of mass consumption should be spared from the purview of the Sales Tax.

In the end, I would recommend that coal, kerosene and matches should not be taken by the Delhi Administration and they should be included in the Third Schedule for the purpose.

RAILWAY ACCIDENT INVESTIGATION REPORT ON THE FIRE ON 311 UP SEALDAH-SAMASTIPUR FAST PASSENGER BETWEEN RAMPUR DUMRA AND HATIDAH LINK CABIN ON DANAPUR DIVISION OF EASTERN RAILWAY ON 12TH NOVEMBER, 1974[1]

One Man Commission Shri S.K. Mojumdar
Officers Present Shri R.K. Basu; Shri M.K. Sinha

Appointment

The Commission was constituted under Rule 4 of the Statutory Investigation into Railway Accidents Rule 1973 issued by the Ministry of Tourism and Civil Aviation vide their Notification No. RS 13.T(8)/71 dated 19th April, 1973.

Terms of Reference

To inquire into the fire on 311 UP Sealdah-Samastipur Fast Passenger between Rampur Dumra and Hatidah Link Cabin on Danapur Division of Eastern Railway on 12th November, 1974.

Conclusions

After considering all the material, factual and circumstantial evidence I have come to the conclusion that the fire which occurred in coach No. GSY 3558 of 311 Up Sealdah-Samastipur Fast Passenger between Rampur Dumra and Hatidah Link Cabin of the

---

1. Ministry of Tourism and Civil Aviation, (Commission of Railway Safety), Government of India, New Delhi, 1980, [i] + 14 p.

Eastern Railway at about 23.40 hrs. on 12-11-74 was caused due to some inflammable material carried in the coach by passengers having been ignited by a lighted matchstick thrown carelessly or by a lighted 'Dhibri' which may have been carried by any of the passengers in the coach which was without lights.

Responsibility

No railway staff is held responsible for this accident. The passengers who were carrying inflammable articles violated the rules under section 59(1) of Indian Railways Act 9 of 1890 and Rules No. 605 of IRCA Coaching Tariff No. 21, Part I (reported in Annexure I of the Report)

Relief Measures

Apropos para 6, medical attention given to the injured persons is considered to be as satisfactory as could be expected in the circumstances. The 3 injured persons who had been admitted in the Nazarcth Mission Hospital were properly looked after.

Recommendations

33. There was considerable difference in the time of departure of 311 Up from Rampur Dumra recorded by the Assistant Station Master, Switchman West Cabin, the Driver and Guard of the train. It appears that the watches of different staff are not synchronized with the clock at the Control office as per extant rules.

34. It would be impracticable to check all the passengers' luggages in order to detect whether any inflammable articles are bcing carried in the trains. Further, under the existing authorisation, the ticket checking staff could not insist on opening the passengers luggages for such examination. In the circumstances, the best preventive method would be to educate the passengers constantly through the Public Address System regarding the danger of carrying inflammable materials and this should be intensified at all stations where this facility exists. More careful watch should also be maintained by the ticket checking staff.

35. The maintenance of electric lights in coaches is far from satisfactory. It was observed that Kent couplers were missing throughout the entire rake of 311 Up. Temporary wire connections

are highly unsatisfactory as they are prone to theft and are likely to get disconnected on the run and the train had only 5 coaches with lights of 13 when it started from Jhajha. Adequate attention should, therefore, be given to improving the lighting arrangements of trains.

36. It is observed from the notification of the Chief Operating Superintendent, Eastern Railway that the alarm chain apparatus on 19 Mail and Express trains have been rendered inoperative up to 15-11-74. In addition, all passenger trains running on Eastern Railway on their entire run and all suburban trains on Sealdah and Howrah Divisions of their entire run are having the alarm chain apparatus rendered inoperative. Only the ladies compartment and the Postal Vans are continuing to have the apparatus in working conditions. Such large scale blanking off of alarm chain apparatus is not desirable and the Board may consider whether any improvement in the situation could be made.

37. The train crew deserve commendation for having promptly isolated the burning coach thus preventing the spread of fire to the adjacent ones.

Railway Board Comments on Various Paras of the Report

Para 33: Suitable action has been taken by railway administration.

Para 34: Suitable instructions have been issued to the railways vide latter No. 74/Tkt. Checking/54 dated 23-4-1975.

Para 35: As suggested by the CRS, trials to standardise new types of dynamos are already in progress. It will take some time to determine the performance-worthiness of the equipment which have been supplied.

According to the extant policy, end-on/mid-on generation are to be adopted gradually. End-on-generation requires a number of modifications in the coaches, which in turn affects workshop turn over, etc. This system is, therefore, adopted on a restricted scale.

Code of practices issued by the RDSO has already been sent to the Railways who are expected to ensure that these are available in the maintenance depots, and in the appropriate language/s if required. This is being reiterated.

With regard to action to check thefts of electrical material, it may be pointed out that security of passenger trains and investigation of such cases of thefts is the responsibility of the Government Railway Police. Action is, however, being taken by the Railway to reduce such thefts to the minimum and pin-point the areas where such thefts are taking place so that effective action could be taken against the criminals in co-ordination with the GRP and the local Police. The matter is also being followed up with the Police authorities for improving the investigation of cases of such thefts. The question of conferment on the RPF of additional powers of investigation of cases relating to railway property is also under consideration of the Government.

As regards training and refresher courses for maintenance staff it may be mentioned that additional recommendations of the CRS are of a general nature. Minimum educational qualifications and experience where necessary have been laid down for direct recruitment. Direct recruits are given initial training before they are put to working posts. They are also given refresher training periodically. The syllabi for initial, promotional and refresher training have been drawn up for most of the technical and operational categories. Staff rendered surplus, before absorption in alternative categories, are given conversion training where necessary.

As a rule, minimum educational qualifications are not prescribed for promotion once staff with the requisite qualifications are recruited. Rules for promotions have been laid down. In the artisans cadre, promotion to skilled and highly skilled grades is made only after a trade test. The standards prescribed for recruitment, promotion and training are considered adequate.

Para 36: Blanking off of alarm chain apparatus has been necessitated on account of large scale indiscriminate alarm chain pulling resulting, in serious dislocation in the running of trains. However the alarm chain apparatus in ladies compartments and coaches carrying mail are not blanked off. The trains and the sections over which blanking off is done are kept under periodical review by the Railway Administrations, taking into account their experience in regard to the misuse of alarm chain on individual trains and section.

Special drives have been launched on all the railways during the current emergency which have substantially brought down the incidence of unauthorised chain pulling. A watch in this regard is being maintained so that follow up action could be taken wherever increase in such incidents is noticed again.

Para 37: Suitable action has been taken by the railway administration.

19

WAGE REVISION COMMITTEE FOR PORT AND DOCK WORKERS AT MAJOR PORTS, 1974 – REPORTS[1]

Chairman Shri B.N. Lokur
Retired Judge of the Allahabad High Court, New Delhi
Members Shri T.S. Sankaran; Dr. B.V. Mehta
Secretary Shri T.R. Malhotra

Appointment

The Government of India in the Ministry of Shipping and Transport, by their Resolution No. PLO/94/74, dated the 11th December, 1974, set-up the Wage Revision Committee to enquire into and recommend as to what revision is necessary in the existing wage structure of the employees, other than Class I and Class II Officers, in the major ports of Bombay, Calcutta, Madras, Visakhapatnam, Cochin, Mormugao, Kandla and Paradip.

Terms of Reference

(a) The Committee will be required to enquire into and recommend as to what revision is necessary in the existing "wage structure" of the "Employees" specified in sub-para (d) below.

(b) In making their recommendations, the Committee will have regard among other relevant factors, to the following.

(i) The obligation of Port and Dock undertakings to provide adequate and efficient port and dock facilities at a reasonable cost;
(ii) the capacity of Port authorities and Dock Labour Boards to

---

1. New Delhi, Ministry of Shipping and Transport, Government of India, December 11, 1974 — January 24, 1977, iv + 354 p.

pay the wage bill, keeping in view the character of the Port transport industry;

(iii) the need for uniformity in the rates of emoluments and benefits of employees doing similar jobs at various major ports;

(iv) the total monetary accrual to the workers, inclusive of basic wage, allowances, payment of *ex-gratia*, etc.;

(v) duties and responsibilities of various posts, including the skills and hazards involved;

(vi) the need for adjusting wage differentials in such a manner as to provide incentive to workers for advancing their skills;

(vii) the economic conditions in the country, and all other related factors;

(viii) the requirements of social justice; and

(ix) extending the system of payment by results; i.e., linking wages to output.

Explanation:

In applying the system of payment by results, the Committee shall keep in view the need for fixing a minimum (fall-back) wage and also to safeguard against over-work and undue speed.

(c) Keeping in view the existing level of wages and variations in dearness allowance from time to time as per the formula evolved by the Central Wage Board for Port and Dock Workers, 1969, the Committee will submit its recommendations regarding demand for relief of an interim character within three months from the date the Committee starts its work. In the event of the Committee advising any interim relief, the date from which this relief should take effect will be indicated by the Committee.

(d) The term "wage structure" as mentioned above would include pay, special pay and allowances.

The term "Employees" mentioned in sub-para (a) above will cover the following, excluding Class I and Class II Officers:

(i) Persons employed by the major port trust of Bombay, Madras, Visakhapatnam, Cochin, Mormugao, Kandla and Paradip and the Commissioners for the Port of Calcutta;

(ii) Persons employed by the Dock Labour Boards and their Administrative Bodies at Bombay, Calcutta, Madras, Visakhapatnam, Cochin, Mormugao and Kandla; and

(iii) Persons covered under the schedules of various schemes framed under the Dock Workers (Regulation of Employment) Act, 1948.

(c) The Committee may also look into the cases of such other categories of workers covered by the Central Wage Board for Port and Dock Workers, 1969, but not included herein, if and when referred to by the Ministry of Labour on receipt of requests on behalf of these categories. Such references to the Committee will be made by the Ministry of Labour only.

Pursuant to para 3(e) of the terms of reference, the Ministry of Labour, having regard to the demand received by it from and on behalf of some of the categories of workers covered by the Wage Board but not included within the purview of the Committee and the possibility of similar demands being received subsequently from and on behalf of other excluded categories, by their Resolution No. V-24027(5)/74-WB, dated the 17th June, 1975, requested the Committee "to include, within its purview, all categories of workers who were covered by the recommendations of the Central Wage Board for Port and Dock Workers, excepting those to whom wage increases have been given or whose pay scale/wage structures have been revised under any arrangements outside the framework of the Wage Board's recommendations."

Contents

Introductory; Interim Relief; Evolution of Existing Wage Structure; Major Ports—Some Basic Facts; Wage Structure—Basic Considerations; Port Finances; Proposed Wage Structure; Allowances and Fringe Benefits; Piece-rate and Incentive Schemes; Alleged Anomalies and Special Representations; Miscellaneous Matters; Financial Impact of our Recommendations; Acknowledgements; Summary of Recommendations; Appendices from I to XXX.

Recommendations

I. *Introductory*

1. In evolving the wage structure, the main object we placed

before us was the need for doing justice to workers and to employers alike in the light of the factors spell out in our terms of reference, in the light of the changed circumstances and also in the light of Directive Principles in the Constitution in relation to labour matters. (Para 1.16)

2. The area of difference between the viewpoints of employers and workers was no doubt large; but we have, in a spirit of objectivity, attempted to evolve a rational synthesis, keeping in mind that while the demands of workers are somewhat exaggerated, the resistance of employers of any increase in wages is equally unjustified. (Para 1.16)

II. *Wage Structure—Basic Considerations*

3. While we ought necessarily to seek guidance from high policy statements in the matter of fixation of wages, we should, in determining the wage structure, follow the general principles and practices which have been authoritatively laid down in the reports of the various committees and commissions, decisions of the Supreme Court of India and awards of Industrial Tribunals. (Para 5.10)

4. The concepts of minimum wage, fair wage and living wage are not static and immutable; they change from time to time and from country to country; in determining fair wage, we should not look to wages prevailing in other countries and should confine ourselves to Indian conditions. (Paras 5.11 and 5.12)

5. We are unable to agree with the proposition that any increase in wages will increase the cost of services which will render them uneconomic to the users of the ports; the proposed increase in wages would not impose any unbearable burden on ports or users thereof; besides, the legitimate needs of workers are entitled to high priority. (Para 5.13)

6. The character and activities of major ports as non-profit-making service organisations have no relevance in the fixation of wages. Whoever may be the employer and whatever his activities, he must pay a reasonable wage to his employees. (Para 5.14)

7. A fundamental object of the wage fixing machinery is to strive to promote the welfare of workers by securing, as effectively as possible, social and economic justice. Betterment of the service conditions of industrial labour not only provides for them the ordinary amenities of life consistent with the advancing national standards but also, in that process, promotes industrial peace which would ac-

celerate productivity resulting in prosperity. (Para 5.14)

8. Our present economy is not in a position to provide a living wage to workers; only a fair wage is in the practical realm. What would be fair wage has to be determined on a consideration of the totality of circumstances. While we are not in favour of a sharp upward movement of wages which would contribute to inflationary forces and render the increase in wages ineffective and illusory, we should evolve, consistently with the capacity of major ports to pay and the legitimate aspirations of workers, a fair wage which would be 'a step towards the progressive realisation of living wage'. (Para 5.15)

9. The wage structure evolved by us does not fall very much short of the need-based minimum wage of the concept of the Indian Labour Conference; however, having regard to the capacity of major ports to pay, we are unable to persuade ourselves to fix for employees in major ports a need-based minimum wage at the levels demanded by workers' representatives. (Para 5.22)

10. We do not find it possible to invoke the industry-cum-region principle in evolving a wage structure for the major port industry for more reason than one. We have formulated a uniform wage structure for all the eight major ports. (Para 5.26)

11. In any attempt at wage fixation, the capacity of the employer to pay is a major consideration. (Para 5.29)

12. We do feel that if any rise in rates or levies cannot be avoided due to escalation in wages as a result of our recommendations, the impact thereof on port users would not be significant. (Para 5.32)

13. We do not subscribe to the view that any upward revision in wages would result in diversion of traffic to nearby minor or intermediate ports. (Para 5.33)

14. The expensive and large scale development works planned or undertaken in the various major ports must be presumed to be in the expectation of an increasing trend in traffic. (Para 5.34)

15. The finances of major ports have considerably improved after the revision of rates and charges in July, 1975. The wage structure which we are recommending would not be beyond the means of major ports. (Para 5.35)

16. There has been considerable improvement in productivity, at least after the Proclamation of Emergency, if not even earlier, and we have strong hopes that the momentum gathered will not be relaxed. (Para 5.40)

17. Our recommendations for the revision of pay scales, particularly at the lower levels, are influenced by the experience of productivity during the last year and our optimism for the years to come. (Para 5.40)

18. The industrial worker, like any other citizen, is entitled to claim a share in the progressive growth of the national economy, particularly as he also has a hand in shaping the economic destiny of the country. (Para 5.42)

19. If a male worker is to be deemed the sole wage earner for the family, his total wages as on the Ist January, 1974, should not fall below Rs. 312.37 to sustain his family of four persons at the national income level, based on the average of the *per capita* national income for 1973-74 and 1974-75. (Para 5.48)

20. The principle of social justice is important in fixing wages. Social and economic upliftment is a legitimate aspiration of the present day worker. (Para 5.49)

21. Our concept of social justice is that though certain levels have to be maintained between the highest and the lowest, the objective should be not to pull down the high-ups but to push up the lowly. (Para 5.50)

22. Fluctuations in consumer prices have an impact on fair wage. A worker can justifiably claim protection of the real wage. The dearness allowance formula is devised for the purpose. (Para 5.51)

23. When the general cost of living goes up, every employee has to make some sacrifice and such sacrifice should be comparatively higher at level of earnings, but we ought to make an exception in the case of the lowest wage earner who, at his level of wages, should not be called upon to make such sacrifice and neutralisation in his case should be 100 per cent. (Para 5.57)

24. We do not subscribe to a flat rate of dearness allowance at all wage levels and the principle of a sliding scale appears to us to be reasonable. (Para 5.58)

25. We have merged into basic pay, dearness allowance admissible under the Wage Board formula at the selected Index Number and provided for variable dearness allowance for its rise. (Para 5.60)

26. We do not favour the Wage Board scheme of fixed Dearness Allowance and Additional Dearness Allowance. (Para 5.60)

27. Merger of dearness allowance into basic pay increases the financial burden of major ports in the form of other benefits determined on the basis of basic pay. But that is inevitable whenever any

portion of dearness allowance is merged into basic pay, and the port administrations should not grudge it. (Para 5.60)

28. We have not taken into consideration the monetary value of fringe benefits in devising the wage structure. We believe that these fringe benefits help considerably in bridging the gap between fair wage and living wage and also that in a Welfare State, every employer ought to deem it his duty and responsibility to provide these benefits in addition to fair wage. (Para 5.65)

29. Since the quantum of *ex gratia* depends upon Government orders, we cannot foresee the amount of *ex gratia* which would be admissible to port and dock workers for the years to follow. It has, therefore, not been possible for us to take into account *ex gratia* payment in formulating our wage structure. (Para 5.70)

30. On the basis of representations received by us and on a close examination made by us independently after discussions with the concerned interests, we have tried to ensure that the rates of emoluments of employees doing similar jobs are more or less uniform. We find ourselves unable to even out the emoluments of workers governed by piece-rate and incentive schemes in the various ports, as these schemes differ from port to port and a scientific and systematic study is required to ensure that these workers secure the same emoluments for similar jobs in all the ports. (Para 5.72)

31. In view of overwhelming evidence regarding high rents and scarcity of housing and consequential hardships, we feel that all major ports deserve to be treated alike in the matter of house rent allowance. (Para 5.79)

32. Having regard to the price data available to us, we take the view that all major ports are eligible to a uniform rate of city compensatory allowance. (Para 5.83)

33. If all major ports have to be on same level in regard to house rent allowance and city compensatory allowance, as we think they should be, we are not in favour of treating them as separate and distinct elements and prefer to merge them into basic pay. (Para 5.84)

34. The total number of pay scales at present in vogue at major ports is more than a hundred. We have compressed the existing pay scales into 24 groups. Reduction in the number of scales not only simplifies the wage structure and reduces paper work, but also facilitates better development of various like categories of employees and more efficient use of manpower. (Paras 5.86, 5.92, 5.93)

35. We are in agreement with the general thinking on the sub-

ject of wage differentials that the disparity should not be unduly large. (Para 5.98)

36. In the pay scales recommended by us, we have proposed a differential ratio of 1 : 2.77 at the start of the lowest and the highest scales. This differential ratio works at the end of the two pay scales to 1 : 2.89. These differentials, we believe, provide not only for adequate incentives for advancement of skills but also serve the ends of social justice. (Para 5.99)

37. We are in favour of relating the wage structure to the 1960 series of the All India Consumer Price Index Numbers for Industrial Workers, as it is the latest available series. (Para 5.99)

38. We have devised a wage structure related to Index Number 250 of the 1960 series, which is the average for the three months of August to October, 1973. We are of the view that the Index Number would not fall below 250. (Para 5.102)

39. We feel that there is no compelling reason to establish parity between the wage structure of port and dock workers and that of Central Government employees. (Para 5.104)

III. *Major Port Finances*

40. A review of major port finances during the period prior in the Fourth Five Year Plan reveals that reliance of major ports on external funds, particularly Government loads, had been increasing in their capital structure and the relative share of internal funds had declined; most of the ports had low levels of return which left very little surplus to finance increasing investments required for development programmes, particularly after the Second Five Year Plan. Nevertheless, upto 1968-69 the net worth position of all the ports together in relation to borrowed funds was not unsatisfactory. (Para 6.17)

41. During the period from 1969-70 to 1974-75, the operating surplus continuously increased upto 1971-72. In 1972-73, the surplus was insignificant and thereafter there has been deficit for the next two years. The net surplus after taking into account income and expenditure relating to finance and miscellaneous items was reduced and the deficit was accentuated. The net surplus of Rs. 15.61 crores accumulated in the first three years of the period was completely wiped out by the deficit of the last three years, the major contributory factor being heavy deficit incurred by Calcutta port. (Para 6.20)

42. The largest revenue during the above period was derived from cargo-handling and storage charges followed generally by port and dock charges (including pilotage fees) and expenditure incurred on providing port and dock services was far in excess of revenue derived from them. (Paras 6.23 and 6.25)

43. The situation changed from July, 1975, when there was a substantial upward revision in port rates and charges. The figures for 1975-76 and our perusal of the budget estimates for 1976-77 show that even after this revision, certain services at some ports would still be unremunerative. (Para 6.26)

44. The ratios of net surplus to capital employed and of operating surplus to capital employed in major ports during the years 1969-70 to 1974-75 reveal a story of unmixed gloom so far as the productivity of investment in the major port industry as a whole is concerned. Both the ratios show a little improvement in the first three years but during the last three years they are negative. (Para 6.28)

45. Failure to give effect to the financial objectives recommended by the Commission on Major Ports, namely, a rate of return of not less than 12 per cent on the capital employed, has resulted in the financial plight of major ports over the years. (Paras 6.31 and 6.32)

46. The overall picture that emerges about the major port finances for the period 1969-70 to 1974-75 is not altogether a happy one. (Para 6.42)

47. The year 1975-76 marks the turning point in the finances of major ports. Largely as a result of the revision of the rate structure in July, 1975, every port experienced a substantial rise in its revenue during 1975-76 and the total revenue of major ports increased from Rs. 126.6 crores in 1974-75 to Rs. 178.8 crores in 1975-76, a rise over Rs. 52 crores. Operating expenditure also increased from Rs. 110.50 crores in 1974-75 to Rs. 126.55 crores in 1975-76 including expenditure arising out of Interim Relief recommended by us). Even then the operating surplus in 1975-76 was Rs. 29.56 crores. Even after taking into account the income and expenditure under the head 'Finance and Miscellaneous Expenditure', the surplus in 1975-76 comes to Rs. 24.79 crores. (Paras 6.43, 6.44 and 6.45)

48. We have reason to believe that the future of major ports is bright, as the budget estimates for the year 1976-77 indicate and also in view of the expected increase in traffic, all-round improvement in productivity, steps taken to reduce unproductive expenditure and

surplus labour, and overtime bill brought under control. With further tightening up of the administration, substantial economy could be effected. Our optimism that these healthy developments will continue in the years to come has influenced our view that the wage structure formulated by us would not impose any under burden on the finances of the ports. (Paras 6.46 and 6.47)

49. The outlay for the last two years of the Fifth Five Year Plan is quite substantial and major ports will have to depend heavily on Government loans notwithstanding operating surpluses. (Para 6.46)

50. The recent revision of the rate structure should not be regarded as the last word; the need for constant watch and, if necessary, further review of the rate structure is obviously indicated as even with the recent increase in the rate structure, the revenue from certain services does not cover their cost. (Para 6.46)

IV. *Proposed Wage Structure*

Minimum Wage

51. A total wage of Rs. 325 corresponding to Index Number 250 of the 1960 series, equivalent to Index Number 303 of the 1949 series, would be a fair wage for the lowest paid worker of ports and docks on the 1st January, 1974. (Para 7.11)

Pay Scales

52. In building up pay scales, skill alone cannot be made their basis; there are other factors also which have to be taken into consideration, e.g., strain of work, environmental conditions of work, hazard involved, disagreeableness of work, etc. (Para 7.13)

53. It would be equitable and reasonable to work out our pay scales with reference to the Wage Board pay scales after rationalising them by appropriate grouping. (Para 7.13)

54. Having regard to the minimum basic wage of Rs. 325, our pay scale for each of the 24 groups of the existing scales formed by us is given in paragraph 7.13. (Para 7.13)

55. Our proposed scales include House Rent Allowance and City Compensatory Allowance as well as (fixed) Dearness Allowance and Additional Dearness Allowance admissible on the 1st January, 1974. No House Rent Allowance or City Compensatory Allowance will therefore be payable at any major port with effect from the 1st

January, 1974, and no Dearness Allowance also will be payable except on rise above the Index Number 250 of 1960 series according to the formula given by us. (Para 7.14)

56. The Special Allowance of the nature of Compensatory Allowance being paid at present to employees in Paradip port shall be discontinued with effect from the 1st January, 1974. (Para 7.15)

57. To avoid cumbersome calculations of salary for parts of the month in consequence of increments accruing on different dates of the month, the increments should be given on the 1st of the month in which they fall due. (Para 7.17)

58. If an employee is assured that he would always, without any let or hindrance, go up to the maximum of the scale, he is apt to relax not only in efficiency but also in discipline and conduct. We have, therefore, provided for Efficiency Bars generally at a stage where there is an increase in the rate of increment to give an opportunity to the employer to review the performance of the employee periodically. We do hope that the authorities concerned will adopt objective standards in enforcing the Efficiency Bars. (Para 7.18)

59. As stagnation at the maximum of a scale for a long time adversely affects the morale and efficiency of the employee, an employee stagnating at the maximum of our proposed scale for three years should be given personal pay equal to one increment in that scale and if he further stagnates for a further period of three years, he should be given a second increment by way of additional personal pay, such increment being the increment last drawn by him. The personal pay so granted should count for all purposes.

This benefit shall not be available to employees who have not been promoted to the next higher grade due to their not passing the requisite test or are otherwise found unfit or against whom disciplinary proceedings are pending; it shall also not to be available to employees on a basic pay of Rs. 1200 in our proposed scales. (Para 7.20)

60. The existing scheme regarding skilled artisans need not be maintained separately as at present. Our proposed long scales, with a span of 20 years or more, should not prevent the holding of trade test at some stage and promotion to a higher scale, irrespective of existence of vacancies but within the totality of the skilled posts. It may be decided at the local level, having regard to the present practice, as to at what stage in the first two scales the trade tests should be held. (Para 7.23)

Fitment in our Proposed Pay Scales

61. If at all there are any employees who are not on Wage Board Scales, they should be brought on to our proposed scales by the process of determining first their corresponding Wage Board scales and thereafter fixing them in our appropriate proposed scales in accordance with our fitment formula. (Para 7.26)

62. We are not in favour of giving to employees as many increments in our proposed scales as they had already earned in their existing scales on the 1st January, 1974, as this would amount to retrospective introduction of our proposed pay scales. (Para 7.27)

63. Our general fitment formula is given in paragraph 7.29. (Para 7.29)

64. Piece-rated workers shall be brought on our proposed scales in accordance with our fitment formula on the basis of their notional pay in the existing scales as on the 1st January, 1974; however, processing wage and other features of the various piece-rate schemes shall not undergo any change as a consequence, pending a comprehensive review thereof. (Para 7.30)

65. Employees appointed to any grade or promoted to a higher grade on or after the 1st January, 1974, shall be brought over to our appropriate proposed scale from the date of their appointment or promotion, as the case may be, and their pay in that scale shall be fixed in accordance with the rules prevailing in the port concerned. (Para 7.31)

Increments

66. After fixing the pay of an employee in our proposed scale, his next increment shall be due on the anniversary of the last increment drawn by him in the existing scale subject, however, that the date of increment shall be the first of the month in which the increment was last due.

Where the pay of two employees of the same category in the same department is fixed in the same proposed scale at the same stage and the date of increment of the senior of the two employees falls due after the date of increment of the junior of the two employees, the date of increment of the senior employee shall be advanced to coincide with the date of increment of the junior employee. (Para 7.32)

Option

67. An employee shall be given option to come over to our proposed scale on the date of earning one or more increments falling due during the period from the 1st January, 1974 to 1st April, 1977. Until he opts to come over to our proposed scale, the employee shall remain on the existing scale and his emoluments shall be determined in accordance with the existing wage structure plus Interim Relief.

Such option shall be exercised within two months of the orders of Government on our recommendations. The option once exercised shall be final.

For the purpose of fixing in our proposed scale the pay of an employee who has exercised the option—

(i) total emoluments shall be arrived at by totalling up basic pay and (fixed) Dearness Allowance admissible to him on the date from which he opts to come over to our proposed scale and House Rent Allowance, City Compensatory Allowance and Additional Dearness Allowance as admissible to him on the 1st January, 1974; and

(ii) compensatory amount and fitment money shall be determined on the basis of his basic pay in the existing scale as on the 1st January, 1974. (Para 7.33)

Dearness Allowance

68. We are in favour of a graduated scale of dearness allowance on the basis of a percentage of basic pay. (Para 7.45)

69. The rates of Dearness Allowance for variations in Index Number above 250 of the 1960 series shall be as follows:

Pay slab	*Percentage of basic pay for variations above Index Number 250 of the 1960 series*
Rs.	
325-399	0.40% with a minimum of Rs. 1.30 per point
400-499	0.35% with a minimum of Rs. 1.60 per point
500-599	0.30% with a minimum of Rs. 1.75 per point
600-799	0.25% with a minimum of Rs. 1.80 per point
800 and above	Rs. 2 per point

(Para 7.46)

70. We are in favour of a quarterly review of Dearness Allowance. For reviewing for the quarter beginning on the 1st January, the average Index Number for the months of August, September and October of the preceding year should be taken into consideration and for subsequent quarters, the average Index Number of subsequent quarters of three months should be taken into account. (Paras 7.49 and 7.50)

71. Review of Dearness Allowance need not be undertaken unless there is a change of five or more points in the quarterly average after the last adjustment. (Para 7.51)

72. In computing quarterly average of Index Numbers, fraction of 0.5 and above should be rounded off to the next higher integer and fraction below 0.5 be ignored. (Para 7.52)

V. *Allowances*

73. The emoluments of employees in major ports include in many cases various types of special pay, personal pay and special allowance paid locally. Port authorities should closely examine each of these items and their rates with a view to satisfying themselves that their continuation is justified having regard to the changed circumstances and the nature of duties and responsibilities of the post concerned. (Paras 8.1 and 8.2)

74. Pending such examination, the amount of special pay, personal pay and special allowance which are at present being paid, whether in a lump sum or as a percentage of basic pay, should not be revised but be maintained at the existing level. (Para 8.2)

Weightage for Night Work

75. Compensation for night work should be regulated either by the night weightage formula of 10 minutes per hour or by reduction of working hours at night, whichever may be found convenient by port authorities, having regard to local conditions and circumstances. If ports in which there exists the practice of payment of a lump sum as shift differential do not find it feasible or practicable to introduce either of these two alternatives, the present practice may continue. However, with effect from the date of Government orders on our recommendations, the minimum amount so payable shall be 50 paise per shift. (Para 8.12)

Attendance Allowance

76. With effect from the date of Government orders on our recommendations, Attendance Allowance shall be paid uniformly in all major ports to such workers as are entitled to this allowance at present, at the rate of 1/60 of the monthly wage comprising basic pay in our proposed scales and Dearness Allowance according to our formula. (Para 8.24)

Overtime

77. We are of the firm opinion that there is considerable scope for reducing the quantum of overtime work, particularly as it has been stated before us that almost all ports are carrying surplus manpower. (Para 8.36)

78. At present, there is no uniformity in regard to payment of overtime and we feel that uniformity should be brought about in this respect in all ports. (Para 8.37)

79. Payment of overtime work is, to some extent, regulated by statutory provisions in respect of those categories of workers to whom the said provisions are made applicable and to that extent, payment for overtime work to such categories of employees shall have to be made in accordance with those provisions. Our recommendations are in respect of payment for overtime work not covered by statutory provisions and in respect of employees to whom such provisions do not apply. (Para 8.38)

80. The general recommendations regarding payment for overtime work are set out in paragraph 8.39. (Para 8.39)

81. Exceptions to the general recommendations are set out in paras 8.41 and 8.42. (Paras 8.41 and 8.42)

Weekly Day of Rest or Holidays

82. Our recommendations for payment for work on a weekly day of rest or on a festival or national holidays are set out in paragraph 8.43. (Para 8.43)

House Rent Allowance and Recovery of House Rent

83. Only a small percentage of the total employees in major

ports have been provided with quarters and there is urgent need for building more houses for employees. (Para 8.52)

84. In view of merger of House Rent Allowance in our proposed scales, House Rent Allowance is inadmissible from the 1st January, 1974. Section 4(1) of the West Bengal Workmen's House Rent Allowance Act, 1974, requires every employer to pay to every workman 3.5 per cent of his wages by way of House Rent Allowance. Employers in Calcutta port should seek exemption from this provision under Section 8 of the said Act. In the event of the exemption not being granted for any reason, employers in Calcutta port should split basic pay in our proposed scales and show 3.5 per cent thereof separately as House Rent Allowance, which should, however, be counted for purposes of Dearness Allowance, retirement benefits, etc. (Para 8.57)

85. Our recommendations for recovery of rent from allottees of accommodation are set out in paragraph 8.58. (Para 8.58)

86. We have refrained for more than one reason from stipulating that rent payable should not exceed 'standard rent' determined under Fundamental Rules. (Para 8.59)

Dust Allowance—Special Washing Allowance

87. Potentialities of some hazard to health on account of iron ore dust do exist but monetary payment by way of an allowance like dust allowance cannot be antidote for such hazard. (Para 8.62)

88. Port management ought to adopt adequate preventing measures against hazards arising out of iron ore dust. Ports where no such measures have been taken should take steps to reduce iron ore dust in the plants, supply protective equipment and arrange for regular medical check up and treatment of workers connected with iron ore handling. (Para 8.63)

89. Workers connected with iron ore handling operations whose body and clothes are soiled by iron ore dust in the performance of their duties, shall be paid a Special Washing Allowance of Rs. 10 per month or 40 paise per shift during the period of such employment. This allowance should be paid throughout the year.

Employees who would be paid Special Washing Allowance should not be paid any other washing allowance or dust allowance. (Paras 8.66 and 8.67)

90. Workers in Calcutta port who are eligible for coal handling

allowance at the rate of Rs. 7.50 per month should be paid at the increased rate of Rs. 10 per month or in the alternative 40 paise per shift. (Para 8.68)

91. The recommendations in paras 89 and 90 above shall take effect from the date of Government orders on our recommendations. (Para 8.69)

Running Allowance

92. In view of the decisions of the Supreme Court of India, we feel that the demand of port railway employees for running allowance has no merit; however, the feasibility of introducing suitable incentive schemes as in Madras port should be considered by ports where no such scheme exists. (Paras 8.47 and 8.75)

Outdoor Work

93. There is no justification in the demand for reduction in the working hours of outdoor clerical staff, nor is there any justification for payment of overtime or special allowance to them for extra hours of work. Where such a practice obtains, the same should be discontinued with effect from the date of Government orders on our recommendations. (Para 8.82)

Uniforms and Uniform Allowance

94. Port administration should consider the demand for uniforms to all outdoor staff in the light of the principles enunciated by the Central Governments Industrial Tribunal at Calcutta, presided over by Shri A. Das Gupta, with the addition made in 1970 by the Central Government Industrial Tribunal, Calcutta, presided over by Shri B.N. Banerjee. (Paras 8.83 to 8.88)

95. If a uniform allowance is paid in lieu of supply of uniforms in any port, we do not consider it necessary to require employers to supply uniforms instead of paying uniform allowance. (Para 8.89)

Washing Allowance

96. In view of the increased cost of soap and detergents, a sum of Rs. 5 per month should be given as Washing Allowance to all

those categories of employees who are entitled to this type of allowance. Other categories of employees whose duties involve continuous contact with dirty or dusty cargo (other than those workers handling iron ore covered by our proposed Special Washing Allowance and workers in Calcutta port who are given coal handling allowance) should also be paid Rs. 5 per month as Washing Allowance; actual categories of employees who would be entitled to this allowance may be determined by port administrations. (Para 8.90)

Conveyance Allowance

97. Port administrations should review the scales of conveyance allowance and the categories eligible therefore, keeping in view the increased cost of travelling and of maintaining a conveyance as well as the extent of travelling required in the performance of duties. (Para 8.91)

Island Allowance in Cochin Port

98. There is no justification for Island Allowance for employees in Cochin port. Island allowance presently being paid to dock workers should be discontinued with effect from the date of Government orders on our recommendations. (Para 8.94)

VI. *Piece-Rate and Incentive Schemes*

99. In view of the criticism of port employers and workers that the existing piece-rate and incentive schemes need to be reviewed and in view of our proposed wage structure, the various existing piece-rate and incentive schemes should be reviewed comprehensively and the desirability of extending these schemes or introducing new schemes for other categories of workers and introducing integrated schemes for cargo-handling workers be also considered. (Para 9.24)

100. A suitable central machinery should be set up to work out broad principles and guidelines for adoption of piece-rate and incentive schemes by the various ports, for providing assistance to them in the revision of their schemes and also for scrutinising and monitoring from time to time the schemes evolved at the local levels. (Para 9.25)

VII. *Attitude Anomalies and Special Representations*

101. It has not been possible for us to undertake any scientific job evaluation of the innumerable posts in the various major ports; that is a task which would have taken many years to complete. We have, in the circumstances, proceeded on the basis that the conclusions of the Classification and Categorisation Committee are generally sound. However, we have, in dealing with the representations made to us, borne in mind the fact that the situation today is not the same it was when that Committee formulated its recommendations. (Para 10.10)

102. Some of the alleged anomalies and demands are resolved by our grouping of the existing scales. (Para 10.13)

103. We have made recommendations relating to some common categories in all major ports and also certain individual categories in each port in respect of which only we considered that a change is called for. Our recommendations must be understood subject to the following clarifications:

(i) Wherever provision has been made by us for more than one scale for a specific category, it should not be considered obligatory for the employer to create posts in each one of these scales;
(ii) If the existing scale of an employee is higher than our proposed scale for his category, he will be entitled to the protection of his existing scale and should accordingly be brought over to our proposed scale corresponding to his existing scale, which would be personal for him. (Para 10.14)

Our Recommendations

104. On a consideration of the alleged anomalies and special representations:

(a) Our recommendations in respect of pay scale of loco-firemen, shunting staff, loco drivers, train examining staff, serangs, inland masters, engine drivers (marine), tide gauge readers, winch drivers/winchmen, tally clerks, cargo-handling workers of B category, nursing staff, laboratory assistants/laboratory technicians (medical department), junior clerks, telephone operators, motor drivers, sainiks/security guards and school teachers in all ports are set out in paragraphs 10.15 to 10.31; and

(b) Our recommendations in respect of pay scales of certain specified categories of employees in individual ports are set out in paragraphs 10.32 to 10.40. (Paras 10.15 to 10.40)

VIII. *Miscellaneous Matters*

Applicability of Our Recommendations

105. Our recommendations will apply to employees as defined in our terms of reference and to all other categories of workers covered by the recommendations of the Wage Board, except such of them who fall outside the framework of those recommendations consequent upon the revision of their pay scales/wage structure. (Para 11.7)

106. In view of pending court proceedings at the instance of bargemen in Calcutta port, we express no opinion on the question whether bargemen who operate both within and without the port area are covered or not by the recommendations of the Wage Board. (Para 11.8)

Unified Cargo-Handling Agency

107. In formulating our proposed scales, we have taken in mind not only the observations of the Commission on Major Ports and the Chatterjee Committee regarding the need for a unified cargo handling agency but also the fact that the question is under the active consideration of Government. Our grouping of scales, read with our recommendations made in Chapter X and paragraphs 11.14 to 11.19, would facilitate integration and interchangeability of cargo-handling workers. (Para 11.13)

108. On the integration of shore and stevedore cargo-handling workers in the ports of Bombay, Calcutta and Madras, Equation Allowance payable to shore workers in the port concerned shall be discontinued. (Para 11.14)

Deployability of Manpower

109. Port administrations should attempt, in consultation with the

representatives of workers concerned, introduction of arrangements for inter-changeability and improved deployability, keeping in view qualifications required, nature of duties and responsibilities, promotional opportunities, etc. (Para 11.26)

Labour Inspectors/Section Officers and Accountants under Calcutta Dock Labour Board.

110. There is no sufficient justification for recommending for the posts of Labour Inspectors, Section Officers and Accountants under Calcutta Dock Labour Board a pay scale higher than the maximum of Class III posts.

It would, however, be unjust to deprive the present incumbents of these posts of the status and benefits enjoyed by them since 1957 and hence they may be treated as Class II officers, but future incumbents should be placed in Class III on our proposed scale of Rs. 900-1200. (Paras 11.29 to 11.31)

Typists at Calcutta and Visakhapatnam Ports

111. Employees in the three grades of typists at Calcutta and Visakhapatnam ports, who are qualified and are fit for duties in the clerical cadre, should be considered for a change over to or for promotion in the clerical cadre at the appropriate level. (Para 11.33)

Other Matters

112. Appropriate authorities should consider the several representations listed in paragraph 11.35. (Para 11.35)

IX. *Financial Impact of Our Recommendations*

113. Since reliable data about the number of employees engaged by employers other than Port Trusts and Dock Labour Boards are not available, the estimate of financial impact of our recommendations is confined to Port Trusts and Dock Labour Boards only. (Para 12.2)

114. The recurring annual increase in the wage bills of Port Trusts and Dock Labour Boards with effect from the 1st January, 1977, would be about Rs. 9.60 crores for 1.05 lakh workers in Port

Trusts and Rs. 3.60 crores for 38,000 workers under Dock Labour Boards with effect from the 1st January, 1977. This includes the current liability of Rs. 8.58 crores in respect of Interim Relief. (Paras 12.3 and 12.4)

115. As regards arrears from the 1st January, 1974 to the 31st December, 1976, payments already made on account of *ex gratia*, overtime, leave, salary, children's education allowance and other benefits, except retirement benefits, need not be recalculated. (Para 12.7)

116. Our estimate of the total arears to be paid for the three years, 1974, 1975 and 1976 is about Rs. 17 crores for Port Trusts and about Rs. 7 crores for Dock Labour Boards. (Para 12.8)

20

ANOMALIES COMMITTEE FOR RAILWAYS, 1974 – REPORT[1]

Chairman Shri D.B. Vohra

Members Shri A.B. Lal; Shri A.V. Poulose; Shri K.S. Haravu; Shri G.D. Sud; Shri Keshav H. Kulkarni; Shri Shashi Bhushan Rao; Shri P.N. Sharma; Shri J.N. Chaki, Shri Priya Gupta; Shri J.P. Chaubey; Shri Umraomal Purohit

Appointment

An Anomalies Committee for Railways was set-up at the level of the Departmental Council under the Scheme of Joint Consultative Machinery. This Committee was composed of representatives of the official side as well as of both the Labour Federations, viz. National Federation of Indian Railwaymen and All India Railwaymen's Federations in 1974.

Terms of Reference

To look into the anomalies arising out of the implementation of the recommendations of the Third Pay Commission. Not only the anomalies in the pay scales of non-gazetted staff but also allied matters required for consideration.

Contents

Report; Recommendations; Record of discussions between Staff and Official sides in regard to issues where no agreement has been arrived at; Record of discussions between the staff and the official side

---

1. New Delhi, Ministry of Railways (Railway Board), 1976, 2, 3, 16, 2 p.

in regard to matters other than anomalies, arising out of the implementation of the recommendations of the Third Pay Commission.

Recommendations

It was agreed to submit the following recommendations for the consideration of Government.

(1) *Senior Trains Clerks*
(2) *Claim Tracers*
(3) *Senior Signallers*
(4) *Message Checkers.*

The revised scale of Rs. 330-480 allotted to these categories of staff in lieu of the existing scales of Rs. 130-280 (in the case of Message Checkers) and Rs. 150-240 (in the case of the other three categories) should be modified to Rs. 330-560.

(5) *Gatemen/Trolleymen*

The scale of Rs. 200-250 allotted to Gangmen should be made applicable also to Gatemen and Trolleymen of the Civil Engineering Department who are presently in the revised scales of Rs. 196-232 and Rs. 200-240. Since this would result in Trolleymen and Head Trolleymen being in the same pay scale, a special pay of Rs. 10 per month is proposed for Head Trolleymen. These modifications would apply equally to Gatemen and Trolleymen in other departments.

(6) *Head Shroffs/Head Cash Clerks*

The revised scale of Rs. 425-600 allotted to Head Shroffs and Head Cash Clerks in place of the existing scale of Rs. 210-320 should be modified to Rs. 425-640.

(7) *Ministries on the Open Line in the Civil Engineering Department*

The scale of Rs. 380-560 (RS) should be allotted to all the Ministries in the Civil Engineering Department, and not only to those who supervise Highly Skilled Grade I Workmen or are promoted from Highly skilled Grade II workers.

(8) *Loco/Fuel Inspectors*

The revised scales of Rs. 550-750 and Rs. 700-900 (existing scales Rs. 370-475 and Rs. 450-575) as recommended by the Pay Commission should be modified to Rs. 700-900 and Rs. 840-1040 respectively in order to allow them the same revised scales as have been notified for Loco Foremen. This would be equally applicable to corresponding Inspectorial categories on the Diesel and Electric Sides. This modification would not, however, be applicable to Inspectors who do not have a specified field jurisdiction and are attached to the Chief Mechanical Engineer/Divisional Mechanical Engineer.

(9) *Technical Supervisors of Loco Sheds*

(a) All Maintenance/Mechanical Foremen or Inspectors as well as all Boiler-Maker Foremen or Inspectors in the existing scale of Rs. 450-575 should be allotted the revised scale of Rs. 840-1040.

(b) All Boiler-Maker staff in the existing scale of Rs. 370-475 should be allotted the revised scale of Rs. 700-900.

This would be equally applicable to corresponding categories in Diesel and Electric Sheds. This modification would not, however, be applicable to Supervisors who do not have a specified field jurisdiction and are attached to the Chief Mechanical Engineer/Divisional Mechanical Engineer.

(10) *Cypher Operators*

The revised scale of Cypher Operators should be improved from Rs. 425-640 to Rs. 425-700.

(11) *Head Proof Readers in Printing Presses*

The revised scale of pay of Head Proof Readers should be modified from Rs. 425-600 to Rs. 425-700 and the designation changed to Chargeman (Proof Reading).

(12) *Machineman/Litho Machineman*

The semi-skilled Grade allotted to this category of staff on the Eastern Railway should be raised to skilled grade.

[Instructions have already been issued notifying the skilled grade of Rs. 260-400 as personal to Machinemen/Litho Machinemen.]

(13) *Voucher Issuers*

The scale of Rs. 210-270 for Voucher Issuers on the Eastern Railway should be raised to Rs. 225-308 to bring them on par with Bill Issuers on other Railways.

[Instructions have already been issued notifying the revised scale of Rs. 225-308 for Voucher Issuers and redesignating their posts as Bill Issuers.]

(14) *Mistries in Workshops, Production Control Organisations, Printing Presses, Sheds and Depots*

A single revised scale of Rs. 380-560 should be allotted to Mistries in Workshops, Production Control Organisations, Printing Presses, Sheds and Depots, instead of the two revised scale of Rs. 380-560 and Rs. 330-480, without attaching the conditions that those mistries who are required to supervise Highly Skilled Grade I workmen as a general rule or wherever the promotion to the grade is made from Highly Skilled Grade II workers may be allotted the Scale of Rs. 380-560, and others the lower scale of Rs. 330-480.

[Instructions have already been issued notifying a single revised scale of Rs. 380-560 for these Mistries.]

CHAIRMAN INDEX OF COMMITTEES & COMMISSIONS IN INDIA 1947-74 Volumes 1 to 12

CONTENTS SURVEY OF COMMITTEES & COMMISSIONS IN INDIA 1947-74 Volumes 1 to 12